KU-609-033

T. S. Eliot
Four Quartets

A CASEBOOK

EDITED BY

BERNARD BERGONZI

WITHDRAWN

M

...an Sixth Form College
Library

Selection and editorial matter © Bernard Bergonzi 1969

All rights reserved. No part of this publication
may be reproduced or transmitted, in any form
or by any means, without permission.

First edition 1969
Reprinted 1975, 1977, 1979

Published by
THE MACMILLAN PRESS LTD
London and Basingstoke
Associated companies in Delhi Dublin
Hong Kong Johannesburg Lagos Melbourne
New York Singapore and Tokyo

ISBN 0 333 02863 5

Printed and bound in Great Britain by
UNWIN BROTHERS LIMITED
Old Woking, Surrey

30553   0002564 7

This book is sold subject to the standard conditions of the
Net Book Agreement.

The paperback edition of this book is sold subject to the
condition that it shall not, by way of trade or otherwise,
be lent, resold, hired out, or otherwise circulated without
the publisher's prior consent, in any form of binding or
cover other than that in which it is published and without
a similar condition including this condition being imposed
on the subsequent purchaser.

CONTENTS

ACKNOWLEDGEMENTS

T. S. Eliot, 'The Genesis of *Four Quartets*' from 'T. S. Eliot talks about himself and the Drive to Create' in *New York Times Review*, 29 November 1953 (John Lehmann); T. S. Eliot, 'Dante and "Little Gidding"' from 'What Dante means to me' in *To Criticize the Critic* (1965) (Faber & Faber Ltd); D. W. Harding, 'A Newly Created Concept' from *Experience into Words* (1963) pp. 107–10 (Chatto & Windus Ltd); 'Mr. T. S. Eliot's Confession' (*Times Literary Supplement*); James Johnson Sweeney, '"East Coker": a reading' from *Southern Review*, VI (1941) 771–91 (Louisiana State University Press); Curtis Bradford, 'Footnotes to "East Coker"' from *Sewanee Review*, LII, no. 1 (1944) (Professor Curtis Bradford); D. W. Harding, 'We Have Not Reached Conclusion' from *Scrutiny*, XI (1943) 216–19 (Cambridge University Press), reprinted in *Experience into Words* (1963) (Chatto & Windus Ltd); R. N. Higinbotham, 'Objections to a Review of "Little Gidding"' and F. R. Leavis, 'Reflections on the above' from *Scrutiny*, XI (1943) 259–61, 261–7 (Cambridge University Press); George Orwell, 'T. S. Eliot' from *Poetry London*, no. 7 (Oct–Nov 1942) (Miss Sonia Brownell); F. O. Matthiessen, 'The *Quartets*', chapter viii of *The Achievement of T. S. Eliot*, 3rd ed. (Oxford University Press Inc.; © F. O. Matthiessen 1958); R. W. Flint, 'The *Four Quartets* Reconsidered' from *Sewanee Review*, LVI, no. 1 (1948) (*Sewanee Review*); Helen Gardner, 'The Music of *Four Quartets*' from *The Art of T. S. Eliot* (1949) (The Cresset Press Ltd and E. P. Dutton & Co. Inc.); Morris Weitz, 'T. S. Eliot: time as a mode of salvation' from *Sewanee Review*, LX, no. 1 (1952) (*Sewanee Review*); Donald Davie, 'T. S. Eliot: the end of an era' from *Twentieth Century*, April 1956 (Twentieth Century Magazine Ltd); Hugh Kenner, 'Into Our First World' from *The Invisible Poet: T. S. Eliot* (1959) pp. 247–76 (Mr Hugh Kenner and W. H. Allen & Co.); C. K. Stead, 'The Imposed Structure of the *Four Quartets*' from *The New Poetic* (1964) pp. 170–85 (Hutchinson & Co. (Publishers) Ltd); Denis Donoghue, 'T. S. Eliot's

Quartets: a new reading' from *Studies* (1965) pp. 41–62 (The Editor, *Studies*); Marshall McLuhan, 'Symbolic Landscape' from *Essays in Criticism*, I (1951) reprinted in *Critical Essays on the Poetry of Tennyson*, ed. J. Killham (Routledge & Kegan Paul and the University of Windsor *Review*, Ontario); A. Alvarez, 'A Meditative Poet' from *The Shaping Spirit* (in U.S.A. *Stewards of Excellence*) (Chatto & Windus Ltd and Charles Scribner's Sons; © A. Alvarez 1958); Karl Shapiro, 'Poetic Bankruptcy' from *In Defense of Ignorance*, pp. 54–7 (Random House Inc.; © Karl Shapiro 1960); William F. Lynch, S.J., 'Dissociation in Time' from *Christ and Apollo* (© Sheed & Ward Inc. 1960); David Perkins, 'Rose-garden to Midwinter Spring: achieved faith in the *Four Quartets*' from *Modern Language Quarterly*, XXIII (1962) (Professor David Perkins and *Modern Language Quarterly*).

GENERAL EDITOR'S PREFACE

EACH of this series of Casebooks concerns either one well-known and influential work of literature or two or three closely linked works. The main section consists of critical readings, mostly modern, brought together from journals and books. A selection of reviews and comments by the author's contemporaries is also included, and sometimes comments from the author himself. The Editor's Introduction charts the reputation of the work from its first appearance until the present time.

What is the purpose of such a collection? Chiefly, to assist reading. Our first response to literature may be, or seem to be, 'personal'. Certain qualities of vigour, profundity, beauty or 'truth to experience' strike us, and the work gains a foothold in our mind. Later, an isolated phrase or passage may return to haunt or illuminate. Where did we hear that? we wonder – it could scarcely be better put.

In these and similar ways appreciation begins, but major literature prompts to very much more. There are certain facts we need to know if we are to understand properly. Who were the author's original readers, and what assumptions did he share with them? What was his theory of literature? Was he committed to a particular historical situation, or a set of beliefs? We need historians as well as critics to help us with this. But there are also more purely literary factors to take account of: the work's structure and rhetoric; its symbols and archetypes; its tone, genre and texture; its use of language; the words on the page. In all these matters critics can inform and enrich our individual responses by offering imaginative recreations of their own.

For the life of a book is not, after all, merely 'personal'; it is more like a tripartite dialogue, between a writer living 'then', a reader living 'now', and whatever forces of survival and honour link the two. Criticism is the public manifestation of this dialogue, a witness to the continuing power of literature to arouse and excite. It illuminates the possibilities and rewards of the dialogue, pushing 'interpretation' as far forward as it can go.

And here, indeed, is the rub: how far can it go? Where does 'interpretation' end, and nonsense begin? Why is one interpretation superior to another, and why does each age need to interpret for itself? The critic knows that his insights have value only in so far as they serve the text, and that he must take account of views differing sharply from his own. He knows that his own writing will be judged as well as the work he writes about, so that he cannot simply assert inner illumination or a differing taste.

The critical forum is a place of vigorous conflict and disagreement, but there is nothing in this to cause dismay. What is attested is the complexity of human experience and the richness of literature, not any chaos or relativity of taste. A critic is better seen, no doubt, as an explorer than as an 'authority', but explorers ought to be, and usually are, well equipped. The effect of good criticism is to convince us of what C. S. Lewis called 'the enormous extension of our being which we owe to authors'. This Casebook will be justified only if it helps to promote the same end.

A single volume can represent no more than a small selection of critical opinions. Some critics have been excluded for reasons of space, and it is hoped that readers will follow up the further suggestions in the Select Bibliography. Other contributions have been severed from their original context, to which some readers may wish to return. Indeed, if they take a hint from the critics represented here, they certainly will.

A. E. DYSON

INTRODUCTION

'Burnt Norton', the first of the *Quartets*, appeared unostenta-
tiously as the final poem in T. S. Eliot's *Collected Poems 1909–
1935*, published by Faber in 1936. A characteristically trenchant
editorial comment in *New Verse* (June–July 1936) remarked on
'Mr Eliot's new long poem, "Burnt Norton", rather a dull meditation on time and God and love, which breaks only a few times
from a thin monotony into richness'. But D. W. Harding, re-
viewing the *Collected Poems* in the September issue of *Scrutiny*,
singled 'Burnt Norton' out for special praise: he referred to the
mature Eliot's mastery of language, describing the poem as a
newly created concept of infinitely rich meaning. This early
polarisation of critical response was to characterise the reception
of later *Quartets*. As the material collected in this volume shows,
the *Quartets* have been the occasion of sharp and even violent
disagreement. To some extent the reasons were ideological: critics
who sympathised with Eliot's Christianity and his general cultural position were naturally disposed to applaud the *Quartets* –
there is a substantial body of writing about the *Quartets*, which
I have not attempted to represent, that treats them largely as
material for religious exegesis – whilst left-wing and agnostic
critics were correspondingly inclined to deplore what they regarded as the obscurantism and pessimism of the poems. For
such readers the *Quartets* offered melancholy evidence of Eliot's
final betrayal of the radicalism evinced in *The Waste Land*, a process begun with his notorious pronouncement in 1928 that he
was a supporter of Anglo-Catholicism in religion, royalism in
politics and classicism in literature. George Orwell's exasperated
attack on the later Eliot, published in 1942,* can be regarded as
typical of this left-wing response. It should be remembered that

* References indicated with an asterisk are included in this volume.

the three *Quartets* following 'Burnt Norton' were published
during the Second World War, and were readily assimilated to
the conspicuous atmosphere of Christian literary revival (mostly
Anglican) of the wartime years, associated with such names as
C. S. Lewis, Dorothy Sayers, and Charles Williams; and, in
poetry, Norman Nicholson and Anne Ridler, with Kathleen
Raine and David Gascoyne as unorthodox outriders. The whole
movement was subject to a hostile analysis some years later by
Kathleen Nott in *The Emperor's Clothes* (1953).

Not all disagreement about the *Four Quartets* has been ideological, however, or at least not directly so. Critics who are
careful to keep within literary terms of reference have shown
marked variations in their response. Some have regarded the
frequently abstract language and the relative decorum of the
verse as evidence of a slackening of poetic intensity on Eliot's
part, whilst others, such as D. W. Harding and F. R. Leavis, see
the *Quartets* as a major achievement, showing a marvellous flexi-
bility and subtlety of language and rhythm, and a new mastery
of complex experience. After 'Little Gidding' appeared in 1942
and the design of the complete *Quartets* was revealed, a good
deal of critical activity was devoted to explicating the five-
movement structure of each of the constituent poems, and tracing
interrelations between the various sections throughout the *Quartets*. The most recent phase of criticism, which can be regarded
as having begun with Donald Davie's essay in 1956,* though
admiring much of the sequence, is less inclined to accept its
essential and triumphant unity, and tends to regard the separate
poems, and their individual movements, as discrete elements that
show varying degrees of poetic success.

'Burnt Norton' was originally intended to stand as a separate
poem, and as placed at the end of the *Collected Poems 1909-1935*
it made an effective conclusion to that volume. Eliot himself has
described how 'Burnt Norton' was a by-product of the imaginative effort that went into writing *Murder in the Cathedral*;* its
origin lay in lines and fragments discarded from the play in the
course of production. It was only with the outbreak of the
Second World War in 1939 that Eliot turned again to writing

purely lyric poetry: the result was 'East Coker', which followed
the formal pattern of 'Burnt Norton'. It was then that he conceived of writing a set of four poems that would incorporate
the first two into a larger unity (according to Grover Smith, Eliot
at one time thought of calling them the South Kensington
Quartets, after the part of London in which he was living).[1]
'East Coker' was printed in the *New English Weekly* in the spring
of 1940, and published as a shilling Faber pamphlet in September 1940. It was reviewed at length, urbanely though quite
unsympathetically, in the *Times Literary Supplement*,* which
deplored the bleakness of its language and the fatalism and
detachment of Eliot's attitudes. The interest of this review is that
it shows that as late as 1940 it was still possible for doubts to be
uttered about the ultimate worth of Eliot's poetic achievement,
even though individual felicities might be acknowledged. (John
Wain has discussed the case of an academic who even in 1943
could refer patronisingly to 'an American critic, Mr T. S. Eliot').[2]
The *TLS* review of 'East Coker' was followed by a sharp protest
in its correspondence columns from F. R. Leavis, who was at
that time still an unqualified admirer of Eliot's achievement. The
TLS was, however, to continue to be cool in its treatment of the
subsequent *Quartets*. When 'Burnt Norton' was reissued as a
pamphlet in 1941, the reviewer noted, 'The reader feels that the
boarhound and the boar, the pattern and the reconciliation are
full of significance – but he may be hard put to it to say what
precisely they signify.' 'The Dry Salvages' appeared later in
1941, and the *TLS* observed that, 'A new note has crept into
this poetry, a note of quiescence, even of bleak resignation. But
it has lost that spice of wit which was woven into the logic of the
earlier poems.' The review of 'Little Gidding', published in
December 1942, was more appreciative but remained critical of
many of the qualities of the poem:

Mr Eliot's expression of this theme is, at its best, impressive,
because he realises to the full how hard and costly the choice

[1] Grover Smith, *T. S. Eliot's Poetry and Plays* (Chicago, 1956)
p. 255.
[2] John Wain, *Preliminary Essays* (1957) p. 189.

between the two fires is. But while this gives a tension to his utterance and a winter starkness to his imagery, which heightens the sense of a second spring breaking in the concluding lines, it also tends to reduce the music of poetry to the dry discourse of the moralist and the intellectual. His characteristic and recurrent use of the paradox, too, is almost becoming a trick.

One of the first sustained critical discussions of any of the *Quartets* was James Johnson Sweeney's essay on 'East Coker', published in the *Southern Review* in 1941.* Sweeney clearly sympathised with Eliot's Christian-conservative position, and he saw the poem as a wartime elegy for secular and progressive attitudes. He was the first critic to identify various central allusions in the poem. He traces the source of the passage about 'daunsinge, signifying matrimonie' to Sir Thomas Elyot's *The Boke named The Gouvernour* of 1531. Sweeney sees the earlier Elyot as a spokesman for the assertive individualism of the Renaissance that was to lead, ultimately, to the overwhelming disasters of the twentieth century; this traditionalist approach is supported with references to Eliot's *The Idea of a Christian Society* and invokes the names of Christopher Dawson and T. E. Hulme. Sweeney also picks up the allusions to St John of the Cross, which Helen Gardner was to discuss subsequently. He refers in passing to resemblances between passages in 'East Coker' and 'Burnt Norton', but misses the larger thematic and structural relationship between the two poems. In 1944 Curtis Bradford, in his 'Footnotes to "East Coker",'* published in the *Sewanee Review*, enlarged on Johnson's discussion, and drew out more of the parallels with 'Burnt Norton'.

In 1942 several English critics offered a progress report on the first three of the *Quartets*. I have referred to George Orwell's angry outburst; on the positive side were Helen Gardner, whose essay, 'The Recent Poetry of T. S. Eliot', published in *New Writing*, formed the basis for her book *The Art of T. S. Eliot* (1949); and F. R. Leavis, whose 'T. S. Eliot's Later Poetry', published in the Summer 1942 number of *Scrutiny*, praised the first three *Quartets* on literary rather than ideological grounds, and concluded of Eliot that 'it should by now be impossible to doubt that he is among the greatest poets of the English language'. (Unfortunately it was not possible to obtain permission to reprint this important essay; it can be most conveniently consulted in Leavis's *Education and the University* (1943), where it appears as Appendix 1.) The publication of 'Little Gidding' provoked a lively and significant debate in the pages of *Scrutiny* in 1943.* Following a laudatory review by D. W. Harding, R. N. Higinbotham wrote in protest, using the customary critical language of *Scrutiny* to dissent from the high valuation of the *Quartets*, arguing that 'the unevenness and lack of homogeneity in these four poems from "Burnt Norton" onwards are therefore the result of disequilibrium in the author's feelings'. The last word was spoken by F. R. Leavis, who vehemently defended the *Quartets* and Harding's assessment of them.

Following the appearance of 'Little Gidding' and the subsequent publication of the four poems in one volume under the title of *Four Quartets*, criticism became increasingly concerned with reading the quadripartite work as a single poem. The first essay on the work as a whole that I have encountered is F. O. Matthiessen's 'The *Quartets*',* published in the *Kenyon Review* in 1943 and incorporated into the later editions of his book *The Achievement of T. S. Eliot* (1947, 1958). Matthiessen's lucid exegesis of the *Quartets* is representative of many later discussions: allusions are noted, the complexities of structure are unravelled (although Matthiessen went into less detail than subsequent commentators), and Eliot's intentions are sympathetically summarised. There were many such explications published in articles and books during the 1940s and early 1950s, and although there may be differences of nuance from one to another, the general impression they leave is of much the same thing being said over and over again. At the same time, the 'adversary tradition' of opposition to the *Quartets* was apparent. There is a relevant passage in Karl Shapiro's long literary-critical poem, *Essay on Rime* (1947), which modulates from comment into parody:

                                                            Eliot
            Himself in the *Quartets* (in my opinion

> His most depressing prosody) makes shift
> Of rhythms one thought he had exhausted ten
> Or fifteen years before. Symptoms of doubt
> Lie in reiteration; we sense confusion,
> The anxiety of the sensitive to mistakes.
> Rather a false step in the right direction
> Than circumspect retreat, procrastination.

Shapiro later adopted an even sharper tone in his *In Defense of Ignorance* (1960),* which hammered at the *Quartets* in a spirit compounded of leftist sentiment and American cultural nationalism.

Two useful positive accounts of the *Quartets* from the late 1940s are included in this collection. R. W. Flint's 'The *Four Quartets* Reconsidered' (1948)* is frankly a work of critical consolidation: 'it becomes more and more apparent that the *Quartets* have worn well'. It does, however, make some original points, correcting Matthiessen on aspects of Eliot's religious attitudes, and displaying a vigorous scepticism about the value of describing the work in terms of its supposed musical form. Helen Gardner, on the other hand, in 'The Music of *Four Quartets*' (chapter II of *The Art of T. S. Eliot*),* devotes a long and sensitive discussion to the work's musical organisation. She also asserts, in contradiction to other commentators, that the sources of the poem are not particularly important – 'No knowledge of the original context is required to give force to the new context' – thus emphasising the difference in poetic method between the *Quartets* and *The Waste Land*. From James Johnson Sweeney onwards, critics have picked up the references to Heraclitus in the *Quartets* and have stressed the importance of Heraclitean ideas about time in Eliot's treatment. But in 'T. S. Eliot: time as a mode of salvation' (1952),* Morris Weitz, writing as a philosopher, claims that Eliot's sense of time is not Heraclitean, but is that of a Christian Neo-platonist.

As I have suggested, the criticism of the *Quartets* took on a new sense of direction with the publication of Donald Davie's essay in 1956,* suggesting that other positions were possible than the total endorsement or the equally total rejection that had so far been manifested. Davie's argument is that the third Quartet, 'The Dry Salvages', is, on the face of it, a thoroughly bad poem. He explores the possibility that its badness may be deliberate, relating it in a parodistic way to the other *Quartets*; in which case, Davie concludes, the *Four Quartets* must represent 'the end of an era' of neo-symbolist complexity and indirection. Hugh Kenner, in the remarkably subtle and sophisticated chapter on the *Quartets* in his *The Invisible Poet* (1959),* tends to make most earlier criticism look very simple. Kenner implies that in the first two *Quartets* Eliot advances opposed elements of 'recurrent illumination' and 'pervasive sombreness', which are falsely reconciled in 'The Dry Salvages' (whose unsatisfactoriness he admits), then truly reconciled at the end of 'Little Gidding'. There is another incisive discussion in C. K. Stead's important book on the making of modern poetry, *The New Poetic* (1964).* Stead analyses the repeated fivefold structure of the *Quartets* with considerable rigour, and his conclusion is temperately unfavourable. He sees the *Quartets* as an attempt at an uneasy compromise between the language of discourse and the 'music of images' of *The Waste Land*, with a corresponding lowering of poetic intensity, despite the presence of many distinguished passages. The most recent essay included in this collection is that by Denis Donoghue, which was published after Eliot's death in 1965.* Like Stead, he offers an analysis of the recurring five-movement structures, though he sees their significance differently, and his judgement on the *Four Quartets* as a whole is a largely positive one. Nevertheless, he admits the weaknesses in some of the separate elements, and like Davie and Kenner he is aware of the problem of 'The Dry Salvages'; in fact, he provides a helpful continuation of their own accounts. Like several earlier commentators on the *Quartets*, Donoghue writes as a Christian; at the same time he offers genuine criticism and not mere exegesis.

The essays by Davie, Kenner, Stead and Donoghue do not provide any kind of a consensus, and they throw out more questions about the ultimate meaning and status of the *Quartets* than they resolve. Critical arguments about the work are certain to go on for a long time, but they will not be able to ignore the conclusions of these critics, however much they dissent from them. Nor will it be possible to assume that the *Quartets* are a seamless unity, all of whose parts are equally well realised and harmoniously interrelated, as was often done in earlier discussions. Recent criticism has perhaps left the *Quartets* less perfect as achieved works, but more interesting as literature.

At the same time, there are signs of emerging agreement on questions of detail, on the actual strengths and weaknesses of the four poems. Section IV of 'East Coker' (which begins 'The wounded surgeon plies the steel') offers an instructive example. Curtis Bradford called it the 'finest section' of the poem, and Helen Gardner has said that 'the grave heavy beat of the lines, the rigid stanza form, the mood, the paradoxes, the sense of tragic triumph, which the rhythm gives, make this lyric very like an early Passion hymn'. More recently, Northrop Frye has referred to 'the bleak hospital imagery, the pedantic allegory, the concentration on Good Friday, and the harsh whether-you-like-it-or-not dogmatism'.[1] Frye implies, without quite saying, that this section is an unattractive piece of writing that may nevertheless be acceptable in its poetic context. Donald Davie has been more outspoken: he refers to 'the much-elaborated skull-and-cross-bones conceit' in section IV of 'East Coker', which he calls 'strained and laboured', and assumes that the passage can be justified only as a parody of true reconciliation: 'should we not take it that the strain and the labouring are deliberate, a conscious forcing of the tone, a *conscious* movement towards self-parody?' C. K. Stead, who does not regard the *Quartets* as an ultimately successful achievement, and Denis Donoghue, who does, show an interesting measure of agreement about this section:

There is, however, another operation of the 'meddling intellect' for which neither his poetic practice nor his experience as a lecturer have prepared Eliot: the conscious working up into verse, through a series of intellectual analogies and paradoxes, of a 'metaphysical' idea. Section IV of 'East Coker' is an example of this; and the result is one of the few sections which not merely

[1] Northrop Frye, *T. S. Eliot* (Edinburgh, 1963) p. 85.

fail to be good poetry, but succeed in being thoroughly bad. . . .
Eliot works these paradoxes out, through a demanding verse
form, with the rigorous exactness of a compiler of crossword
puzzles. The result is a piece of ingenuity, a synthetic poem,
quite without feeling or life. (Stead)

In 'East Coker' the lyric of purgation hovers over Adam's curse,
Original Sin. The tone is strangely crude; indeed, this is one of
the weaker parts of the poem. The analogies of health and
disease, surgeons, patients, and hospitals are marginally appropriate, and far too dependent upon our reading 'the wounded
surgeon' as Christ, 'the dying nurse' as the Church, the hospital
as the earth, the briars as the thorns of Christ. When we have
effected these translations little remains but the satisfaction of
having done so. (Donoghue)

It is reasonable to conclude that this section of 'East Coker' is
unlikely to recover the esteem in which it was held by early
critics of the *Four Quartets*. On the other hand, there has been
pretty uniform agreement about the excellence of section II of
'Little Gidding', particularly the long Dantean passage beginning
'In the uncertain hour before the morning' in which the poet
walks the streets of London after an air-raid. (Eliot describes the
problem of its composition in a passage included in this volume,
and A. Alvarez examines its poetic quality in an extract from
The Shaping Spirit.*) Even an early hostile critic like R. N.
Higinbotham specifically excluded this section from his stric-
tures on the *Quartets*: 'the most noteworthy success is the second
part of section II of "Little Gidding", applied to which Mr Harding's praises are accurate'. Kathleen Nott is another writer ideo-
logically opposed to Eliot who has singled this section out for
high praise.[1]
    The reader of the critical material collected in this volume may
well be disconcerted by the degree of disagreement between
critics of established reputation, but he should not fall into
despair or pure relativism. The *Four Quartets* have been available for a comparatively short time, scarcely long enough for a

[1] Kathleen Nott, *The Emperor's Clothes* (1953) p. 218.

true critical perspective to have formed. As the last substantial work by a poet of major but still somewhat problematical reputation their own status has reflected a number of uncertainties. The ideological element intervenes in a way that it did not in Eliot's earlier poetry: agnostics, for instance, can read *The Waste Land* (as I. A. Richards once did) as a poem indicating a severance with all possible beliefs; whilst Christians can read it as a poem of pre-conversion; and both sets of readers can be in substantial agreement about its poetic merits. But the *Quartets* force 'the problem of belief' on the reader with some insistence, although such critics as Harding and Leavis have shown that it is possible to admire the *Quartets* without in any way endorsing their doctrinal attitudes. Again, in purely literary terms, critics may agree that the *Quartets* represent a distinct movement on from *The Waste Land*, whilst not agreeing at all whether this movement is a progressive or a regressive one. As I have suggested, the later essays collected in this book point the way forward to further critical debate: my own feeling is that with the passing of time Eliot's earlier poetry is likely to endure rather better than the *Quartets*, notwithstanding their several magnificent passages, and to this extent I find myself in agreement with Mr Stead. But that is very far from implying that he has said the last word.

POSTSCRIPT (1979)

I have written more about *Four Quartets*, modifying some of the ideas expressed in this Introduction, in 'Ghostly Voices' (*Encounter*, July 1978): a review article on Helen Gardner's important book, *The Composition of 'Four Quartets'* (1978).

BERNARD BERGONZI

PART ONE

Two Statements
by T. S. Eliot

THE GENESIS OF
FOUR QUARTETS

I REMEMBER once more feeling I'd written myself out just before *The Rock* was commissioned. I had to write it – I had a deadline – and working on it began to make me interested in writing drama, and led directly to *Murder in the Cathedral*. That was dramatic poetry, of course, and I thought pure unapplied poetry was in the past for me, until a curious thing happened. There were lines and fragments that were discarded in the course of the production of *Murder in the Cathedral*. 'Can't get them over on the stage', said the producer, and I humbly bowed to his judgement. However, these fragments stayed in my mind, and gradually I saw a poem shaping itself round them: in the end it came out as 'Burnt Norton'.

Even 'Burnt Norton' might have remained by itself if it hadn't been for the war, because I had become very much absorbed in the problems of writing for the stage and might have gone straight on from *The Family Reunion* to another play. The war destroyed that interest for a time: you remember how the conditions of our lives changed, how much we were thrown in on ourselves in the early days? 'East Coker' was the result – and it was only in writing 'East Coker' that I began to see the Quartets as a set of four.

(*New York Times Book Review*, 29 November 1953)

DANTE AND 'LITTLE GIDDING'

TWENTY years after writing *The Waste Land*, I wrote, in 'Little Gidding', a passage which is intended to be the nearest equivalent to a canto of the *Inferno* or the *Purgatorio*, in style as well as content, that I could achieve. The intention, of course, was the same as with my allusions to Dante in *The Waste Land*: to present to the mind of the reader a parallel, by means of contrast, between the Inferno and the Purgatorio, which Dante visited and a hallucinated scene after an air-raid. But the method is different: here I was debarred from quoting or adapting at length – I borrowed and adapted freely only a few phrases – because I was *imitating*. My first problem was to find an approximation to the *terza rima* without rhyming. English is less copiously provided with rhyming words than Italian; and those rhymes we have are in a way more emphatic. The rhyming words call too much attention to themselves: Italian is the one language known to me in which exact rhyme can always achieve its effect – and what the effect is, is for the neurologist rather than the poet to investigate – without the risk of obtruding itself. I therefore adopted, for my purpose a simple alternation of unrhymed masculine and feminine terminations, as the nearest way of giving the light effect of the rhyme in Italian. In saying this, I am not attempting to lay down a law, but merely explaining how I was directed in a particular situation. I think that rhymed *terza rima* is probably less unsatisfactory for translation of the *Divine Comedy* than is blank verse. For, unfortunately for this purpose, a different metre is a different mode of thought; it is a different kind of *punctuation*, for the emphases and the breath pauses do not come in the same place. Dante *thought* in *terza rima*, and a poem should be translated as nearly as possible in the same

Luton Sixth Form College
Library

thought-form as the original. So that, in a translation into blank verse, something is lost; though on the other hand, when I read a *terza rima* translation of the *Divine Comedy* and come to some passage of which I remember the original pretty closely, I am always worried in anticipation, by the inevitable shifts and twists which I know the translator will be obliged to make, in order to fit Dante's words into English rhyme. And no verse seems to demand greater literalness in translation than Dante's, because no poet convinces one more completely that the word he has used is the word he wanted, and that no other will do.

I do not know whether the substitute for rhyme that I used in the passage referred to would be tolerable for a very long original poem in English: but I do know that I myself should not find the rest of my life long enough time in which to write it. For one of the interesting things I learnt in trying to imitate Dante in English, was its extreme difficulty. This section of a poem – not the length of one canto of the *Divine Comedy* – cost me far more time and trouble and vexation than any passage of the same length that I have ever written. It was not simply that I was limited to the Dantesque type of imagery, simile and figure of speech. It was chiefly that in this very bare and austere style, in which every word has to be 'functional', the slightest vagueness or imprecision is immediately noticeable. The language has to be very direct; the line, and the single word, must be completely disciplined to the purpose of the whole; and, when you are using simple words and simple phrases, any repetition of the most common idiom, or of the most frequently needed word, becomes a glaring blemish.

(1950)

PART TWO

Reviews and Early
Criticism 1936-44

D. W. Harding

A NEWLY CREATED CONCEPT

A Note on 'Burnt Norton'

IN parts of the later poems Eliot's 'meaning', what he intends his words to do, is so complex and difficult that direct explicit statement is ruled out. Much of 'Burnt Norton', for instance, is not using current concepts to make a statement, not even a subtle statement. Instead, it is exploring possibilities of meaning that lurk in the interstices of familiar ideas.

Ordinarily our abstract ideas are over-comprehensive and include too wide a range of feeling to be of much use by them-selves. If our words 'regret' and 'eternity' were exact bits of mosaic with which to build patterns much of 'Burnt Norton' would not have had to be written. But

> Words strain,
> Crack and sometimes break, under the burden,
> Under the tension, slip, slide, perish,
> Decay with imprecision, will not stay in place,
> Will not stay still.

One could say, perhaps, that the poem takes the place of the ideas of 'regret' and 'eternity'. Where in ordinary speech we should have to use those words, and hope by conversational trial-and-error to obviate the grosser misunderstandings, this poem is a newly created concept, equally abstract but vastly more exact and rich in meaning. It makes no statement. It is no more 'about' anything than an abstract term like 'love' is about anything: it is a linguistic creation. And the creation of a new concept, with all the assimilation and communication of experience that that involves, is perhaps the greatest of linguistic achievements.

In this poem the new meaning is approached by two methods. The first is the presentation of concrete images and definite events, each of which is checked and passes over into another before it has developed far enough to stand meaningfully by itself. This is, of course, an extension of a familiar language process. If you try to observe introspectively how the meaning of an abstract term – say 'trade' – exists in your mind, you find that after a moment of blankness, in which there seems to be only imageless 'meaning', concrete images of objects and events begin to occur to you; but none by itself carries the full meaning of the word 'trade', and each is faded out and replaced by another. The abstract concept, in fact, seems like a space surrounded and defined by a more or less rich collection of latent ideas. It is this kind of definition that Eliot sets about here – in the magnificent first section for instance – with every subtlety of verbal and rhythmical suggestion.

And the complementary method is to make pseudo-statements in highly abstract language, for the purpose, essentially, of putting forward and immediately rejecting ready-made concepts that might have seemed to approximate to the concept he is creating. For instance:

> Neither from nor towards; at the still point, there the dance is,
> But neither arrest nor movement. And do not call it fixity,
> Where past and future are gathered. Neither movement
>   from nor towards,
> Neither ascent nor decline.

Or

> Not the stillness of the violin, while the note lasts,
> Not that only, but the co-existence,
> Or say that the end precedes the beginning,
> And the end and the beginning were always there
> Before the beginning and after the end.
> And all is always now.

In neither of these methods is there any attempt to state the meaning by taking existing abstract ideas and piecing them together in the ordinary way. Where something approaching this more usual method is attempted the result is a little less interesting; for instance:

> The inner freedom from the practical desire,
> The release from action and suffering, release from the inner
> And the outer compulsion, yet surrounded
> By a grace of sense, a white light still and moving,
> *Erhebung* without motion, concentration
> Without elimination, both a new world
> And the old made explicit, understood
> In the completion of its partial ecstasy,
> The resolution of its partial horror.

There, abstract concepts already available are being used, for an individual purpose, it is true, but tending towards generalization away from, rather than through, particularities of experience.

(*Scrutiny*, 1936; reprinted in *Experience Into Words*, 1963)

Times Literary Supplement

MR T. S. ELIOT'S CONFESSION

'EAST COKER' is not a pastoral in the Somerset dialect, nor in the dialect of 'pure poetry', which Mr Eliot, not for the first time, scorns as a device outworn, the pretty plaything of times when poets had nice manners but only trivial themes – such as *Hamlet* and *Lear* and *Paradise Lost*, poems basically misconceived because the motives were insufficient, Hamlet, for instance (no notice need be taken of God and the Devil and the fall of man) not having had sufficient ground for his tragic indecision in such day-to-day incidents as the murder of his father, the betrayal of his mother and the suicide of his lover. We live in more critical days when there is motive enough to set going poets double Shakespeare's size. What is made of it by Mr Eliot, whose proportions are not of that dimension, but are considerable, considerable enough to create a following, a clique, even a claque – who, it should be acknowledged to him, earn his amused disdain?

The critic is saved, by Mr Eliot himself, from exploration of technique and accomplishment, from any attempt to explain the thrill of admiration, or whatever kind of thrill it is he feels. He need only consider the subject, the bare bones of the poem. Why that should apply only to poetry and not to prose and painting and music may be left to the Bare Boners to explain – and no one need doubt their readiness to oblige: the eager ability of the 'modern' to 'explain' what he is after has no counterpart in the history of art. There are always 'movements' in poetry. The poets of the nineties, for instance, wanted to purify poetry of all that was not poetry. Mr Eliot's aim seems to be to purify poetry of all that is poetry. That is not an unfair statement. He has accepted as a dogma something D. H. Lawrence had said about the need for poetry to be bare and stark. It must suit the barren, futile conditions and the misdirected purposes of our prematurely afflicted century – 'poetry', Mr Eliot has said, 'with nothing "poetic" about it . . . poetry so transparent that we should not see the poetry'. In reading it we should be intent on what the poetry *points out* and not on the poetry. 'We should not see the poetry' does sound rather like 'the art that conceals art', but it is almost treasonable to suspect any such outmoded idea can be re-echoed in our more intelligent times.

There's the rub. More intelligent? Mr Eliot despairs of our days and deeds. And he remains a poet in spite of his efforts to break up his splendid incantations with passages of the prosiest of prose:

So here I am, in the middle way, having had twenty years –
Twenty years largely wasted, the years of *l'entre deux guerres* –
Trying to learn to use words, and every attempt
Is a wholly new start, and a different kind of failure
Because one has only learnt to get the better of words
For the thing one no longer has to say, or the way in which
One is no longer disposed to say it.

This is indeed bare enough of poetry, but it is also a confession that he will never try to achieve an *opus consummatum* – a rebuke to the sad ghost of Coleridge who could make only excuses and promises. Mr Eliot has given a fresh and effective cadence to dramatic, lyrical and psychological poetry; and it fails in the long run to satisfy because for the most part it is used as a trick of defiance, an impish gesture, to show he knows all about that kind of thing. And it is unnecessary to say of Mr Eliot, with his rare knowledge of the best that has been done in verse, and his own considerable achievements and bold experiments, that he does know. Even when deploring his 'different kinds of failure' he excites the reader with sudden felicities:

What is the late November doing
With the disturbance of the spring
And creatures of the summer heat,
And snowdrops writhing under feet

And hollyhocks that aim too high
Red into grey and tumble down
Late roses filled with early snow?
Thunder rolled by the rolling stars
Simulates triumphal cars
Deployed in constellated wars
Scorpion fights against the Sun
Until the Sun and Moon go down
Comets weep and Leonids fly
Hunt the heavens and the plains
Whirled in a vortex that shall bring
The world to that destructive fire
Which burns before the ice-cap reigns.

The reader has only just visited East Coker when he is lifted with pleasure into this. But he gets no farther, for Mr Eliot immediately apologizes. 'That', he says (and there is no need, in view of the pressure on our space, to split the lines up into a visual appearance of poetry, as Mr Eliot does), 'that was a way of putting it – not very satisfactory: A periphrastic study in a worn-out poetical fashion, Leaving one still with the intolerable wrestle With words and meanings. The poetry does not matter.'

It does not. Poetry is worn out and is hereby consigned to the relics of a romantic past. We need consider only the bare bones, what 'the poetry points out'. Mr Eliot is disdainful of many things, of most things. His poetry is the poetry of disdain – disdain of the tragic view of life, of the courageous view, of futile sensualists, of poetry, and now even of himself. He is becoming more and more like an embalmer of the nearly dead; he colours their masks with expert fingers to resemble life, but only to resemble. On all their lips is the twisted smile of Prufrock. 'In the beginning is my end', says the poet, and 'in the end is my beginning'. The knowledge gained from experience has only a limited value. We are in a dark wood, in a bramble, our foothold never secure.

The only wisdom we can hope to acquire
Is the wisdom of humility: humility is endless.

Humility is noble, and it is noble to come to it and to proclaim it as a faith. There is a grandeur in the humility of the English religious poets, but there is a lack of their ecstasy in 'East Coker'. Where Vaughan, whose days were as troubled as our own and little less violent, saw eternity the other night and bright shoots of everlastingness, Mr Eliot sees only the dark. 'They all go into the dark', all the people in his vision of a world of bankers, men of letters, statesmen, committeemen, contractors, labourers, who eat and work and go to bed and get out of bed. All are for the dark,

> And we all go with them, into the silent funeral
> Nobody's funeral, for there is no one to bury.

This is a hymn of humility, but a sad one, and somewhat incongruous. For in spite of the animation of his powerful incantations there is more satire than poetry in Mr Eliot's headshaking over a terrible bleak, meaningless world of hollow men, with smell of steaks in passage ways, and satire and humility go strangely together. This is the confession of a lost heart and a lost art. These are sad times, but we are not without hope that Mr Eliot will recover both, finding even that hearts are trumps and that Keats was not far out about the ore in the rift.

(14 September 1940)

James Johnson Sweeney

'EAST COKER':
A READING

SINCE its first appearance in the spring of 1940, T. S. Eliot's 'East Coker' has been widely applauded as his most considerable poetic achievement of the last eighteen years. Since the publication of *The Waste Land* Eliot's use of literary allusion and adapted quotation has become familiar and expected. In spite of this, with the publication of 'East Coker' in book form we again began to hear criticisms and complaints reminiscent of those which greeted *The Waste Land* two decades ago.

In his essay 'Tradition and the Individual Talent' republished in *The Sacred Wood* (1920) we read: 'the historical sense involves a perception, not only of the pastness of the past, but of its presence'. Again in his introduction to Mark Wardle's translation of Valéry's *Le Serpent* (1924) he wrote: 'One of the qualities of a genuine poet . . . is that in reading him we are reminded of remote predecessors, and in reading his remote predecessors we are reminded of him.'

Between the publication of these two statements *The Waste Land* appeared, when the presence and necessity of notes provoked impatience and censure on the part of many critics. But as I. A. Richards put it in his *Principles of Literary Criticism*: 'A more reasonable complaint would have been that Mr Eliot did not provide a larger apparatus of elucidation.'

But it appears that the reviewers are still reluctant to make the effort to read him carefully before passing judgment on him. For example, in the *New Statesman and Nation* of 14 September 1940 we have such a perceptive critic as G. W. Stonier writing in the body of a generally sympathetic review as follows:

Again his [Eliot's] use of quotation, by which he so often imparts a nostalgic flavour to his verse, has curious lapses. In 'East

Coker' there are examples of both success and failure. The section beginning

O dark dark dark. They all go into the dark,
The vacant interstellar spaces, the vacant into the vacant,
The captains, merchant bankers, eminent men of letters . . .

makes excellent use of a well-known passage in Samson ('Dark, dark, dark! The moon . . . hid in her vacant interlunar cave'). But how do the last lines of the following passage, delightful in its scene, strike the reader?

In that open field,
If you do not come too close, if you do not come too close,
On a summer midnight, you can hear the music
Of the weak pipe and the little drum,
And see them dancing around the bonfire
The association of man and woman
In daunsinge, signifying matrimonie –
A dignified and commodious sacrament,
Two and two, necessarye coniunction,
Holding eche other by the hand or the arm
Whiche betokeneth concorde.

There the Elizabethan spelling imparts no flavour save perhaps one of pedantry; its only effect is to make us think, 'Well, I suppose Eliot, when he wrote that, was thinking of passages in Spenser's Epithalamion.' Yet obviously to Eliot the whiff of the antique has an immediate, an emotional effect, like the reminiscences of Haydn in Prokofieff's Classical Symphony. This is a purely literary failure. . . .

Such a conclusion is an injustice. And it is particularly difficult to understand since Stonier concludes this sentence with the words: 'the more odd because of all poets Eliot is in certain directions the most precise in his effects.'

A reader who has the confidence in Eliot's precision that Stonier claims to have and is as familiar with Eliot's allusive technique, should not be satisfied to identify such a pointed emphasis on the archaic as a mere willful infusion of pedantry. He should endeavor to find what specific allusion is embodied in the passage and why the poet sought to underscore these lines in the text by setting them apart from the rest in archaic spelling. In Eliot's manner of doing it there is certainly no attempt at disguise or mystification. We are clearly invited to associate the lines with some specific feature of the literary past. And had Stonier seriously considered this point he would have had to look no further for a cue than the poem's title and the author's name.

Coker is a small village near Yeovil on the borders of Dorsetshire and Somersetshire in England, reputedly the birthplace of Sir Thomas Elyot (?–1546), the author of *The Boke named The Gouvernour* (1531). Chapter XXI of The Firste Boke is entitled 'Wherefore in the good ordre of daunsinge a man and a woman daunseth to gether'. And the opening paragraph of this chapter reads:

It is diligently to be noted that the associatinge of man and woman in daunsinge, they bothe obseruinge one nombre and tyme in their meuynges, was not begonne without a speciall consideration, as well for the *necessarye coniunction* of those *two persones,* as for the intimation of sondry vertues, whiche be by them represented. And for as moche as *by the association of a man and a woman in daunsinge may be signified matrimonie,* I coulde in declarynge *the dignitie and commoditie of that sacrament* make intiere volumes . . .

Then further along we come across a passage: In euery daunse, of a moste auncient custome, there daunseth to gether a man and a woman, *holding eche other by the hande or the arme, whiche betokeneth concorde.*'

Here we have clearly the source of those lines. Their roots turn out to be Tudor not Elizabethan. And thanks to that 'flavour of pedantry', or more exactly archaism, to which Stonier objects, one aspect of Eliot's approach to his theme in 'East Coker' begins to take shape for us.

The Boke named The Gouvernour was one of the first of those works partly on politics, partly on education, which the study of the classics and more particularly that of Plato, multiplied at the end of the Renaissance throughout Europe. *The Gouvernour* has been described as the earliest treatise on moral philosophy in the English language.

Sir Thomas Elyot was an ardent monarchist, a scholar deeply influenced by the writings of such continental humanists as Pico della Mirandola and Erasmus, and a thorough churchman – at one time the intimate of Sir Thomas More, but always a loyal adherent to the Church of his sovereign. We are at once struck by the link between Sir Thomas Elyot's interests and T. S. Eliot's famous declaration of faith as a 'Classicist in literature, royalist in politics, and anglo-catholic in religion' which appeared in his 1928 preface to *For Lancelot Andrewes*. A common emphasis is apparent in the title of T. S. Eliot's essay *The Idea of a Christian Society* and Elyot's translation of Pico della Mirandola's *Rules of a Christian Life*; just as we find a community of viewpoint between T. S. Eliot's later poems and Sir Thomas Elyot's work entitled *Cyprianus, a Swete and Devoute Sermon of the Holy Saynt Cyprian on the Mortality of Man*.

Finally, a fundamental feature of Sir Thomas Elyot's interests was language – words in particular. He was very conscious of the poverty of the Anglo-Saxon of his time as compared with other languages and desired above all things to augment its vocabulary. In 1536 he undertook the compilation of a dictionary, the *Bibliotheca Eliotae* subsequently known as *Eliotes Dictionaire*. And from a purely linguistic viewpoint *The Gouvernour* may be regarded as a connecting link between the English of the time of Chaucer and the English of the time of Bacon. Its style for the period is peculiar; for many of the words or phrases it employed were even then going out of use, while, on the other hand, many new words are recognizable, apparently original importations.

We now see the picture beginning to arrange itself: a twentieth-century Eliot, who feels he has certain spiritual links with a Tudor Elyot, communing with himself in the dark spring following the outbreak of the second world war within little more than two decades. Although Sir Thomas Elyot of Coker may have died without issue, there is a sufficient kinship in their interests to draw the contemporary Eliot to him in thought. Something is amiss with contemporary civilization, its mode of conduct or philosophy of life. The elder Elyot had tried through *The Boke named The Gouvernour* to suggest for his period a pattern of harmonious living and concord based on the Platonic ideals of the Renaissance. The younger man, faced by the darkness of the present moment, feels a certain irony in the parallels which he recognizes between his own interests and those of his precursor. In spite of all the confidence in intellectual progress of Sir Thomas Elyot's time, it is evident, today, that the neo-classical, individualist approach of the Renaissance led to a mechanical view and a spiritual poverty and produced the cataclysm which has overwhelmed the present age. 'In my beginning is my end.'

This is the theme which dominates the whole work. Like a musical phrase it is woven back and forth through the entire texture of the composition, now stated in one key of meaning, now in another.

The actual wording of the theme is possibly an echo of the inscription 'En ma fin est mon commencement' embroidered upon the chair of state of Mary, Queen of Scots. In 1931 Maurice Baring published an historical study of the Scottish queen under this title. In his preface we read:

The title of this book needs some explanation. The inscription:
    'In my End is my Beginning'
was the motto embroidered upon the Chair of State of Mary, Queen of Scots. This inscription perplexed Mr Nicholas White, a friend of Cecil's, who, on his road to Ireland in the spring of the year 1569, paid a visit of curiosity to the Queen of Scots during her captivity at Tutbury, the house of the Earl of Shrewsbury.

He wrote as follows: 'In looking upon her cloth of estate, I noticed this sentence embroidered: 'en ma fin est mon commencement', which is a riddle I understand not' . . .

Baring continues:

Her motto was symbolic in more ways than one. Putting aside the question of whether the death of the Queen of Scots was, as some think, the triumph of a martyred saint awaiting canonization in the future, or a consummate piece of playacting, there is no doubt that practically and politically the end of the Queen of Scots was her beginning; for at her death her son, James Stuart, became heir to the crowns of England and Scotland and he lived to wear both crowns.

A more remote source of the theme, yet a source which has

been rich in suggestion for so much of Eliot's mature poetry, is the philosophical remains of Heraclitus of Ephesus. For example here we read:

The beginning and the end are common. (LXX)
Fire lives in the death of earth, air lives in the death of fire, water lives in the death of air, and earth lives in the death of water. (XXV)

Throughout the poem we find this theme given two contrasting interpretations: a spiritual one, and a material or temporal one. In the spiritual interpretation the 'beginning' is seen as that 'highest type of knowledge – the intuition of pure being' which Christopher Dawson regards as 'the starting point of human progress' in his study *Progress and Religion*; and man's end – goal or purpose – is the knowledge of the Divine Order, or God, which can only come by intuition, through love. The material or temporal interpretation stresses the cyclic nature of history, the temporality of material achievement, and the mortality of man in the spirit of the admonition: 'Remember, man, that thou art dust and unto dust thou shalt return.'

These two interpretations of the dominant theme are played back and forth until their final combination in that victorious reversal of the introductory statement that closes the poem: 'In my end is my beginning.'

I

Man as a physical being has his cycle of life; its opening predicates its close.

Like every other form of animal life man is the creature of environment, heredity and function. 'Consequently his culture is not an abstract intellectual construction, but a material organization of life, which is submitted to the same laws of growth and decay, of "generation and corruption", as the rest of the material world.'[1] As in Heraclitus' view, all is one eternal flux, all is involved in ceaseless round of life, death, growth, and decay.

[1] Christopher Dawson, *Progress and Religion* (1931) p. 74.

The Logos, the element of law or order, is the only stable factor in the ever shifting world:

> In succession
> Houses rise and fall, crumble, are extended,
> Are removed, destroyed, restored . . .

Houses – whether the term be taken literally to signify buildings, the material components of a village such as Coker, or figuratively, as dynasties – houses rise and fall, houses live and die.

> there is a time for building
> And a time for living and for generation
> And a time for the wind to break the loosened pane
> And to shake the wainscot where the field-mouse trots
> And to shake the tattered arras woven with a silent motto.

In the passing of Mary, Queen of Scots, we see the fugitive character of temporal glory and we have its symbolization in the fluttering of the tattered arras embroidered with her motto.

To Eliot, as he looks back from the dark moment after the outbreak of a new, disillusioning war, the village of Coker in its association with Sir Thomas Elyot represents a beginning – the beginning of a period which had looked forward idealistically and hopefully to a future of intellectual achievement and conquest. You can still imagine Sir Thomas Elyot's ideal dancers in their dance 'around the bonfire' symbolizing human harmony and concord, yet at the same time reminding us, through 'the rhythm of their dancing', of the laws of growth and decay, of generation and corruption – 'Eating and drinking. Dung and death.' And the poet is brought back to the reality of the present. For that period is completely behind us,

> Dawn points, and another day
> Prepares for heat and silence.

All that survives, from the period just closed, on which we can hope to build for the future, is what that period already had at its outset – 'the intuition of pure being'.

> Out at sea the dawn wind
> Wrinkles and slides. I am here
> Or there, or elsewhere. In my beginning.

II

So what has the present day to do with these hopes of a younger time? Eliot asks himself in the opening lines of the second section

> What is the late November doing
> With the disturbance of the spring
> And creatures of the summer heat . . . ?

In these 'sproutings' of 'That corpse you planted last year in your garden' we feel an echo of *The Waste Land* and a renunciation of the earlier attitude of that poem and of 'Gerontion'. 'Do not let me hear . . .'. The pattern and content of these poems he sums up in the first seventeen lines of section II of 'East Coker', with subtle echoes of their rhythms and imagery. Late November, like *The Waste Land*'s 'winter dawn', now hears 'thunder rolled by the rolling stars . . . whirled in a vortex that shall bring' the world, eventually, through fire, as preached in the 'Fire Sermon', and through devastation to 'the peace that passeth understanding', even as *The Waste Land* saw this prefigured in

> The sound of horns and motors, which shall bring
> Sweeney to Mrs Porter in the spring.

But 'the poetry does not matter'. To start again is the important thing. As Christopher Dawson says in *Progress and Religion*: 'intellectually, at least, man's development is not so much from the lower to the higher as from the confused to the distinct'. The materialist approach did not help us to this. In spite of Sir Thomas Elyot's enthusiasm, zeal and optimism, things did not work out as they were expected to. The autumn of civilization did not bring the serenity and calm that was expected. Did those quiet-voiced elders, such as Sir Thomas Elyot and the Renaissance leaders, deceive us more with their confidence in man and his powers of intellectual achievement, or the despairful author of 'Gerontion'?

> There is, it seems to us,
> At best, only a limited value

> In the knowledge derived from experience
> The knowledge imposes a pattern, and falsifies,
> For the pattern is new every moment.

For in the Heraclitean saying, no man ever bathes twice in the same stream, just as we may speak of the ever-changing bather the stream receives. Or according to the late F. H. Bradley, for whom Eliot has long had a great admiration: If views are dependent on needs and needs are culturally and individually determined,

the whole Universe seems too subject to the individual knower. What is given counts for so little and the arrangement counts for so much, while in fact the arranger, if we are to have real knowledge, seems so dependent on the world. But the individual who knows is here wrongly isolated, and then, because of that, is confronted with a mere alien Universe. And the individual, as so isolated, I agree, could do nothing, for indeed he is nothing. My real personal self which orders my world is in truth inseparably one with the Universe. Behind me the absolute reality works through and in union with myself, and the world which confronts me is at bottom one thing in substance and in power with this reality. There *is* a world of appearance and there *is* a sensuous curtain, and to seek to deny the presence of this or to identify it with reality is mistaken. But for truth I come back always to that doctrine of Hegel, that 'there is nothing behind the curtain other than that which is in front of it'.

Again we read in Eliot's 1939 essay *The Idea of a Christian Society*:

so long as we consider 'education' as a good in itself ... without any ideal of the good life for society or for the individual, we shall move from one uneasy compromise to another. To the quick and simple organization of society for ends which, being only material and worldly, must be as ephemeral as worldly success, there is only one alternative. As political philosophy derives its sanction from ethics, and ethics from the truth of religion, it is only by returning to the eternal source of truth that we can hope for any social organization which will not, to its ultimate destruction, ignore some essential aspect of reality.

In other words, the solution is clearly not through the accumulation of encyclopaedic knowledge in accord with the ideal of the Renaissance, or a scientific exploration of our physical world in keeping with that of the last two centuries, but through a return to the beginning – through the intuition of pure being – to the eternal source of truth. The increase of human knowledge only brings us the satisfaction of feeling ourselves undeceived 'Of that which, deceiving, could no longer harm'. At the same time the passionate pursuit of material knowledge which has characterized the last five centuries of European history has steadily more and more discouraged any interest in spiritual values. As a result we find ourselves today like Dante in the opening lines of the *Inferno*:

> In the middle of the journey of our life
> I found myself in a dark wood,
> having lost the straight path.

'Life has become' for us, as it had for Dr Watson in A. Conan Doyle's *The Hound of the Baskervilles*, 'like that great Grimpen Mire, with little green patches everywhere into which one may sink and with no guide to point the track.' And Eliot has both these pictures in mind when he sees himself in 'East Coker'

> In the middle, not only in the middle of the way
> But all the way, in a dark wood, in a bramble,
> On the edge of a grimpen, where there is no secure
>   foothold,
> And menaced by monsters, fancy lights,
> Risking enchantment.

And in this predicament after depending so long on the misleading advice and the empty promises of our elders, Eliot resolves that we should put aside all notions of 'the wisdom of old men'. 'Do not let me hear', he writes, 'Of the wisdom of old men, but rather of their folly', which is their vanity. In reality they are nothing more than infinitesimal details of the Divine pattern. And their notion of their importance as individuals, their dread of losing their imagined spiritual autonomy – their fear 'of belonging to another, or to others or to God' is only

another heritage of the Renaissance individualist approach. At
best it is merely the wisdom of the children of this world in their
generation – a short-term wisdom. For if we face facts frankly
we will realize that

> The only wisdom we can hope to acquire
> Is the wisdom of humility: humility is endless.

This is especially clear today when we consider the emptiness
of the material civilization we have so long adulated. It was a
dream, a delusion even as Eliot's present-day vision of Sir Thomas
Elyot's dancers. And in the concluding lines of section II of
'East Coker' Eliot caustically underscores its fragile passing with
a parody of the line of Stevenson's 'Requiem': 'Home is the
sailor, home from sea, / And the hunter home from the hill' –

> The houses are all gone under the sea.
> The dancers are all gone under the hill.

III

The third section of the poem opens on this note – the darkness
in which the disappearance of these illusions has left the world:

> Oh dark dark dark. They all go into the dark,
> The vacant interstellar spaces, the vacant into the vacant,
> The captains, merchant bankers, eminent men of letters,
> The generous patrons of art, the statesmen and the rulers,
> Distinguished civil servants, chairman of many committees,
> Industrial lords and petty contractors, all go into the dark,
> And dark the Sun and Moon, and the Almanach de Gotha
> And the Stock Exchange Gazette, the Directory of Directors,
> And cold the sense and lost the motive of action.
> And we all go with them . . .

In the present world-crisis Eliot sees illustrated the broader
spiritual problem which faces us. In his editorial valedictory
'Last Words' in the final issue of the *Criterion* (January 1939), he
wrote: 'The period immediately following the war of 1914 is
often spoken of as a time of disillusionment: in some ways and
for some people it was rather a period of illusions.' And in the

concluding paragraph of *The Idea of a Christian Society* published in the autumn of 1939 we read:

I believe that there must be many persons who, like myself, were deeply shaken by the events of September 1938; persons to whom that month brought a profounder realization of a general plight . . . a feeling of humiliation which seemed to demand an act of personal contrition, of humility, repentance and amendment; a doubt of the validity of a civilization. . . . Was our society, which had always been so assured of its superiority and rectitude, so confident of its unexamined premisses, assembled round anything more permanent than a congeries of banks, insurance companies, and industries, and had it any beliefs more essential than a belief in compound interest and the maintenance of dividends?

And in this context – its association with the present eclipse of such formerly powerful sources of information as the Almanach de Gotha, the Stock Exchange Gazette and the Directory of Directors – the line 'And cold the sense and lost the motive of action' affords a subtle, ironic commentary through an echo it brings us of the line from Swinburne's 'The Last Oracle' (*Poems and Ballads – Second Series*): 'Dark the shrine and dumb the fount of song thence welling.'

To Milton's Samson the darkness in his eyes was a source of lamentation:

> O dark, dark, dark, amid the blaze of noon,
> Irrecoverably dark, total Eclipse
> Without all hope of day!

To Eliot, on the contrary, the first closing-in of darkness brings promise of a sounder road to truth and enlightenment. We already have a suggestion of this in the echo of Vaughan's 'Ascension Hymn' – 'They are all gone into the world of light!' – in the first line of section III: 'O dark dark dark. They all go into the dark.' The clearing away of material, distracting ambitions, the blacking-out of the 'fancy lights', open a way to the poet to return to his beginning – to 'the starting point of human progress, the intuition of pure being'.

> I said to my soul, be still, and let the dark come upon you
> Which shall be the darkness of God.

For the poet, this darkness is the darkness of the Isa Upani-
shad:

> Into blind darkness enter they
> That worship ignorance;
> Into darkness, as it were, greater
> They that delight in knowledge.
> Other, indeed, they say, than knowledge!
> Other, they say, than non-knowledge!

It is the transitional stage between periods – Jung's *Night
Journey* of the Rebirth Pattern – with a suggestion of the present
war in the possible ambiguity of interpretation afforded by the
'hollow rumble of wings':

> As, in a theatre,
> The lights are extinguished, for the scene to be changed
> With a hollow rumble of wings, with a movement of
> darkness on darkness . . .

But from a spiritual viewpoint such a darkness and such a
realization of the emptiness of material achievement awaken in
Eliot above all thoughts of *The Dark Night of the Soul*, that
passive night, that intense purification with which God, according to St John of the Cross, visits the soul. To such as desire
purification St John of the Cross says:

Advice must be given to learn to abide attentively and to pay no
heed either to imagination or its workings; for here, as we may
say, the faculties are at rest, and are working not actively but
passively by receiving that which God works in them.

And in this spirit Eliot tells us

> I said to my soul, be still, and wait without hope
> For hope would be hope for the wrong thing; wait without
>   love
> For love would be love of the wrong thing; there is yet faith
> But the faith and the love and the hope are all in the waiting.
> Wait without thought, for you are not ready for thought:
> So the darkness shall be the light, and the stillness the
>   dancing.

In the first half of this line we hear once again an echo of
Milton's *Samson*:

> O first created Beam, and thou great Word,
> Let there be light, and light was over all;
> Why am I thus bereav'd thy prime decree?

And in the concluding clause – 'And the stillness the dancing',
another echo of Sir Thomas Elyot of Coker: 'There daunseth to
gether a man and a woman, holding eche other by the hande or
the arme, which betokeneth concorde.'

To recover purity of vision, which must not be regarded as
hopelessly lost, we must learn from nature the need of under-
going

> the agony
> Of death and birth

– that is to say 'rebirth' – a return through the agony of death
(near at hand for 'old men') to 'the beginning', 'the intuition of
pure being'. The way to this, according to Eliot, is St John of
the Cross's *Dark Night of the Soul* as we have it explained in
the concluding lines of section III:

> In order to arrive there,
> To arrive where you are, to get from where you are not,
> You must go by a way wherein there is no ecstasy.
> In order to arrive at what you do not know
> You must go by a way which is the way of ignorance.

And it is clear that Eliot wants the source of these lines to be
readily recognizable in order that his reference may enjoy the
advantage of all the accumulated commentary and explanation
linked to St John of the Cross's mystical philosophy. We can
see this from the closeness with which he makes them echo a
translation of the saint's own words:

> — In order to arrive at having pleasure in everything,
> Desire to have pleasure in nothing . . .
> — In order to arrive at a knowledge of everything,
> Desire to know nothing.
> — In order to arrive at that wherein thou hast no pleasure,

Thou must go by a way wherein thou hast no pleasure.
— In order to arrive at that which thou knowest not,
Thou must go by a way that thou knowest not.
— In order to arrive at that which thou possessest not,
Thou must go by a way that thou possessest not.
— In order to arrive at that which thou art not,
Thou must go through that which thou art not.

This is clearly not defeatism or apathy. Nor is it a philosophy of escape such as so many critics are constantly seeing in Eliot's writings. To these, Agatha, in Eliot's *Family Reunion* (part II, scene ii), has already replied in her answer to Amy's taunt – 'So you *will* run away':

> In a world of fugitives
> The person taking the opposite direction
> Will appear to run away.

Stonier, in his review of 'East Coker', writes that Eliot 'having abjured ecstasy, allows himself to fall into a mental trance'. What Eliot actually advocates is far from an apathetic passivity. In *Ash Wednesday* he prayed

> Teach us to care and not to care
> Teach us to sit still.

But 'to sit still' in the sense advocated by St John as a necessary step to spiritual purgation. For Eliot feels with St John of the Cross that we must undergo not only the mortification of the flesh by *The Ascent of Mount Carmel* but also the trial of *The Dark Night of the Soul*, before we can hope for that perfect union of the soul with God in love, and for the divinization of all our faculties described by St John of the Cross in *The Spiritual Canticle* and *The Living Flame of Love*.

Then in summing up his conclusions from the advocated approach of St John of the Cross, Eliot returns in the last three lines of section III to Heraclitus, 'The Dark' – the unity of opposition, the harmony of strife:

> And what you do not know is the only thing you know
> And what you own is what you do not own
> And where you are is where you are not.

For among the Heraclitean fragments we read: 'The unlike is joined together, and from differences, results most beautiful harmony, and all things take place by strife' (XLVI).

It is this Heraclitean note combined with echoes of the seventeenth-century English metaphysical poets which will characterize the entire following section of the poem.

IV

There, in the opening lines, the poet sees Christ, with His hands bleeding from the nail wounds, as the wounded surgeon in a similar light to that in which Pascal sees Him: 'Jesus suffers in His passions the torments which men inflict on Him; but in His agony He suffers the torments He inflicts on Himself. (*Pensées*, no. 552.) And at the same time in these lines we have another echo of Heraclitus: 'The physicians, therefore . . . cutting and cauterizing, and in every way torturing the sick, complain that the patients do not pay them fitting reward for thus effecting these benefits – and sufferings' (LVIII).

The soul, according to St John of the Cross, during *The Dark Night* is 'under medical treatment for the recovery of its health, which is God Himself'. The steel that questions the distempered part is God's love; for, as St John of the Cross describes it in *The Living Flame of Love*: 'the soul will be conscious of an assault upon it made by a seraph armed with a dart of most enkindled love, which will pierce the soul . . .'. Still the compassion of the Surgeon is always evident. For the soul 'amidst these gloomy and loving pains, is conscious of a certain companionship and inward strength which attends upon it' (*The Dark Night of the Soul*).

'Our only health is our disease' since the soul must suffer 'that it may become meet for the divine love'. The constant care of God 'is not to please', 'for as God sets the soul in this dark night to the end that He may quench and purge its sensual desire, He allows it not to find attraction or sweetness in anything whatsoever.'

Furthermore, 'To be restored, our sickness must grow worse'

for only through the most complete suffering can we hope for complete purgation.

Throughout all these stanzas we see the Heraclitean play of opposites persevering. But an echo which this line brings up gives us another key to the undercurrent thought of this section: the vital need to put aside the blinding, confining interests of the body and of the world. For here, rhythm and figures both are clearly intended to recall those of Marvell's 'A Dialogue between the Soul and the Body' in which the soul complains of its imprisonment in the confining flesh:

> *Soul.* O Who shall, from this Dungeon, raise
> A Soul inslav'd so many wayes? . . .
> Here blinded with an Eye; and there
> Deaf with the drumming of an Ear . . .
> Constrain'd not only to indure
> Diseases, but what's worse, the Cure:
> And ready oft the Port to gain
> Am Shipwrackt into Health again.

'The whole earth is our hospital endowed by the ruined millionaire', Adam, with original sin. As T. E. Hulme put it in a passage quoted by T. S. Eliot in his introduction to Baudelaire's *Journaux Intimes*, 'in the light of these absolute values, man himself is judged to be essentially limited and imperfect. He is endowed with Original Sin.'

The cure is a fever cure – through the fever of love which is kindled in burning away impurities until the ascending chill will bring a calm similar to that which will be brought into the world by

> that destructive fire
> Which burns before the ice-cap reigns.

The purgation must grow from a purgation of the flesh to a purgation of the mind.

> The chill ascends from feet to knees,
> The fever sings in mental wires.

We are reminded of the 'trilling wires of the blood' in 'Burnt Norton'. But here the experience has to do with the spirit rather than with the flesh. And we remember that Eliot feels that 'the great mistake made about Christianity is to suppose it primarily a religion and emotion when it is primarily dogma and intellectual' (*The Idea of a Christian Society*).

Suffering is the basis of our cure – a penitential suffering and a thorough period of trial. We try constantly to blind ourselves to the need for humility and penance with notions of the importance of man and with materialistic emphases –

> we like to think
> That we are sound, substantial flesh and blood

– but at bottom we recognize the necessity of penance, and the fact that even our own penance would be feeble without the divine atonement made by Christ on our behalf. This is the reason that we 'call this Friday good' – the day on which the anniversary of Christ's sufferings is observed. And just as we saw Eliot in *Ash Wednesday* commemorating a victory over the temptation in the wilderness and announcing his spiritual entrance upon a penitential period, this Good Friday note in 'East Coker' celebrates the culmination of suffering and purgation, and an anticipation of the Resurrection to the light.

v

So now the poet feels, 'here I am, in the middle way', returning to his earlier echo of 'nel mezzo del cammin'. He feels lost in the dark wood

> having had twenty years –
> Twenty years largely wasted, the years of *l'entre deux guerres* –
> Trying to learn to use words.

He has come to feel with Pico della Mirandola, one of the exemplars of his precursor, Sir Thomas Elyot, that:

We shall live for ever, not in the school of word-catchers, but in the circle of the wise, where they talk not of the mother of Andromache or of the sons of Niobe, but of the deeper causes of things human and divine; he who looks closely will see that even the barbarians had intelligence not on the tongue, but in the breast.

In 'Burnt Norton' Eliot had already expressed a similar sentiment:

> Words move, music moves
> Only in time; but that which is only living
> Can only die. Words, after speech, reach
> Into the silence.

But, in the opening chorus of *The Rock*,

> The endless cycle of idea and action,
> Endless invention, endless experiment,
> Brings knowledge of motion, but not of stillness;
> Knowledge of speech, but not of silence;
> Knowledge of words, and ignorance of the Word.

Again in 'Burnt Norton':

> Only by the form, the pattern,
> Can words or music reach
> The stillness, as a Chinese jar still
> Moves perpetually in its stillness . . .

Today the poet has come to realize that each venture in 'trying to learn to use words' is merely

> a new beginning, a raid on the inarticulate
> With shabby equipment always deteriorating
> In the general mess of imprecision of feeling,
> Undisciplined squads of emotion.

He feels with Heraclitus that 'It is a weariness to labour at the same things and to be always beginning afresh' (LXXXII).

Emotion in Eliot's opinion is primarily a contributor of confusion. In *The Idea of a Christian Society* we read, 'It is not enthusiasm, but dogma, that differentiates a Christian from a pagan society.' And Eliot feels with T. E. Hulme, whom he quotes substantially in the closing paragraph of his preface to Baudelaire's *Journaux Intimes*, that a man 'can only accomplish anything of value by discipline – ethical and poetical. Order is thus not merely negative, but creative and liberating. Institutions are necessary.' Emotion upsets order. The lack of order, or discipline overwhelmed by emotion, only throws us back into 'the general mess of imprecision of feeling'. Whenever and wherever this occurs, according to Eliot, ground is lost.

> What there is to conquer
> By strength and submission, has already been discovered
> Once or twice, or several times, by men whom one cannot
> hope
> To emulate . . .

Or in Heraclitus' words: 'Much learning does not teach one to have understanding, else it would have taught Hesiod and Pythagoras, and again Xenophanes and Hecataeus' (LVI).

> There is only the fight to recover what has been lost
> And found and lost again and again: and now, under conditions
> That seem unpropitious. But perhaps neither gain nor loss.
> For us, there is only the trying. The rest is not our business.

Humility outweighs individualism and material achievement. In the end it is only 'the still point' of which 'Burnt Norton' spoke which matters.

> there the dance is,
> But neither arrest nor movement. And do not call it fixity.
> . . . Except for the point, the still point,
> There would be no dance, and there is only the dance.
> I can only say, *there* we have been: but I cannot say where.
> And I cannot say, how long, for that is to place it in time.

With the opening line of the second half of section v we have a restatement of the main theme in a new wording, 'Home is where one starts from'. But

> As we grow older
> The world becomes stranger, the pattern more complicated
> Of dead and living. Not the intense moment
> Isolated, with no before and after,
> But a lifetime burning in every moment

> And not the lifetime of one man only
> But of old stones that cannot be deciphered.

We are assailed increasingly by distractions and interests of the world about us, whereas

> Love is most nearly itself
> When here and now cease to matter.

'Old men ought to be explorers': they should not be satisfied with the world at hand, but be ready to 'put off the old man and put on the new'. Whether we are 'Here or there does not matter' – for love, according to St John of the Cross, 'is like a fire, which ever ascends, hastening to be absorbed in the centre of its sphere' (*The Dark Night of the Soul*).

> We must be still and still moving
> Into another intensity
> For a further union, a deeper communion.

As Pascal urged (*Pensées*, no. 524) 'there must be feelings of humility, not from nature, but from penitence, not to rest in them, but to go on to greatness' –

> Through the dark cold and the empty desolation,
> The wave cry, the wind cry, the vast waters
> Of the petrel and the porpoise.

For, even now,

> Dawn points, and another day
> Prepares for heat and silence. Out at sea the dawn wind
> Wrinkles and slides.

> 'In my end is my beginning.'

Curtis Bradford

FOOTNOTES TO
'EAST COKER'

MR JAMES JOHNSON SWEENEY, by his recent discussion of
'East Coker' in the *Southern Review*, has done a service to those
interested in Eliot. He has found the source of lines 28–33 in Sir
Thomas Elyot's *Boke named The Gouvernour*. He has shown the
influence of Eliot's reading of Heraclitus and of St John of the
Cross, writers to whom Eliot himself has called our attention in
the epigraphs to 'Sweeney Agonistes' and 'Burnt Norton'
respectively. There still remains much to be done before 'East
Coker' is as clear to us as *The Waste Land* or *Ash Wednesday*.
An elucidation of Eliot's images and of the chain of association
responsible for their arrangement is necessary to an understanding of any of his poems; Mr Sweeney does little with the images
and misses a good many links in the chain of association. He
often pushes parallels much further than they will go. Like Mr
Sweeney, I am only interested in understanding 'East Coker';
therefore I shall spend no time confuting his argument where I
think it weak. I shall attribute to him by his initials (JJS) all the
facts and interpretations which I borrow, and proceed to my own
explication of the poem. The full elucidation of a major poem by
Eliot comes only after the work of many commentators can be
combined; perhaps Mr Sweeney and I between us can make a
beginning.

Readers of Eliot's post-*Waste Land* poems have had to face
the fact that Eliot has been more and more drawing away from
the Renaissance tradition. While Eliot's technique grows easier
for the English reader, because based more directly on the
methods of the Elizabethans and the metaphysicals, his poems
become harder to understand. The influence even of Dante seems
since *Ash Wednesday* to have waned. 'Burnt Norton', 'East

Coker' and 'The Dry Salvages' require in particular some knowledge of Heraclitus and of St John of the Cross. The two aspects
of Heraclitus' philosophy which have particularly interested
Eliot are his conception of the experiential world as a constant
flux and his concern with the Logos as the single stable element
in the universe. The use of the Logos in the gospel of John ties
Heraclitus' teaching into Eliot's Christianity. Eliot calls attention to both aspects of Heraclitus in the epigraphs to 'Burnt
Norton'. Eliot himself gives very precise expression to the penitential method he has taken over from St John of the Cross in
lines 117–29 of 'Burnt Norton', and lines 112–28 and 134–47 of
'East Coker' (JJS). These general facts are necessary to an understanding of Eliot's later poetry, but not any very detailed knowledge of the books themselves. Altogether too much has been
made of Eliot's reading; the poems may yet disappear under the
bulk of documentation.

The title 'East Coker' names the town from which the Eliot
family emigrated to America, and to which during the course of
the poem another Eliot now returns. The visit may have been
real or imaginary, in either case it recalls to the poet an event in
his family history which was at once a beginning and an end. The
title, unlike the titles of *The Waste Land* and 'The Hollow Men',
does not call our attention to the main image in the poem. What
is this main image, or objective correlative? There are several and
they have all been made familiar to us by earlier poems. The
decay of western Europe (*Waste Land*, 'Hollow Men'), the idea
of purgation and penitence through the eclipse of earthly desires
(*Ash Wednesday*, 'Burnt Norton'), and the flux of appearances
('Burnt Norton'). Eliot has not needed a new correlative, for
'East Coker' is a summary and re-examination of ideas previously developed. There is no epigraph since 'East Coker'
requires no new knowledge of us. (The passage from Sir Thomas
Elyot need not be pinned down.)

I

Eliot has been playing with time in 'Burnt Norton', very much
as Mann, Joyce, and Virginia Woolf have for a long time been

playing with it. Lines 147–53 of the earlier poem prepare us for the opening of 'East Coker':

> Not the stillness of the violin, while the note lasts,
> Not that only, but the co-existence,
> Or say that the end precedes the beginning,
> And the end and the beginning were always there
> Before the beginning and after the end.
> And all is always now.

In accord with his practice since *Ash Wednesday* there is a protagonist, probably Eliot himself. At any rate we are in somebody's mind; the poem is in the first person. The protagonist has at the outset coalesced his existence in time, 'In my beginning is my end'. This we accept as an expression of how he feels; it is not something we must understand. Next comes an expression of the cyclical nature of all experience (JJS), whether of the individual or the race, which ends with man gone and the field-mouse in possession (the 'Gerontion' and *Waste Land* note). The decay of a house – the original Eliot house? – seems to start the whole chain of association. In the second stanza, after a restatement of the theme 'In my beginning is my end', the poet brings us to the here and now. The body of the stanza tells us that it is summer; the protagonist is in the country, standing in a lane and looking out over an open field. He has probably been visiting the onetime seat of his family. To the here and now the third stanza contrasts the Merrie England that was: the England which the Eliots left. Dancing figures from the long ago are reincarnated by the enchantment of midsummer night. Eliot has already in 'Burnt Norton' contracted life's whole fitful fever into the image 'dance'. We are made aware of Merrie England not by dates, but by the antique flavor of the spelling. (Eliot's chain of association was probably from 'dance' to the passage on dancing in Sir Thomas Elyot's book; Eliot's antique would of necessity be genuine.) These figures of enchantment have kept time, too. They are dead; the flux has rolled them under. They are particular examples of the general statements made in stanza one. We began in the late afternoon; have gone on to midnight. The first section closes with dawn, which traditionally ends midsummer night revelries, and which serves as well to bring us back to the present. The return to the present is marked by a single detail, the dawn wind at sea. The protagonist, having coalesced his existence in time, now expands his existence in space. 'I am here/ Or there, or elsewhere.' Then the refrain 'In my beginning'. He is involved in the flux he is describing.

II

It is now late November; late November historically speaking compared to the England that was (JJS), the late November time-of-life for the poet-protagonist (cf. 'Gerontion' and the 'aged eagle' of *Ash Wednesday*). Two lines of general statement are followed by a rush of details which takes us through the seasons from spring to winter (from snowdrops to roses filled with snow), and which links with section one by a reference to the dancers ('And creatures of the summer heat'). This leads by an easily followed chain of association to the cycle of the Universe. War in heaven, an echo of the present war, rushes the earth to the fire which shall burn out its present life before the second glacial age, a restatement in more general terms of the whole cyclical idea introduced into section one. This portion of the poem is in Eliot's earlier manner. We catch hints of 'Gerontion', *Waste Land*, *Ash Wednesday*; no particular parallels are intended, for when you run them down they add nothing to the meaning. In the stanza which follows, Eliot turns on this earlier manner. 'That was a way of putting it'; a way which he now finds unsatisfactory. He attacks the problem differently, first admitting that he himself has not found the 'Long hoped for calm, the autumnal serenity'. He inquires what the value of age is, and denies the common assumption that the old are wise. Every experience is so new that past experience does not help; the whole of life is a struggle through a dark wood. Old men are fools. They fear passion; they fear surrender (compare lines 95–6 with the dayadhvam–sympathize section of *The Waste Land*). Our only wisdom is the humility of *Ash Wednesday*. At the end the second is linked to the first section by a reference to 'houses' and 'dancers'.

III

The idea of humility is with Eliot associated with the extreme humility of the penitent during the dark night of the soul described by St John of the Cross; this association is the link between sections II and III. The darkness is first used in another way; the dark state of present-day European civilization is pictured. The now familiar flux of appearances returns; much has been whirled away and much more will go. There is a danger that we will all go too. After this statement of the *Waste Land* predicament, the protagonist returns. The darkness of present-day Europe has reminded him of the one hopeful darkness, the dark night of the soul (JJS and others):

> I said to my soul, be still, and let the dark come upon you
> Which shall be the darkness of God.

The poet is describing a mystical state, so he immediately helps us to understand it by three images: a theater darkened for a change of scenery, an underground train stopped between stations, and the activity of the mind under ether. After this attempt to describe quiescent waiting, the poet invokes it for his own soul in words close to St John of the Cross (JJS). Here 'all is always now', time ceases, and activity and quiet coalesce. We are carried back to the first section by similarity of idea with the refrain 'In my beginning is my end' and by a reference to dancing. At line 129 there follows a vignette which evokes all the charm of the world of the senses; it is very like the passage in *Ash Wednesday* beginning 'And the lost heart stiffens and rejoices'. Note a significant difference. There the charm of the sense world distracted the protagonist from the ascent of the mount of purgatory, because he was so recalled he was lost. Here the sense world is:

> Not lost, but requiring, pointing to the agony
> Of death and birth.

The poet acknowledges that he has said all this before (in *Ash Wednesday* and 'Burnt Norton'), but repeats it in a passage which paraphrases St John of the Cross very closely (JJS). Eliot is more difficult than the passage he copies. He seems to say that in order to save your soul you must rest in God with comp͜͜͜ humility. Lines 136–7 are particularly difficult:

> In order to arrive there,
> To arrive where you are, to get from where you are not . . .

Perhaps Eliot means: in order to get to real existence, to escape from non-existence –

IV

In the fourth section, finest in the poem, Eliot uses precise images to restate the less precise language of the section just concluded. He again pictures modern man waiting for salvation. Our plight is movingly and passionately described. Christ, the 'wounded surgeon', identified by the 'bleeding hands' of line 150, works over us (JJS); the Church, now a 'dying nurse', continues to remind us that we are mortal (God first told Adam he was death-bound when he expelled him from Eden) and must perish before we can be saved. Our indifference to Christianity is reflected in the key images 'wounded surgeon' and 'dying nurse'. We lie ill in a hospital of world-size, endowed by the bourgeois society of the last three hundred years (the 'ruined millionaire'); all we are here promised for the future is the maddening paternalism of the totalitarian state ('absolute paternal care'). It is only through suffering in this purgatory, purposive suffering, that we can be warmed by salvation. Here, experiencing a second war of world proportions in a single lifetime, man's whole experience is a horrid travesty of the holy communion ('The dripping blood our only drink, etc.'). The war involves all mankind in a collective sacrifice; it blots out nearly all the good in man, though this somehow persists obstinately. Our sacrifice must still, in spite of everything, remind us of Christ's sacrifice if we are ever to save ourselves ('in spite of that, we call this Friday good').

V

We turn in the final section back to the plight of the poet-protagonist. As an artist Eliot has struggled with words. The problem of the writer, who must make an art-medium out of words worn and battered by their daily use for every type of human intercourse from business letters to prayers, is feelingly stated. The poet realizes that what he is attempting to discover has already been discovered by Dante, Donne, and others – his masters. But he is not competing with them; he is only trying to recover the lost sense of man's spiritual possibilities. Conditions seem unpropitious, but at least the trying is something. 'Home is where one starts from'; our true home is the unknown from which we came and into which we go. As one grows older life becomes increasingly complicated, though certain ideals emerge. We should seek not the moment of individual passion, but a lifetime – a whole cycle – of spiritual passion. Passion anonymous and communal. There is a time for experience and a time for the quiet recollection of experience (starlight and photograph album). True love is spiritual, not temporal. Old men (note the return to section II) should be explorers; they must be still (compare *Ash Wednesday*, section VI) and at the same time be moving on:

> Into another intensity
> For a further union, a deeper communion

even though it must be through the coldness and emptiness of the contemporary world so movingly described in sections III and IV. As the poem is about to end with images of desolation, the poet recollects that his end, his death, is his true spiritual beginning. There has been a triumphant reversal of the statement with which the poem began (JJS).

(*Sewanee Review*, 1944)

'LITTLE GIDDING':
A DISAGREEMENT IN *SCRUTINY*

I

D. W. HARDING: 'We have not reached conclusion'

THE opening of the poem speaks of renewed life of unimaginable splendour, seen in promise amidst the cold decline of age. It offers no revival of life-processes; it is a spring time, 'But not in time's covenant'. If this 'midwinter spring' has such blooms as the snow on hedges,

> Where is the summer, the unimaginable
> Zero summer?

With the sun blazing on the ice, the idea of pentecostal fire, of central importance in the poem, comes in for the first time, an intense, blinding promise of life and (as later passages show) almost unbearable.

The church of Little Gidding introduces another theme of the poem. Anchored in time and space, but for some people serving as the world's end where they can fulfil a purpose outside time and space, it gives contact with spiritual concerns through earthly and human things.

A third theme, important for the whole poem, is also stated in the first section: that the present is able to take up, and even give added meaning to, the values of the past. Here too the pentecostal idea comes in:

> And what the dead had no speech for, when living,
> They can tell you, being dead: the communication
> Of the dead is tongued with fire beyond the language of the
> living.

Section II can be regarded as the *logical* starting-point of the whole poem. It deals with the desolation of death and the futility of life for those who have had no conviction of spiritual values in their life's work. First come three sharply organized riming stanzas to evoke, by image and idea but without literal statement, our sense of the hopeless death of air, earth, fire and water, seen not only as the elements of man's existence but as the means of his destruction and dismissal. The tone having been set by these stanzas, there opens a narrative passage describing the dreary bitterness in which a life of literary culture can end if it has brought no sense of spiritual values. The life presented is one, such as Mr Eliot's own, of effort after clear speech and exact thought, and the passage amounts to a shuddering 'There but for the grace of God go I'. It reveals more clearly than ever the articles in the *Criterion* did, years ago, what it was in 'humanism' that Mr Eliot recoiled from so violently. What the humanist's ghost sees in his life are futility, isolation, and guilt on account of his self-assertive prowess – 'Which once you took for exercise of virtue' – and the measure of aggression against others which that must bring.

The verse in this narrative passage, with its regular measure and insistent alliteration, so effective for combining the macabre with the urbane and dreary, is a way to indicate and a way to control the pressure of urgent misery and self-disgust. The motive power of this passage, as of so much of Mr Eliot's earlier poetry, is repulsion. But in the poem as a whole the other motive force is dominant: there is a movement of feeling and conviction outwards, reaching towards what attracts. The other parts of the poem can be viewed as working out an alternative to the prospect of life presented in this narrative.

Section III sees the foundation for such an alternative in the contact with spiritual values, especially as they appear in the tradition of the past. Detachment (distinguished from indifference) allows us to use both our own past and the historical past in such a way as to draw on their present spiritual significance for us without entangling us in regressive yearning for a pattern which no longer is:

> History may be servitude,
> History may be freedom. See, now they vanish,

The faces and places, with the self which, as it could, loved
 them,
To become renewed, transfigured, in another pattern.

Once we accept the significance of the spiritual motives and intentions of the past, even the factions connected with the church and community of Little Gidding leave us an inheritance; we can be at one with the whole past, including the sinning and defeated past, for its people were spiritually alive,

   All touched by a common genius,
   United in the strife which divided them.

But the humanist's fate cannot be escaped in so gentle and placid a way; a more formidable ordeal is waiting. In contrast to the leisurely meditation of section III, the fourth section is a forceful passage, close-knit with rime, and incisive. Its theme is the terrifying fierceness of the pentecostal experience, the dove bringing fire. This is not the fire of expiation, such as the humanist had to suffer. It is the consuming experience of love, the surrender to a spiritual principle beyond us, and the only alternative to consuming ourselves with the miserable fires of sin and error. This pentecostal ordeal must be met before the blinding promise seen in 'midwinter spring' can be accepted.

The final section develops the idea that every experience is integrated with all the others, so that the fulness of exploration means a return, with better understanding, to the point where you started. The theme has already been foreshadowed in section III where detachment is seen to give liberation from the future as well as the past, so that neither past nor future has any fascination of a kind that could breed in us a reluctance to accept the present fully.

The tyranny of sequence and duration in life is thus reduced. Time-processes are viewed as aspects of a pattern which can be grasped in its entirety at any one of its moments:

   The moment of the rose and the moment of the yew-tree
   Are of equal duration.

One effect of this view of time and experience is to rob the

moment of death of any over-significance we may have given it.
For the humanist of section II life trails off just because it can't
manage to endure. For the man convinced of spiritual values life
is a coherent pattern in which the ending has its due place and,
because it is part of a pattern, itself leads into the beginning. An
over-strong terror of death is often one expression of the fear of
living, for death is one of the life-processes that seem too terrifying to be borne. In examining one means of becoming reconciled to death, Mr Eliot can show us life too made bearable,
unfrightening, positively inviting:

> With the drawing of this Love and the voice of this
>   Calling

> We shall not cease from exploration
> And the end of all our exploring
> Will be to arrive where we started
> And know the place for the first time.

Here is the clearest expression of a motive force other than
repulsion. Its dominance makes this poem – to put it very
simply – far happier than most of Mr Eliot's.

Being reconciled to death and the conditions of life restores
the golden age of unfearful natural living and lets you safely,
without regression, recapture the wonder and easy rightness of
certain moments, especially in early childhood:

> At the source of the longest river
> The voice of the hidden waterfall
> And the children in the apple-tree
> Not known, because not looked for
> But heard, half-heard, in the stillness
> Between two waves of the sea.
> Quick now, here, now, always –
> A condition of complete simplicity
> (Costing not less than everything)

The whole of this last section suggests a serene and revitalized
return from meditation to one's part in active living. It includes
a reaffirmation of that concern with speech which has made up so

much of Mr Eliot's work and which could have been the bitter futility that it is for the ghostly humanist. The reaffirming passage (introduced as a simile to suggest the integrated patterning of all living experience) is an example of amazing condensation, of most comprehensive thinking given the air of leisured speech – not conversation but the considered speech of a man talking to a small group who are going to listen for a time without replying. It is one example of the intellectual quality of this poem. In most of Mr Eliot's poems the intellectual materials which abound are used emotionally. In much of this poem they are used intellectually, in literal statement which is to be understood literally (for instance, the opening of section III). How such statements become poetry is a question outside the range of this review. To my mind they do, triumphantly, and for me it ranks among the major good fortunes of our time that so superb a poet is writing.

•

II

R. N. HIGINBOTHAM: Objections to a review of 'Little Gidding'

THE review of 'Little Gidding' [by D. W. Harding] was an exposition, almost a paraphrase, but hardly a criticism, and crossed, I think, the line which separates the 'abeyance of the critical function' from its favourable exercise. Surely any reviewer should suspect his reactions when he can find nothing better to say than what his poet has already said better? Perhaps the last paragraph represented a hasty concession to the necessity of making some objective remark about the work. But even here, alas, the question raised was 'outside the range of this review'. That gives me a pretext to codify some disturbing impressions – not faked up *ad hoc* – about Mr Eliot's recent verse.

Mr Harding drew a distinction between the emotional and the intellectual use of intellectual material. One between emotional and intellectual material, each used intellectually, is more illuminating. Mr Eliot used to contemplate the conditions, of mind or affairs, which he wished to represent, from the outside, personifying such of himself as was relevant in some as it were dramatic character. He then represented what he saw by consciously assembling fragments of it intense enough to express all he left out. In this way he created poems both evocative and passionate. But at least since 'Burnt Norton' he has stopped being satisfied with the mere representation of conditions in isolation. He now finds them only properly understood or indeed significant when placed in a framework of more important and permanent truth. This is a natural development from earlier work obsessed by the meaninglessness of autonomous mood. But the significance of such qualifications of a condition can only be properly apprehended intellectually, syllogistically. Certainly they can be suffused with emotion, but the raw material is plain, logical argument. Now Mr Eliot's general method, of assembling intense fragments, has not changed. Since, however, many aspects of the conditions as he has come to represent them are thus intellectual, many of his fragments also must be intellectual. Furthermore they must be sufficiently powerful to stand the pressure generated by the emotional fragments.

His only hope of fulfilling this last necessity would be to feel what he thinks as intensely as he feels what he feels. Then the intellectual material would go about with him as constantly as the emotional and, like that, would pick up the diverse associations and occurrences which somehow make poetry. With certain exceptions, however, it has not done so. It lacks body, is thin. As for method, there is sometimes the crass, palpable expression of it which Mr Harding notes at the beginning of section III of 'Little Gidding'. In themselves such parts escape both censure and praise, except in so far as one may be interested in the skilful arrangement of unimportant rhythms and Mr Eliot's personal redistribution of emphasis among familiar arguments. But he is seldom so uncompromising with the blatancy of direct statement. Usually he resorts to symbols. But, since his intellectual material is not felt enough to be constantly with him and with the whole of him, it has insufficient background and body to produce spontaneous symbols. His symbols have to be thought up and clapped on. Again it is a matter of opinion: I myself cannot believe that these recurrent children in foliage, this silent music, these still dances, these gardens, these roses and yews which have their moments, these flames, that eternal wild thyme unseen and the useful, the universally adaptable, the good old sea, which figures so largely in the similes of our island race, are genuine and necessary expressions of a meaning. They are not existent enough and they are too uniform. They are a poeticising device, a private code, whose cyphers are often determined by the obsolete emotional associations attached to certain words in poetic convention. Kings at nightfall, for instance, really mean nothing; 'king' is a nice, emotive word; so is 'nightfall': that's all, that's all, that's all. Premiers at question-time would be more moving. Kings now can only impinge forcefully on a mind which is playing literary chess. Mr Eliot has even succumbed to the unselfconscious use of old phrases like 'the world's end'; of clichés like 'the enigma of the fever chart', 'transient beauty', 'worshippers of the machine'. Nothing is gained by such paraphrasing. The original meaning's effect is not widened but confined, forced into the compass of a stock-response. Often the meaning is lost; often it does not seem worth finding. Secondary effects of this artificiality are preciousness, disappearance of verbal evocativeness, vagueness and a continual groping after the elusive, with the one authentic word slipping through the enunciation. Finally the straining after effect causes an occasional portentousness, as though Mr Eliot were promulgating, rather than writing, verse: see the opening of sections I and V of 'The Dry Salvages'.

The melancholy of the failure is in the contrast with the successes. The most noteworthy success is the second part of section II of 'Little Gidding', applied to which Mr Harding's praises are accurate. There are others: 'Burnt Norton', most of section III, section IV; 'East Coker', most of section I, section II; 'The Dry Salvages', section II and section IV. They are all seen or felt; they are vivid, real, not existing in an impossible rose-shot, children-tinkled haze. Their material, in fact, is emotional, whereas the failures, as I have tried to show, are in attempts to use intellectual material.

The unevenness and lack of homogeneity in these four poems from 'Burnt Norton' onwards are therefore the result of disequilibrium in the author's feelings. If Mr Eliot's achievements were not so great and his seriousness not beyond question I should use the term 'insincerity' to describe the general effect.

III

F. R. LEAVIS: Reflections on the above

MR HIGINBOTHAM disagrees with D. W. Harding's critical estimate of 'Little Gidding': that is what he means when, ironically quoting me, he speaks of an 'abeyance of the critical function'. And his manner of expressing his disagreement commits him, I think, to an indefensibly restricted view of the ways in which that function may be performed. 'Surely', he asks, 'any reviewer should suspect his reactions when he can find nothing better to say than what his poet has already said better?' To bring out how much better the poet has said it is, of course, the whole point and the conscious critical purpose of Harding's elucidation, and that such elucidation has its essential part in the critical function where 'Little Gidding' and the companion poems are concerned Mr Higinbotham's own criticism serves, I think, to bring out, though the service this time is unintentional. (And Mr Higinbotham's views on Eliot, as a friend remarked to me, are probably shared by many people.)

A value-judgment can't, we all know, be demonstratively enforced; the critic can only attempt to help other readers to an approach by which, freed from inappropriate expectations and preconceptions and adverted as to the kind of thing they have in front of them, they will be able to *take* the poem – take it for what it is: the judging goes with the taking. Mr Higinbotham finds the meaning of 'Little Gidding' so obvious that he can't believe (one gathers) that any reader a critic need bother about will be grateful for such an elucidation as Harding's, and this alone would lead us to doubt the grounds of Mr Higinbotham's confidence ('what the poet has already said better') that he understands well enough what the poet has said. He goes on, of course, to complain that Harding leaves unanswered, having raised it, an important question about the working of the poem. And it is true that if Harding had been able to find the time, and had claimed the space, to elaborate that account of the working which the elucidation demands for its completion, his readers (or most of them) would have found even more cause for gratitude. But the reviewer of an interesting and complex work doesn't, in proposing for his review a limited scope, need to plead the pressure of wartime employments. There have been before in *Scrutiny* relevant discussions of Eliot's poetic methods, and no one who has read Harding's examination of 'Burnt Norton' in his review of *Collected Poems 1909–1935* (see *Scrutiny* for September 1936) is likely to suppose that when he pronounced the question about Eliot's use of intellectual materials to be 'outside the range' of his review of 'Little Gidding' it was because of any uncertainty as to how he would proceed to answer it.

Unfortunately he hasn't been able to contribute to this number of *Scrutiny* at all, and has had reluctantly to renounce the opportunity offered by Mr Higinbotham's letter of going further with the discussion of 'Little Gidding' and of the problems it raises. I myself have had no chance of discussing things with him; he hasn't seen my comments on Mr Higinbotham's criticism of Eliot's poetry, or been consulted about them, and what follows must be taken as coming from me, and me alone.

Mr Higinbotham, offering to correct and supplement Harding, gives his own account of the relation between the 'intellectual material' and the 'emotional' in these late poems of Eliot's. I am bound to say that in so doing he seems to me to show a complete failure to recognize the kind of organization the poems present, and an accompanying failure to appreciate the distinctive genius of the poet. Early in the first paragraph of his argument (the second of the letter) he pulls us up with: 'But at least since "Burnt Norton" he has stopped being satisfied with the mere representation of conditions in isolation.' It seems quite plain from the general context that we are not to take 'at least' as meant to qualify seriously the implication that up to 'Burnt Norton' the poet *was* satisfied with such mere representation. This implication will, I know, have surprised others as much as it surprised me. For some account of the way in which, from the first of the *Ash Wednesday* sequence onwards, Eliot's poems, so far from being preoccupied with 'conditions in isolation' or 'autonomous mood', are preoccupied with establishing, in a constructive exploration of experience, the apprehension of a reality in relation to which life in time has what meaning it can be made to yield, I may perhaps be allowed to refer back to *Scrutiny* for Summer last year. What Mr Higinbotham is constating is the notable presence in 'Burnt Norton' of 'intellectual materials' used, as the review of 'Little Gidding' puts it, intellectually. He thinks that any going beyond 'the mere representation of conditions in isolation' must depend upon such a presence – 'But the significance of such qualifications of a condition can only be properly apprehended intellectually, syllogistically'.

In taking over Harding's phrase, 'intellectual materials', Mr Higinbotham, unconsciously and significantly, gives its meaning a shift into another plane. Harding, in talking of 'materials', is thinking, not of something behind the text, but of what lies on the page before us, to be taken up by us, in the re-creative process of reading, into the organism of the realized poem. For Mr Higinbotham the 'materials' are what we deduce to be behind the text, they are in Mr Eliot and are what he tries, with very incomplete success, to make poetry out of. Or perhaps, it would be better to say that they are what were, on a kind of inner workman's bench, *before* him. A concomitant of this shift is the curious account we are offered of the relation between the two postulated kinds of 'material', the emotional and the intellectual ('each used intellectually'). The passage quoted in my last paragraph continues:

Certainly they can be suffused with emotion, but the raw material is plain, logical argument. Now Mr Eliot's general method, of assembling intense fragments, has not changed. Since,

however, many aspects of the conditions as he has come to represent them are thus intellectual, many of his fragments also must
be intellectual. Furthermore they must be sufficiently powerful to
stand the pressure generated by the emotional fragments.

In this way Mr Higinbotham faces the poet with a very difficult – in fact, an insoluble – problem. Here are the two different
stuffs, the separate rolls or sheets (so to speak), from which fragments have to be selected to go into the poem. The emotional
stuff is 'live' – poetically active, and the fragments carry with
them into the poem a charge derived from the context from
which they have been taken. In this way, though in itself non-
poetical, the intellect (for clearly we have to explain the 'intellectually' of 'emotional and intellectual material, each used intellectually' by correlating it with the 'consciously assembled' of the
sentence I am on the point of quoting) can work to poetic
effect – 'He then represented what he saw by consciously assembling fragments of it intense enough to express all he left out.
In this way he created poems both evocative and passionate.'
But what can the intellect do with the intellectual stuff, the
chosen fragments of which can carry from their context, of its
nature poetically inert, no charge with them?

Just how Mr Higinbotham conceives of this intellectual stuff,
this 'raw material' of 'plain, logical argument', I can't figure to
myself convincingly. Nor do I understand the relation between
thinking and feeling implied here:

His only hope of fulfilling this last necessity [that the intellectual fragments should 'be sufficiently powerful to stand the
pressure generated by the emotional fragments'] would be to feel
what he thinks as intensely as he feels what he feels. Then the
intellectual material would go about with him as constantly as
the emotional, and, like that, would pick up the diverse associations which somehow make poetry.

For the essential argument makes 'thinking' a matter pertaining
to an abstract realm that is insulated from concrete experience,
though the intellect is somehow able, across the insulating boundaries, to take cognizance of 'conditions' outside, and place them
'in a framework of more important and permanent truth' – a

framework the significance of which, one gathers, 'can only be properly apprehended intellectually, syllogistically'.

I shouldn't myself like to have to try and explain to a psychologist or a philosopher my own notions about the relations between 'thinking' and 'feeling', but my acquaintance with poetry as a literary critic is enough to convince me that I am justified in pronouncing Mr Higinbotham's account, in so far as one can gather it, inadequate to the facts. A literary critic can hardly fail to have given a great deal of attention to the problems raised by those two terms, 'thinking' and 'feeling', in company. He certainly can't have failed to do so if he has grappled with Eliot's later poetry, for there the poet's essential preoccupations entail, inseparably, a conscious preoccupation with those problems.

But the problem of inducing intellectual material to 'pick up the diverse associations and occurrences that somehow make poetry', so that fragments can go duly charged into the poem with a chance of holding their own against emotional fragments, coming from an emotional context, was provided by Mr Higinbotham. It is only if you suppose the poet to have been faced with it that you can judge him to have been beaten by it. The passages that Harding instances as exemplifying intellectual materials used intellectually are (I concur in his judgment) poetry because of their context, the poem as a whole – or rather, the sequence as a whole; because, that is, they belong to a vital organization. When Harding says the materials are used intellectually his appositional clause makes quite plain what he means: 'in literal statement which is to be understood literally'. That is, they demand to be taken as if we were for the moment reading a prose treatise, moral or philosophical. As if – but they have a force and a life that no treatise could have given them. Their context, instead of being one of statement and argument, is one that evokes concretely the living experience from which they emerge as the index and summary. We don't feel them as a matter of abstract thinking about or of; the presence in them of the concrete they focus and transmit is too immediate and commanding – if, that is, we have understood the organization and made ourselves capable of taking the poem. What in fact this poetry renders concretely is the exploratory process in which experience is ordered into significance – a process a good deal more inward and organically complex than that envisaged by Mr Higinbotham as being operated by the intellect on 'conditions in isolation' ('He now finds them only properly understood or indeed significant when placed in a framework of more important and permanent truth'). The way in which, in this poetry, intellectual formulation emerges from the experiential matrix clearly has general bearings, and a literary critic can't help believing that those whose business is with intellectual formulation, and those – psychologists or philosophers – whose business is to be interested in the nature of thought, must, if they achieve the approach, find themselves notably indebted to the genius of the poet.

Failing to achieve the approach Mr Higinbotham finds, not only that the passages of intellectual material are 'thin' and 'lack body', but that, since this material, not being felt enough by the poet, 'has insufficient background and body to produce spontaneous symbols', his 'symbols have to be thought up and clapped on'. In this way, a large proportion of the other-than-intellectual material is dismissed as not 'genuine and necessary expression of a meaning':

They are not existent enough and they are too uniform. They are a poeticizing device, a private code, whose cyphers are often determined by the obsolete emotional associations attached to certain words in poetic convention. Kings at nightfall, for instance, really mean nothing; 'king' is a nice, emotive word; so is 'nightfall': that's all, that's all, that's all. Premiers at question-time would be more moving.

This illustration brings home pretty forcibly with what insistence Mr Higinbotham reads the poem as an assemblage of fragments. He not only misses the wider and more recondite organization; he ignores the connections that for any reader, one would have thought, lie obvious on the page in view. Here is the phrase he objects to restored to its immediate context:

> If I think, again, of this place,
> And of people, not wholly commendable,
> Of no immediate kin or kindness,
> But some of peculiar genius,
> All touched by a common genius,
> United in the strife which divided them;
> If I think of a king at nightfall,
> Of three men, and more, on the scaffold
> And a few who died forgotten
> In other places, here and abroad,
> And of one who died blind and quiet,
> Why should we celebrate
> These dead men more than the dying?

The 'place', explicitly enough, is Little Gidding. The associated 'people', plainly, are of the seventeenth century, and so, equally plainly, are the figures in the rest of the sentence, and that one of them should be a king can surely be more naturally and convincingly explained than by invoking a blind need in the poet to clutch at a worn poetical property. These are particular figures of the past that have lodged in the poet's imagination – historic figures very relevant to the theme of the poem. And it will have been noted that the whole 'If I think' passage leads up to the question:

> Why should we celebrate
> These dead men more than the dying?

Even if for a reader who can't take the passage in its place in the whole organization the question has nothing like its due force, the explicit intention as given locally makes Mr Higinbotham's reaction look odd:

> It is not to ring the bell backward
> Nor is it an incantation
> To summon the spectre of a Rose,
>   etc.

For the reader who has, from 'Burnt Norton' on, taken the essential organization and development, the question has behind it that mercilessly resourceful process by which human and historic time is de-realized into a dismaying relativity and his habit-confident sense of present and past and reality routed – the process so disturbingly furthered, in 'The Dry Salvages', by that symbolic and evocative use of the sea to which Mr Higinbotham (in what looks to me like mere petulance) objects. Possessed by this consciousness of evanescence and insignificance, of not-being, why indeed should we celebrate these dead men more than the living (the 'dying') – why should we attribute to them more reality?

The force of the positive answer indicated by Harding is conditioned by the effect of the negative or solvent process. I can imagine it's being said that it depends upon it too much – that the poet creates a vacuum which the duly 'conditioned' reader is drawn in to fill too readily with the hints provided. But from the outset a positive creative process has accompanied the sapping, unsettling and dissolving – a process any account of which must be mainly an enlargement of Harding's account of the 'creation of concepts' in 'Burnt Norton'. I won't attempt such an enlargement here, or recapitulate what I offered last year in the Summer *Scrutiny*. I will merely suggest that Mr Higinbotham ponders the relations in 'Burnt Norton' between the proposition,

> Time past and time future
> What might have been and what has been
> Point to one end, which is always present,

the imagery of 'our first world', 'reality', 'the still point', 'the dance', 'consciousness', 'the form' and 'the pattern', and tries to grasp what kind of co-operation between all these (and a great deal else) is *intended* – a co-operation of which we are given a kind of clinching résumé in the closing section, with its culminating 'Quick now, here, now, always – '.

That he has not really tried is sufficiently shown, I think, by his dismissing 'transient beauty' in section III as a cliché – a reaction as betrayingly arbitrary as his reactions to 'kings at nightfall'. And what would he substitute for 'world's end' in 'Little Gidding'? Does he perhaps think that 'end of the world' means the same thing? If Eliot is to be judged guilty of a weak-

ness for clichés, then no poet who ever wrote can escape conviction. Of course, what we have here is not criticism, but a
patent expression of that curiously strong feeling which per-
vades the note as a whole. I remarked on this feeling to a friend
to whom I showed the note and he replied: 'I think a possible
explanation is that he's one of the many people who like their
poetry miserable. The passage he notes for praise bear this out.
After all, Eliot's earlier work was bound to have a strong appeal
for [people who go to poetry to indulge their sense of grievance
against things], and I can see that they would feel it is a final
outrage if *he* started turning happy on them.'

I ask Mr Higinbotham to believe that it is with my eye on the
'many people' that I quote this. In the general bearing of his
comment my friend was certainly right, and the point he makes
is an important one; it calls attention to another aspect of the
difficulty of Eliot's later poetry. This poetry is difficult by reason
of the discipline of self-knowledge and readjustment it imposes.
To deal with one's miseries in the manner indicated above is
comparatively easy, and it offers by way of satisfaction (at various
possible levels) a sense of superiority and a licence for a measure
of self-congratulation. It involves too the temptation to protect
oneself from effort with sanctioned and respectable clichés of
feeling and attitude. Eliot's later poetry exacts of the reader who
proposes to feel that he has mastered it a far more difficult
emotional and moral readjustment.

Such in fact is the demand under this head made by 'Little
Gidding' that few readers will be quick to feel that they are in a
position to render anything like a final account of what, for
them, the poem is and does. Harding's account seems to me
admirable – admirable in positive definition and admirable in its
patent awareness of the problems of concrete determination it
leaves the assenting reader with. A critical account of any poetry
can only point, or draw a line round. It must always be left to
each reader to grasp for himself what is concretely presented. In
the case of 'Little Gidding' the grasping must be a matter, not
only of much attentive re-reading of the whole sequence, but of
meditation and disciplined self-searching. That what we are

offered is worth these, and in what general ways, ought, I think, to be plain to any qualified reader of poetry who has seriously attempted the approach. But he will be a rare reader who does not go on feeling that he must re-read the whole, and question his experience, again and yet again. 'Detachment (distinguished from indifference)' – yes, one in a sense knows well enough what one ought to have there, though the having will clearly be more than a matter of reading a poem attentively. 'For the man convinced of spiritual values life is a coherent pattern in which the ending has its due place and because it is part of a pattern, itself leads into the beginning': 'the present is able to take up, and even give added meaning to, the values of the past': – just what corresponding to these phrases one actually grasps is a question that, in the stock-taking with which a reading tries to complete itself, leads one back again and again to a re-reading. The poetry and the question – the questions – have to be lived with.

(*Scrutiny*, 1943)

George Orwell

T. S. ELIOT

THERE is very little in Eliot's later work that makes any deep impression on me. That is a confession of something lacking in myself, but it is not, as it may appear at first sight, a reason for simply shutting up and saying no more, since the change in my own reaction probably points to some external change which is worth investigating.

I know a respectable quantity of Eliot's earlier work by heart. I did not sit down and learn it, it simply stuck in my mind as any passage of verse is liable to do when it has really rung the bell. Sometimes after only one reading it is possible to remember the whole of a poem of, say, twenty or thirty lines, the act of memory being partly an act of reconstruction. But as for these three latest poems, I suppose I have read each of them two or three times since they were published, and how much do I verbally remember? 'Time and the bell have buried the day', 'At the still point of the turning world', 'The vast waters of the petrel and the porpoise', and bits of the passage beginning 'O dark dark dark. They all go into the dark'. (I don't count 'In my end is my beginning', which is a quotation.) That is about all that sticks in my head of its own accord. Now one cannot take this as proving that 'Burnt Norton' and the rest are 'worse' than the more memorable early poems, and one might even take it as proving the contrary, since it is arguable that that which lodges itself most easily in the mind is the obvious and even the vulgar. But it is clear that something has departed, some kind of current has been switched off, the later verse does not *contain* the earlier, even if it is claimed as an improvement upon it. I think one is justified in explaining this by a deterioration in Mr Eliot's subject-matter. Before going any further, here are a couple of extracts, just near enough to one another in meaning to be comparable. The first is the concluding passage of 'The Dry Salvages':

> And right action is freedom
> From past and future also.
> For most of us, this is the aim
> Never here to be realised;
> Who are only undefeated
> Because we have gone on trying;
> We, content at the last
> If our temporal reversion nourish
> (Not too far from the yew-tree)
> The life of significant soil.

Here is an extract from a much earlier poem:

> Daffodil bulbs instead of balls
> Stared from the sockets of his eyes!
> He knew how thought clings round dead
>   limbs
> Tightening its lusts and luxuries.
>
> He knew the anguish of the marrow,
> The ague of the skeleton;
> No contact possible to flesh
> Allayed the fever of the bone.

The two passages will bear comparison since they both deal with the same subject, namely death. The first of them follows upon a longer passage in which it is explained, first of all, that scientific research is all nonsense, a childish superstition on the same level as fortune-telling, and then that the only people ever likely to reach an understanding of the universe are saints, the rest of us being reduced to 'hints and guesses'. The keynote of the closing passage is 'resignation'. There is a 'meaning' in life and also in death; unfortunately we don't know what it is, but the fact that it exists should be a comfort to us as we push up the crocuses, or whatever it is that grows under the yew-trees in country churchyards. But now look at the other two stanzas I have quoted. Though fathered onto somebody else, they probably express what Mr Eliot himself felt about death at that time, at least in certain moods. They are not voicing resignation. On the contrary, they are voicing the pagan attitude towards death, the belief in the next world as a shadowy place full of thin, squeaking ghosts, envious of the living, the belief that however bad life may be, death is worse. This conception of death seems to have been general in antiquity, and in a sense it is general now. 'The anguish of the marrow, the ague of the skeleton', Horace's famous ode *Eheu fugaces*, and Bloom's unuttered thoughts during Paddy Dignam's funeral, are all very much of a muchness. So long as man regards himself as an individual, his attitude towards death must be one of simple resentment. And however unsatisfactory this may be, if it is intensely felt it is more likely to produce good literature than a religious faith which is not really *felt* at all, but merely accepted against the emotional grain. So far as they can be compared, the two passages I have quoted seem to me to bear this out. I do not think it is questionable that the second of them is superior as verse, and also more intense in feeling, in spite of a tinge of burlesque.

What are these three poems, 'Burnt Norton', 'East Coker' and 'The Dry Salvages', 'about'? It is not so easy to say what they are about, but what they appear on the surface to be about is certain localities in England and America with which Mr Eliot has ancestral connections. Mixed up with this is a rather gloomy musing upon the nature and purpose of life, with the rather indefinite conclusion I have mentioned above. Life has a 'meaning', but it is not a meaning one feels inclined to grow lyrical about; there is faith, but not much hope, and certainly no enthusiasm. Now the subject-matter of Mr Eliot's early poems was very different from this. They were not hopeful, but neither were they depressed or depressing. If one wants to deal in antitheses, one might say that the later poems express a melancholy faith and the earlier ones a glowing despair. They were based on the dilemma of modern man, who despairs of life and does not want to be dead, and on top of this they expressed the horror of an over-civilised intellectual confronted with the ugliness and spiritual emptiness of the machine age. Instead of 'not too far

from the yew-tree' the keynote was 'weeping, weeping multi-
tudes', or perhaps 'the broken fingernails of dirty hands'.
Naturally these poems were denounced as 'decadent' when they
first appeared, the attacks only being called off when it was
perceived that Eliot's political and social tendencies were reactionary. There was, however, a sense in which the charge of
'decadence' could be justified. Clearly these poems were an end-
product, the last gasp of a cultural tradition, poems which spoke
only for the cultivated third-generation rentier, for people able
to feel and criticise but no longer able to act. E. M. Forster praised
'Prufrock', on its first appearance because 'it sang of people who
were ineffectual and weak' and because it was 'innocent of public
spirit' (this was during the other war, when public spirit was
a good deal more rampant than it is now). The qualities by which
any society which is to last longer than a generation actually has
to be sustained – industry, courage, patriotism, frugality, philo-
progenitiveness – obviously could not find any place in Eliot's
early poems. There was only room for rentier values, the values
of people too civilised to work, fight or even reproduce themselves. But that was the price that had to be paid, at any rate at
that time, for writing a poem worth reading. The mood of lassi-
tude, irony, disbelief, disgust, and not the sort of beefy enthusiasm demanded by the Squires and Herberts, was what sensitive
people actually felt. It is fashionable to say that in verse only the
words count and the 'meaning' is irrelevant, but in fact every
poem contains a prose-meaning, and when the poem is any good
it is a meaning which the poet urgently wishes to express. All art
is to some extent propaganda. 'Prufrock' is an expression of
futility, but it is also a poem of wonderful vitality and power,
culminating in a sort of rocket-burst in the closing stanzas:

> I have seen them riding seaward on the waves
> Combing the white hair of the waves blown back
> When the wind blows the water white and black.
>
> We have lingered in the chambers of the sea
> By sea-girls wreathed with seaweed red and brown,
> Till human voices wake us, and we drown.

There is nothing like that in the later poems, although the rentier despair on which these lines are founded has been consciously dropped.

But the trouble is that conscious futility is something only for the young. One cannot go on 'despairing of life' into a ripe old age. One cannot go on and on being 'decadent', since decadence means falling and one can only be said to be falling if one is going to reach the bottom reasonably soon. Sooner or later one is obliged to adopt a positive attitude towards life and society. It would be putting it too crudely to say that every poet in our time must either die young, enter the Catholic Church, or join the Communist Party, but in fact the escape from the consciousness of futility is along those general lines. There are other deaths besides physical death, and there are other sects and creeds besides the Catholic Church and the Communist Party, but it remains true that after a certain age one must either stop writing or dedicate oneself to some purpose not wholly aesthetic. Such a dedication necessarily means a break with the past:

> every attempt
> Is a wholly new start, and a different kind of failure
> Because one has only learnt to get the better of words
> For the thing one no longer has to say, or the way in which
> One is no longer disposed to say it. And so each venture
> Is a new beginning, a raid on the inarticulate
> With shabby equipment always deteriorating
> In the general mess of imprecision of feeling,
> Undisciplined squads of emotion.

Eliot's escape from individualism was into the Church, the Anglican Church as it happened. One ought not to assume that the gloomy Pétainism to which he now appears to have given himself over was the unavoidable result of his conversion. The Anglo-Catholic movement does not impose any political 'line' on its followers, and a reactionary or austro-fascist tendency had always been apparent in his work, especially his prose writings. In theory it is still possible to be an orthodox religious believer without being intellectually crippled in the process; but it is far from easy, and in practice books by orthodox believers usually

show the same cramped, blinkered outlook as books by orthodox Stalinists or others who are mentally unfree. The reason is
that the Christian churches still demand assent to doctrines which
no one seriously believes in. The most obvious case is the immortality of the soul. The various 'proofs' of personal immortality which can be advanced by Christian apologists are psychologically of no importance; what matters, psychologically, is that
hardly anyone nowadays *feels* himself to be immortal. The next
world may be in some sense 'believed in' but it has not anywhere
near the same actuality in people's minds as it had a few centuries ago. Compare for instance the gloomy mumblings of these
three poems with 'Jerusalem my happy home'; the comparison is
not altogether pointless. In the second case you have a man to
whom the next world is as real as this one. It is true that his
vision of it is incredibly vulgar – a choir practice in a jeweller's
shop – but he believes in what he is saying and his belief gives
vitality to his words. In the other case you have a man who does
not really *feel* his faith, but merely assents to it for complex
reasons. It does not in itself give him any fresh literary impulse.
At a certain stage he feels the need for a 'purpose', and he wants
a 'purpose' which is reactionary and not progressive; the immediately available refuge is the Church, which demands intellectual absurdities of its members; so his work becomes a continuous nibbling round those absurdities, an attempt to make
them acceptable to himself. The Church has not now any living
imagery, any new vocabulary to offer:

> the rest
> Is prayer, observance, discipline, thought and action.

Perhaps what we need is prayer, observance, etc., but you do not
make a line of poetry by stringing those words together. Mr
Eliot speaks also of

> the intolerable wrestle
> With words and meanings. The poetry does not matter.

I do not know, but I should imagine that the struggle with meanings would have loomed smaller, and the poetry would have
seemed to matter more, if he could have found his way to some

creed which did not start off by forcing one to believe the incredible.

There is no saying whether Mr Eliot's development could have been much other than it has been. All writers who are any good develop throughout life, and the general direction of their development is determined. It is absurd to attack Eliot, as some left-wing critics have done, for being a 'reactionary' and to imagine that he might have used his gifts in the cause of democracy and Socialism. Obviously a scepticism about democracy and a disbelief in 'progress' are an integral part of him; without them he could not have written a line of his works. But it is arguable that he would have done better to go much further in the direction implied in his famous 'Anglo-Catholic and Royalist' declaration. He could not have developed into a Socialist, but he might have developed into the last apologist of aristocracy.

Neither feudalism nor indeed Fascism is necessarily deadly to poets, though both are to prose-writers. The thing that is really deadly to both is Conservatism of the half-hearted modern kind.

It is at least imaginable that if Eliot had followed whole-heartedly the anti-democratic, anti-perfectionist strain in himself he might have struck a new vein comparable to his earlier one. But the negative Pétainism which turns its eyes to the past, accepts defeat, writes off earthly happiness as impossible, mumbles about prayer and repentance and thinks it a spiritual advance to see life as 'a pattern of living worms in the guts of the women of Canterbury' – that, surely, is the least hopeful road a poet could take.

(A review of 'Burnt Norton', 'East Coker' and 'Dry Salvages' in *Poetry London,* 1942)

F. O. Matthiessen

THE QUARTETS

a white light still and moving.

IN the course of an artist's development certain phases may detach themselves and challenge comprehension as completed wholes. Eliot rounded out such a cycle with 'Little Gidding' (1942), and we are now able to see the full significance of the experiments with structure which he inaugurated in 'Burnt Norton' eight years previously. He speaks of the four poems which form this cycle as 'quartets', and has evolved for them all the same kind of sequence of five parts with which he composed 'Burnt Norton'. *The Waste Land* was also composed in this fashion, but the contrast is instructive. In his earlier desire for intense concentration the poet so eliminated connectives that *The Waste Land* might be called an anthology of the high points of a drama. It was as though its author had determined to make his poem of nothing but Arnold's 'touchstones', or had subscribed to Poe's dictum that no longer poem could exist than one to be read at a sitting. In the intervening years Eliot has given further thought to the problem, and he has recently concluded that 'in a poem of any length there must be transitions between passages of greater and lesser intensity, to give rhythm of fluctuating emotion essential to the musical structure of the whole'. He has also enunciated 'a complementary doctrine' to that of Arnold's 'touchstones': the test of a poet's greatness by 'the way he writes his less intense but structurally vital matter'.

None of the four quartets is much more than half as long as *The Waste Land*, but he has included in them all transitional passages that he would previously have dismissed as 'prosaic'. His fundamentally altered intention is at the root of the matter. The dramatic monologues of Prufrock or Gerontion or of the

various *personae* of *The Waste Land* have yielded to gravely
modulated meditations of the poet's own. The vivid situations
of his *Inferno* have been followed by the philosophic debates of
his *Purgatorio*. He has made quite explicit the factors condition-
ing his new structures in the essay from which I have just quoted
'The Music of Poetry'. As is always the case with Eliot, this
essay throws the most relevant light upon his poetic intentions,
and is thus a further piece of refutation to those who persist in the
fallacy that there is no harmony between his 'revolutionary'
creative work and his 'traditionalist' criticism.

Looking back now over the past generation, he finds the
poetry of our period to be best characterized by its 'search for a
proper modern colloquial idiom'. He develops the same theme
near the close of 'Little Gidding' where he envisages the right
equilibrium between 'the common word' and 'the formal word'.
Only through their union of opposites do we get 'The complete
consort dancing together'. Eliot, no less than the later Yeats, has
helped to restore to poetry the conversational tones which had
been muffled by the ornamental forms and diction of the end of
the century. But now Eliot is thinking of the other partner to the
union, and remarks that 'when we reach a point at which the
poetic idiom can be stabilized, then a period of musical elabora-
tion can follow'. Just as Donne, in his later work, returned to the
formal pattern of the sonnet which he had mocked in the broken
rhythms of his early lyrics, so Eliot now believes that there is
such a 'tendency to return to set, and even elaborate patterns'
after any period when they have been laid aside.

The present phase of his own return seems to have started
with 'New Hampshire' and 'Virginia', the short musical evocations which grew out of his renewed impressions of America in
the early 1930s. The impulse to write a series of such place-
name poems led on in turn to the more ambitious 'Burnt Norton', which borrows its title from a Gloucestershire manor near
which Eliot has stayed. The titles of the other three quartets
indicate more intimate relationships: East Coker, in Somerset,
is where the Eliot family lived until its emigration in the
mid-seventeenth century to the New England coast; the Dry

Salvages, a group of rocks off Cape Ann, mark the part of that coast which the poet knew best as a boy; Little Gidding, the seat of the religious community which Nicholas Ferrar established and with which the names of George Herbert and Crashaw are associated, is a shrine for the devout Anglican, but can remind the poet also that 'History is now and England'.

The rhythmical pattern of 'Burnt Norton' is elaborated far beyond the delicate melodies of the brief 'Landscapes'. Eliot seems to have found in the interrelation of its five parts a type of structure which satisfied him beyond his previous experiments. For he has adhered to it with such remarkably close parallels in the three succeeding quartets that a description of the structure of one of them involves that of all, and can reveal the deliberateness of his intentions. In each case the first part or movement might be thought of as a series of statements and counterstatements of a theme in lines of an even greater irregularity than those of the late Jacobean dramatists. In each of these first movements a 'landscape' or presented scene gives a concrete core around which the poet's thoughts gather.

The second movement opens with a highly formal lyric: in 'The Dry Salvages' this is a variant of a sestina, rising from the clang of the bell buoy; in 'Little Gidding' each of the three eight-line stanzas ends with a refrain – and thus does Eliot signalize his own renewal of forms that would have seemed played out to the author of 'Prufrock'. In the other two poems he has also illustrated a remark which he has been repeating in his recent essays, that 'a poem, or a passage of a poem, may tend to realize itself first as a particular rhythm before it reaches expression in words'. The lyric in 'Burnt Norton' – which is echoed perhaps too closely in 'East Coker' – is as pure musical incantation as any Eliot has written. Not only does its opening image, 'Garlic and sapphires in the mud', take its inception from Mallarmé's line 'Tonnerre et rubis aux moyeux'; but the rhythm of the poem in which that line occurs, 'M'introduire dans ton histoire', seems also to have haunted Eliot's ear until it gave rise to a content which, with the exception of its opening line, is wholly different from Mallarmé's.

Following the lyric in the second movement, Eliot has relaxed
his rhythms for a sudden contrast; and in 'The Dry Salvages',
and especially in 'East Coker', has carried his experiment with
the prosaic virtually over the border into prose:

> That was a way of putting it – not very satisfactory:
> A periphrastic study in a worn-out poetical fashion,
> Leaving one still with the intolerable wrestle
> With words and meanings. The poetry does not matter.
> It was not (to start again) what one had expected.

The sharp drop from incantation is designed to have the virtue
of surprise; but it would seem here to have gone much too far,
and to have risked the temporary collapse of his form into the
flatness of a too personal statement. The variant in 'Little Gidding' substitutes for such a sequence a modified *terza rima*, where
the poet uses instead of rhyme a sustained alternation of masculine and feminine endings, in a passage that makes the strong-
est testimony for the value of formal congruence.

What the third parts have in common is that each is an account
of movement. In 'Burnt Norton' it is a descent into the London
Underground, which becomes also a descent into the dark
night of the soul. In 'East Coker' the allusion to St John of the
Cross is even more explicit. The poet's command to his soul to

> be still, and wait without hope,
> For hope would be hope for the wrong thing,

borrows its sequence of paradoxes directly from the text of the
sixteenth-century Spanish mystic. In 'The Dry Salvages' where
the concluding charge is

> Not fare well
> But fare forward, voyagers,

the doctrine of action beyond thought of self-seeking is, again
explicitly, what Krishna urged to Arjuna on the field of battle;
and we recall Eliot's remarking, in his essay on Dante, that 'the
next greatest philosophical poem' to *The Divine Comedy* within
his experience was the *Bhagavad-Gita*. In 'Little Gidding' the
passage of movement is the *terza rima* passage at the close of the
second part, and the deliberately prosaic lines open the third

section. The movement described is the 'dead patrol' of two air-raid wardens.

The versification in these third parts is the staple for the poems as a whole, a very irregular iambic line with many substitutions, of predominantly four or five beats, but with syllables ranging from six to eighteen. The fourth movement, in every case, is a short lyric, as it was in *The Waste Land*. The fifth movement is a resumption and resolution of themes, and becomes progressively more intricate in the last two poems, since the themes are cumulative and are all brought together at the close of 'Little Gidding'.

It seems doubtful whether at the time of writing 'Burnt Norton', just after *Murder in the Cathedral*, Eliot had already projected the series. His creative energies for the next three years were to be largely taken up with *The Family Reunion*, which, to judge from the endless revisions in the manuscript, caused him about as much trouble as anything he has done. With 'East Coker' in the spring of 1940 he made his first experiment in a part for part parallel with an earlier work of his own. Again Donne's practice is suggestive: when he had evolved a particularly intricate and irregular stanza, he invariably set himself the challenge of following it unchanged to the end of his poem. But in assigning himself a similar problem for a poem two hundred lines long, Eliot has tried something far more exacting, where failure could be caused by the parallels becoming merely mechanical, and by the themes and rhythms becoming not subtle variations but flat repetitions. 'East Coker' does indeed have something of the effect of a set piece. Just as its high proportion of prosaic lines seems to spring from partial exhaustion, so its resumption of themes from 'Burnt Norton' can occasionally sound as though the poet was merely imitating himself. But on the whole he had solved his problem. He had made a renewal of form that was to carry him successively in the next two years through 'The Dry Salvages' and 'Little Gidding'. The discrimination between repetition and variation lies primarily in the rhythm; and these last two poems reverberate with an increasing musical richness.

A double question that keeps insisting itself through any discussion of these structures is the poet's consciousness of analogies with music, and whether such analogies are a confusion of arts. One remembers that Eliot, in accepting Lawrence's definition of 'the essence of poetry' as a 'stark, bare, rocky directness of statement', drew an analogy with the later quartets of Beethoven. This does not mean that he has ever tried to copy literally the effects of a different medium. But he knows that poetry is like music in being a temporal rather than a spatial art; and he has by now thought much about the subject, as the concluding paragraph of 'The Music of Poetry' shows:

I think that a poet may gain much from the study of music: how much technical knowledge of musical form is desirable I do not know, for I have not that technical knowledge myself. But I believe that the properties in which music concerns the poet most nearly, are the sense of rhythm and the sense of structure. I think that it might be possible for a poet to work too closely to musical analogies: the result might be an effect of artificiality.

But he insists – and this has immediate bearing on his own intentions – that 'the use of recurrent themes is as natural to poetry as to music'. He has worked on that assumption throughout his quartets, and whether he has proved that 'there are possibilities of transitions in a poem comparable to the different movements of a symphony or a quartet', or that 'there are possibilities of contrapuntal arrangement of subject-matter', can be known only through repeated experience of the whole series. All I wish to suggest here is the pattern made by some of the dominant themes in their interrelation and progression.

'Burnt Norton' opens as a meditation on time. Many comparable and contrasting views are introduced. The lines are drenched with reminiscences of Heraclitus' fragments on flux and movement. Some of the passages on duration remind us that Eliot listened to Bergson's lectures at the Sorbonne in the winter of 1911 and wrote an essay then criticizing his *durée réelle* as 'simply not final'. Other lines on the recapture of time through consciousness suggest the aspect of Bergson that most stimulated Proust. But the chief contrast around which Eliot constructs this poem is that between the view of time as a mere continuum, and the difficult paradoxical Christian view of how man lives both 'in and out of time', how he is immersed in the flux and yet can penetrate to the eternal by apprehending timeless existence within time and above it. But even for the Christian the moments of release from the pressures of the flux are rare, though they alone redeem the sad wastage of otherwise unillumined existence. Eliot recalls one such moment of peculiar poignance, a childhood moment in the rose-garden – a symbol he has previously used, in many variants, for the birth of desire. Its implications are intricate and even ambiguous, since they raise the whole problem of how to discriminate between supernatural vision and mere illusion. Other variations here on the theme of how time is conquered are more directly apprehensible. In dwelling on the extension of time into movement, Eliot takes up an image he had used in 'Triumphal March': 'at the still point of the turning world'. This notion of 'a mathematically pure point' (as Philip Wheelwright has called it) seems to be Eliot's poetic equivalent in our cosmology for Dante's 'unmoved Mover', another way of symbolising a timeless release from the 'outer compulsions' of the world. Still another variation is the passage on the Chinese jar in the final section. Here Eliot, in a conception comparable to Wallace Stevens' 'Anecdote of the Jar', has suggested how art conquers time:

> Only by the form, the pattern,
> Can words or music reach
> The stillness, as a Chinese jar still
> Moves perpetually in its stillness.

'Burnt Norton' is the most philosophically dense of the series, and any adequate account of Eliot's development of his themes would demand detailed analysis. With the opening phrase of 'East Coker', 'In my beginning is my end', he has extended his meditation on time into history. In such a phrase, which is close to Heraclitus' 'The beginning and the end are common', the poet has also indicated the recurrent attraction he feels to the reconciliation of opposites which characterizes that pre-socratic philosopher. Eliot is using these words in a double sense. He is thinking historically – as the first section goes on to make clear, he is thinking back to the conception of order and harmony as propounded by a sixteenth-century Thomas Elyot in his *Boke named The Gouvernour*. And near the close of the poem, the overtones of history and of family are blended in the phrase, 'Home is where one starts from'. But the continuity with which he is concerned is not simply that of race. He is also thinking in religious terms – in my beginning, in my birth, is implied my end, death; yet, in the Christian reversal of terms, that death can mean rebirth, and the culminating phrase of 'East Coker' is 'In my end is my beginning'.

As his thought becomes involved with the multiple meanings of history, with how the moments of significance and illumination bisect 'the world of time', he dwells also on the course of the individual history, and his reflections become deeply personal as he confronts the disappointments of old age. He weighs the 'limited value' of what can be learned from experience, since its accustomed pattern may restrict and blind us to what comes with the 'new and shocking' moment. When the soul is sick, it can learn only through humility, only if it accepts the paradox which is developed both by St John of the Cross and by Marvell in his 'Dialogue between the Soul and Body', that 'Our only health is the disease'. Man may come to the end of his night of dark vacancy only if he learns that he 'must go by the way of dispossession'.

The three middle sections of 'East Coker' are as sombre as anything Eliot has written, and culminate in his pronouncing his career which has fallen between two wars as 'twenty years largely wasted'. The danger of such a declaration is that it risks false humility, and the inertness of these lines contrasts unsatisfactorily with the comparable passage in 'Burnt Norton' on what is gained through form. But the contrast is structurally deliberate, and with the phrase, 'Home is where one starts from', there comes the quickening reflection that old men should be explorers 'into another intensity / For a further union'. What they must pass through is such 'empty desolation' as the sea's, and in developing that image in the concluding lines of 'East Coker', the poet prepares the most thrilling transition of the whole series. For 'The Dry Salvages' opens with a contrast between the river and the sea, between the two forces that have most conditioned Eliot's sense of rhythm. For nationalist critics of the Van Wyck Brooks school who declare that Eliot has broken away from his roots since he has not included in his poems realistic details from the Middle West, it could be profitable to note that the river is 'the big river' – at first the frontier, then the 'useful, untrustworthy' conveyor of shipping, then a problem to be solved by the bridge builder, and at last 'almost forgotten' by city dwellers. This passage gives an insight into the sources of a poet's rhythm; and into how he penetrates for his material beneath all surface details, in order to repossess his essential experience. The significance of the river for Eliot shows in what he wrote to a St Louis paper in 1930:

I feel that there is something in having passed one's childhood beside the big river, which is incommunicable to those who have not. Of course my people were Northerners and New Englanders, and of course I have spent many years out of America altogether; but Missouri and the Mississippi have made a deeper impression on me than any other part of the world.

The contrapuntal balance of sea and river reinforces, throughout 'The Dry Salvages', the themes of time and movement. And yet the underlying changelessness of the sea beneath its tides, with its tolling bells measuring 'time not our time', underscores also the contrasting theme of the timeless. History is again dwelt on, and is now discerned as not just the blind corridor it seemed to Gerontion, since 'Time the destroyer is time the preserver'. This perception gives foundation for Krishna's counsel of disinterested action. Then, after the bell buoy's 'perpetual angelus' has resounded through the lyrical fourth movement, as it had in the sestina at the opening of the second, Eliot makes his most complete articulation of what can be involved in 'the intersection of the timeless with time'. By allusions to the rose-garden and to the other moments of illumination that he has symbolized in the three poems so far, he suggests the common basis of such moments in their 'hints' of grace. He goes farther, and states that such 'hints' lead also to the central truth in his religious convictions:

> But to apprehend
> The point of intersection of the timeless
> With time, is an occupation for the saint –
> No occupation either, but something given
> And taken, in a lifetime's death in love,
> Ardour and selflessness and self-surrender.
> For most of us, there is only the unattended
> Moment, the moment in and out of time,
> The distraction fit, lost in a shaft of sunlight,
> The wild thyme unseen, or the winter lightning
> Or the waterfall, or music heard so deeply
> That it is not heard at all, but you are the music
> While the music lasts. These are only hints and guesses,
> Hints followed by guesses; and the rest
> Is prayer, observance, discipline, thought and action.
> The hint half guessed, the gift half understood, is Incarnation.
> Here the impossible union
> Of spheres of existence is actual,
> Here the past and future
> Are conquered and reconciled . . .

The doctrine of Incarnation is the pivotal point on which Eliot's thought has swung well away from the nineteenth-century's romantic heresies of Deification. The distinction between thinking of God become Man through the Saviour, or of Man becoming God through his own divine potentialities, can be at the root of political as well as of religious belief. Eliot has long affirmed that Deification, the reckless doctrine of every great man as a Messiah, has led ineluctably to Dictatorship. What he has urged in his *Idea of a Christian Society* is a re-established social order in which both governors and governed find their completion in their common humility before God. The above passage, therefore, compresses, at the climax of 'The Dry Salvages' the core of Eliot's thought on time, on history, and on the destiny of man.

The content of 'Little Gidding' is most apparently under the shadow of the war. But it underlines what Eliot declared in an essay on 'Poetry in Wartime', that the more permanently valuable poetry of 1914–18 was 'more of sadness and pity than of military glory'. The secluded chapel enforces thoughts of pilgrimage and prayer, but a further reflection on history carries the poet to the realization that

> We cannot restore old policies
> Or follow an antique drum.

If 'history may be servitude, history may be freedom', and

> Here, the intersection of the timeless moment
> Is England and nowhere. Never and always.

In the final movement he resumes successively all his major themes, opening with 'The end is where we start from'. This leads into another passage on words and form, since 'every sentence is an end and a beginning', 'every poem an epitaph'. Comparably, every action is a step towards death, but may likewise be a step towards redemption. Once again we have a recognition of the potentialities of history far more resolute than what was seen in the tired backward look in 'East Coker'. For now the poet affirms that

> We shall not cease from exploration
> And the end of all our exploring
> Will be to arrive where we started
> And know the place for the first time.

What we will know is adumbrated through allusions that take us back through the series, back to 'the source of the longest river', back, indeed, to the moment of release that he evoked in 'New Hampshire', to 'the children in the apple tree'. But the completion of that glimpsed vision, as was the case with Dante's childhood love for Beatrice, must be sought through full maturity, through

> A condition of complete simplicity
> (Costing not less than everything).

The value of Eliot's device of incremental repetition hinges most on this final section of 'Little Gidding', since there is hardly a phrase that does not recall an earlier passage in the series. Some readers may object that this makes too much for a circular movement, with insufficient resolution at the close. In one sense this is true, but only in as much as the questions on which the poet is meditating are endless in their recurrent urgency. And such structural recurrence of themes, as Proust also found, is the chief device by which the writer can convey the recapture of time. The concluding lines mount to finality in their enunciation that all

> shall be well
> When the tongues of flame are in-folded
> Into the crowned knot of fire
> And the fire and the rose are one.

Out of their context these lines may seem to be merely a decorative allusion to Dante's paradise. But once you have observed the central role that fire plays, intermittently through the series and dominantly in 'Little Gidding', the potential reconciliation of the flames of destruction with the rose of light is weighted with significance. A glance at Eliot's varied symbolic use of fire can also give us an opportunity to examine more closely than we have so far the texture of the poetry he has developed through the structures of his quartets.

The lyric at the opening of the second part of 'Little Gidding' recounts the successive death of the elements. It versifies, with amplification, a sentence of Heraclitus that dwells both on the ceaseless flux and on the reconciliation of opposites, 'Fire lives in the death of air, and air in the death of fire; water lives in the death of earth, and earth in the death of water.' We can observe again the lasting impression made on the poet's consciousness by this philosopher, concerning whom he recorded in his student's notebook of thirty years ago: 'By God he meant fire'. But the fire in this lyric, and in the *terza rima* lines which follow it, is not the fire of creation:

> In the uncertain hour before the morning
> Near the ending of interminable night

> At the recurrent end of the unending
> After the dark dove with the flickering tongue
> Had passed below the horizon of his homing . . .

The 'dark dove' is the bird that haunts now all our skies; its 'flickering tongue' is the airman's fire of destruction. The figures who meet 'between three districts when the smoke arose' and who tread 'the pavement in a dead patrol' need no annotation of their function. But Eliot is occupied here with other meetings as well. It is no usual fellow warden whom he encounters but 'a familiar compound ghost'. This 'ghost' is akin, as some phrases show, to Brunetto Latini, whose meeting with Dante in Hell is one of the passages which has impressed Eliot most. A characteristic of Eliot's poetic thought ever since *Ash Wednesday* has been to make free transitions from the *Inferno* to the *Purgatorio*; and the last words spoken in this 'disfigured street' as the day is breaking, are advice to the poet that he cannot escape from the 'exasperated spirit' of old age,

> unless restored by that refining fire
> Where you must move in measure, like a dancer.

And here, in the image of the dance – as Theodore Spencer has remarked to me – one also moves in anticipation beyond the searing flames of purgatory to the radiant spheres of paradise.

The other chief passage on fire in 'Little Gidding' is the fourth movement, as impressive a lyric as any Eliot has produced:

> The dove descending breaks the air
> With flame of incandescent terror
> Of which the tongues declare
> The one discharge from sin and error.
> The only hope, or else despair
>   Lies in the choice of pyre or pyre –
>   To be redeemed from fire by fire.
>
> Who then devised the torment? Love.
> Love is the unfamiliar Name
> Behind the hands that wove

> The intolerable shirt of flame
> Which human power cannot remove.
> We only live, only suspire
> Consumed by either fire or fire.

The control of the range of meanings here is masterly. On one level, the choice in the first stanza is between destruction and destruction, for as 'the tongues' on both sides declare it is either 'we' or 'they', the 'incandescent terror' must blot out either London or Berlin. But the descending dove is, more profoundly, that of annunciation, and 'the tongues' of prophecy declare the terms of our possible redemption. The poem reaches the heart of its meaning in the heavily stressed end-word of the opening line of the second stanza. That most familiar word is yet unfamiliar to mankind, which 'cannot bear very much reality'. We can hardly face the fact that love is essentially not release but suffering; and that the intolerable burden of our desires – our Nessus shirt – can be removed by nothing within our power, but solely through grace. All we have is the terms of our choice, the fire of our destructive lusts or the inscrutable terrible fire of divine Love.

The poetry of purgation, as Eliot has observed, is ordinarily less exciting than that of either damnation or beatitude, but this lyric transcends such limitation through its fervour. The encounter between the air-raid wardens is the other most dramatic passage in the poem. Since it marks Eliot's first experiment with *terza rima*, it carries further the long series of his debts to Dante. But its method follows more particularly the lesson of another master. The 'forgotten, half-recalled' figure is evoked by the device of multiple reference which Henry James used in his 'ghost' stories. The figure, 'too strange . . . for misunderstanding', suggests not only Brunetto Latini or Arnaut Daniel. When he reminds Eliot how their common concern with speech impelled them 'to purify the dialect of the tribe', he virtually translates from Mallarmé's 'Le Tombeau d'Edgar Poe' ('donner un sens plus pur aux mots de la tribu'), and indicates that he may be thought of as any of Eliot's dead masters. When he proceeds to disclose 'the gifts reserved for age', it is interesting to recall that

Eliot's bitter 'Lines for an Old Man' contain in the manuscript the epigraph, 'to Stéphane Mallarmé'.

It may be objected that such a range of suggestion detracts from dramatic singleness. It is more certainly true – as we noted in relation to his plays – that Eliot, from the time of his earliest poems, has been more successful in posing a dramatic moment than in developing a sustained action. It may also be charged that he betrays a limitation of content in comparison with some of the other strange meetings that he recalls. Whereas the lines spoken by Brunetto Latini are, as Eliot himself has said, Dante's 'testimony of a loved master of arts'; and Wilfred Owen's hallucinated pitiful encounter was with no less than the enemy he had killed; the main burden that Eliot's 'ghost' has to convey is the impotent lacerations of growing old.

But to the charge that has been brought against Eliot that ever since his conversion his content has been tenuous, the range of reflection and feeling in the quartets should serve to give a persuasive refutation. The trouble has been that whereas Eliot's earlier poetry was difficult in form, his later work is difficult in thought. The reader of 'Gerontion' had to learn how to supply the missing connectives. The reader of the quartets finds a sufficiently straightforward logic, but is confronted with realms of discourse largely unfamiliar to a secular age. Sustained knowledge of the dark night of the soul is a rare phase of mystical experience in any age; and it is at that point that agnostic and atheist readers have been most severe in demanding whether Eliot's lines express anything more than mere literary allusions. The severity is desirable, but it should not be forgotten that authentic poetry often takes us into experiences equally remote from our ordinary hours, as in Oedipus' vision at Colonos, in Rilke's *Duino Elegies*, or in almost the whole *Paradiso*. Misconceptions of Eliot's content may be avoided if we remain aware, at least, of what he is aiming to do. As our examination of the structures of his quartets has borne out, the greatest change from his earlier poems is that his intentions now are only intermittently dramatic. Or rather, he has tried to concentrate his desire for drama into his two plays; and what he has produced in his quartets is what in the seventeenth century would have been called meditations. Yet the most striking change in the texture of his verse is his abandonment of the devices that he learned from Donne and the other metaphysicals. The qualities for which he now aspires are those of a less popular seventeenth-century master, Lancelot Andrewes, whose 'spiritual discipline' he has contrasted with Donne's broken intensity. The three attributes of Andrewes's style that Eliot singled out for praise can belong to poetry as well as to prose: 'ordonnance, or arrangement and structure, precision in the use of words, and relevant intensity'. Those attributes seemed very far from the poetical aims of 'The Hollow Men', which he had written the year before his essay on Andrewes; but something comparable to the 'purely contemplative' emotion he found in Andrewes is what he now wants most to express.

The measure of an author's attraction for Eliot can always be read in what that author has taught him about the development of his medium; and it is notable that the passage which Eliot cited to show how Andrewes's spiritual reflections can force 'a concrete presence upon us', provided him with the starting-point of his own 'Journey of the Magi'. Another sentence ('Let us then make this so accepted a time in itself twice acceptable by our accepting . . .'), which illustrated how Andrewes did 'not hesitate to hammer, to inflect, even to play upon a word for the sake of driving home its meaning', gave Eliot a similar word-play in 'Burnt Norton' ('There they were as our guests, accepted and accepting'), and stimulated him to such an independent development as the startling 'Distracted from distraction by distraction'.

Those who demand that a poet's content should be immediately useful will take no satisfaction in Eliot's belief that the poet in wartime should as a man 'be no less devoted to his country than other men', but that 'his first duty as a poet' is still to the preservation and development of his 'native language'. To the nationalist critics that will seem to beg the question of content altogether. But the cheapness of Van Wyck Brooks's opinion that Eliot is a poet of little hope, less faith, and no charity, should

be substantially refuted by the lyric on the kinds of love alone.
But such a lyric does not exist alone; it rises organically as the
summation of one of Eliot's profoundest themes. And those who
are suspicious of the inertness of the passages which urge the
soul to wait in the dark without hope, should remember that the
final declaration, even in 'East Coker' is that 'We must be still
and still moving'. The reconciliation of opposites is as fundamental to Eliot as it was to Heraclitus. Only thus can he envisage
a resolution of man's whole being. The 'heart of light' that he
glimpsed in the opening movement of 'Burnt Norton' is at the
opposite pole from the 'Heart of Darkness', from which he took
the epigraph for 'The Hollow Men'. Essential evil still constitutes more of Eliot's subject-matter than essential good, but
the magnificent orchestration of his themes has prepared for that
paradisal glimpse at the close, and thereby makes it no decorative
allusion, but an integrated climax to the content no less than to
the form. Such spiritual release and reconciliation are the chief
reality for which he strives in a world that has seemed to him
increasingly threatened with new dark ages.

(*Kenyon Review*, 1943; reprinted in
The Achievement of T. S. Eliot, 1947)

PART THREE

Later Criticism

R. W. Flint

THE *FOUR QUARTETS*
RECONSIDERED (1948)

It becomes more and more apparent that the *Quartets* have worn well. Instead of remaining an indigestible lump outside of modern thought and experience, as some critics predicted they would, they have proved themselves as poetry and as a valuable record of modern religious experience. Because they are genuine in a time of much facile religiosity, they have gained for us an authority roughly analogous to the authority of *In Memoriam* for the Victorians. They refuse to be shunted in the name of a militant secularism, along with Plotinus, Thomas à Kempis, or St John of the Cross, to some side track reserved for pure mysticism. Why? – because they are not primarily meditations of personal justification in terms of a well-defined spiritual dogma (although they are partially that), nor a body of esoteric metaphysical speculations (although they are partly that also), but, rather, a poet's attempt to enlighten and justify his whole spiritual climate, his 'clerisy', to use Arnold's word. In this he assumes the classic prophetic function and must be thought of as a prophet as well as what Delmore Schwartz calls a 'culture hero'. It has become commonplace to find quotations from the *Quartets* in religious journals and newspaper supplements, a fact which might seem on the surface to reinforce Maugham's suspicions about Anglo-American longevity worship (*Cakes and Ale*: suspicions largely justified in his case). In reality it is a tribute to Eliot's feat in managing to be both a good poet and a prophet in a time like ours.

In recent years several exegetical accounts of these poems have appeared, excellent studies in this magazine [*Sewanee Review*] as

well as Raymond Preston's sensitive sleuthing and Professor
Matthiessen's comprehensive study in the *Kenyon Review* (Spring
1943). I make no attempt to improve on these, but hope, if I can,
to clarify somewhat Eliot's position in the religious and philosophical controversies which have become more real to us since
the *Quartets* first appeared. Just as, in order to overcome in our
own minds the negativity of the secular existentialism of Sartre
(if we choose to overcome it), we have to understand something
of the other less negative forms of existentialism as well as the
kind of philosophizing to which existentialism is the antithesis,
we must likewise determine where the *Quartets* stand in relation
to the other possibilities of religious expression in our literature
before dismissing them out of hand as too esoteric, difficult,
traditional, undemocratic, or whatever. Since they are poems
they must be enjoyed as such. That, after all, is the first and great
commandment: but they are nevertheless the poetry of a philosopher and a philosopher who has less fear of the hobgoblin consistency than some of his colleagues and disciples.

The *Quartets* are philosophical to a degree that is unusual in
Eliot and unique for modern English poetry. An exaggerated
legend of their difficulty has consequently grown up among
careless readers. They turn away from the mordant study of
contemporary decay which formed the substance of the principal poems before *Ash Wednesday* (a study that was oracular
rather than analytical) toward a wrestling with the final implications of his faith. Comparison with Auden is patent: Auden has
absorbed philosophy into his verse while Eliot has made poetry
out of his philosophy. Like Koestler, Auden has treated ideas
journalistically, simplifying them into slogans, but retaining a
vocabulary and a tendency to abstraction that gives the impression of abstruse argument. In this respect he has debauched the
genre and made many readers impatient with the rigorous but
ultimately more rewarding speculations of Eliot's well-trained,
orderly, and passionately honest mind. Auden's method is epi-
grammatic: Eliot's is dramatic and therefore intrinsically more
poetic. (It is discouraging, with Dostoevski only a half century
in the grave, to note that a book like *The Death of Vergil* can be

hailed as great 'philosophical fiction'. No wonder Auden is also taken for a sage.) The *Quartets* are difficult poems, of course, compared with Tennyson's 'Ulysses' or even 'The Hollow Men', but the difficulty is not primarily of belief itself but of the concentration with which this belief is expressed, developed, and insisted upon. We are in the great *faith-for* period of our own intellectual history. We hear a great deal about faith-for-living, faith-for-working, and more often about faith-for-faith's-sake. Generally speaking, we have not yet developed, or rediscovered, that intellectual thirst to explore the boundaries of speculation beyond which faith has its meaning. Without at least Spinoza's 'intellectual love of God' or Paul's feeling for dialectics, without any real concern for the foundations of being expressed in the only categories in which they can be expressed, an intellectual only mouths words in talking about the need for faith. Simple people have had real faith and complicated people have had simple faith, but faith is not itself *intellectually* simple.

It should not be necessary to go over the ground pioneered by Eliot in explaining how a poem may be both good philosophy and good poetry, but neither without the other. We learned to understand and enjoy his early poetry in the light of his criticism of the metaphysicals and certain French poets: now we find his latter case argued in the essays on Marvell, Bradley, Pascal, Bishop Andrewes, Bishop Bramhall, the Lambeth Conference, etc., or in the polemic against Arnold, Donne, Milton, or the New Humanism. In his later favorites he has singled out the qualities of intellectual passion, immediacy and consistency; in his official *bêtes noires* he has found fuzzy, sentimental, or turgid thinking. A few sentences from the Dante essay should recall the part of his argument that concerns us.

You are not called upon to believe what Dante believed, for your belief will not give you a groat's worth more understanding or appreciation; but you are called upon more and more to understand it. If you can read poetry as poetry, you will 'believe' in Dante's theology just as you believe in the physical reality of his journey; that is, you suspend both belief and disbelief. I will not deny that it may be in practice easier for a Catholic to grasp the meaning, in many places, than for an ordinary agnostic, but that is not because the Catholic believes but because he has been instructed. It is a matter of knowledge and ignorance, not of belief and scepticism.

We have tended to allow our poets a good deal of latitude in their philosophical ventures and not demanded too much integrity in that direction. It so happens, however, that Eliot has courted and achieved that kind of integrity to a remarkable degree. Despite its increasing reliance on tradition, his poetry has been all of a piece. That is, the religious experience of later years was implicit in his drastic rejection of the conventional modern beatitudes in his youth. The poets whose methods he adapted became the tools of his intellectual need at each stage in the search for a basis of faith rather than the logical steps in an aesthetic progression. It is quite possible by studying Eliot's avowed favorites to instruct oneself in the articles of his belief to the point where belief on the reader's part is unnecessary for enjoyment of his poems. The early poems did not require this labor: the *Quartets* do. But even here Eliot has made an effort to be accessible to the layman and to avoid the appearance of dogmatism. He has, indeed, insisted many times on his layhood. After his passionate defense of Anglicanism in *Murder in the Cathedral* he makes what may seem to the purist a curious return to the aesthetic indirection and indecision of *Ash Wednesday*. We must bear in mind in this connection a point that most critics (who, thinking faith the easy way out of any situation, expect it to be at least a perfect faith) have neglected; that they are wrestling with the spiritual obligations that Eliot himself, not Thomas à Becket, assumed in joining the Church of England, and that, as such, they cannot embrace the same certainties with the same ardor. In taking the role of philosopher seriously, Eliot has given his faith a dramatic interest that is lacking in the work of poets who, like Auden and Shapiro, want, if possible, to be all things to all men. There is in these latest poems a lack of sops to curiosity and the will to be mystified that constitutes a special kind of difficulty for some readers.

II

Eliot's epiphanies continue to be somewhat tenuous in content
and doggedly secular, at least in outward appearance. Familiar
symbols of fulfilled time – the children's voices, whether in the
apple tree or 'chantant dans la coupole', the rose-garden, and
the voice of the bird ('Quick now, here, now, always') – all re-
appear, preserving a certain symbolic continuity with the earlier
poems that is indicative of a deeper continuous concern. Readers
of Augustine, Kierkegaard, Barth and others who have conditioned the modern radical Christian sensibility will ask: Where
is the Cross and the Passion? Where is the 'offense'? Where is
Hopkins's ecstatic cry to the 'Thou mastering me God . . .'?
Murder in the Cathedral, the work closest to the *Quartets* in time,
not only invoked the Passion but saw it re-enacted by St Thomas,
consciously eager for the 'qualitative leap'.

> It is not in time that my death shall be known;
> It is out of time that my decision is taken
> If you call that decision
> To which my whole being gives entire consent.
> I give my life
> To the law of God above the law of man.

In dramatizing the life of an English saint, Eliot minced no matters. The Christian story is exploited in its starkest colors with no
shying from the overtones of blood-sacrifice, spiritual pride, and
obscurantism which have scared others of Eliot's turn of mind
into equivocal humanisms. But if the faith of St Thomas is Eliot's
ideal, there is no reason to assume that he has himself attained it.
If he still wants to speculate as to whether Krishna meant that
'the future is a faded song, a Royal Rose or a lavender spray / Of
wistful regret . . .', that is his privilege at which a dogmatic
purism has no right to cavil. He has strained to keep his private
resolutions within secular reach and he wants us to remember
that he went to school with Santayana and William James. In the
Quartets, the mystical speculations, tenuous as they may seem,
are deeply embedded in social and psychological observation.

Eliot's pattern of experience borrowed from the classical

mystics has been well explained by other writers. As the cycle
begins, we are referred back to the familiar bleak Eliot landscape
– 'Tumid apathy with no concentration / Men and bits of paper,
whirled by the cold wind'. Having fixed our locus, we move
from this recognition of external emptiness through the traditional emptying of the inner life preceding spiritual regeneration.
When Eliot mentions the epiphanies that illuminate this 'darkness of God' and adds that 'the rest is prayer, observance, discipline, thought and action', we recall the three criteria that
William James set down for all mystical experience – immediate
luminousness, moral helpfulness, and philosophical reasonable-
ness. Eliot's is a higher grade of religion than Arnold's or Babbitt's, but it is also not the theology of Tillich, Niebuhr, or
Brunner, which is to say it is not consistently Biblical or prophetic in the Biblical-prophetic tradition, although his stance
vis-à-vis modern society is often prophetic. I can best illustrate
this point, perhaps, by comparing Eliot and Robert Lowell in the
matter of eschatology which has lately become a dramatically
pertinent subject. Niebuhr says that we must take the Biblical
eschatology 'seriously but not literally'; we must act, that is, as if
the world were on the verge of extinction. Lowell goes him one
better by asserting that all covenants are abrogated and the end
is really here – 'All the doves are sold'. But Eliot, although he
may meditate like Heraclitus on the death of the elements, has no
real sense of final things. In his Bradley essay he writes that 'we
fight to keep something alive rather than in the expectation that
anything will triumph'. Eliot has been slightly in advance of his
time but not too much to prevent him from being thoroughly of
it. A New England streak of diffidence as to self-commitment
marks the very human and familiar shortcomings of the philosophical climate in which he grew up. Eliot has never been more
explicitly a New Englander than in the Quartets.

III

These late poems of Eliot's are not as exotic or contrived as the
earlier poems, but they are not lacking in lines and lyrics of a

stabbing, sensuous beauty – lines like 'After the kingfisher's wing / Has answered light to light, and is silent, the light is still / At the still point of the turning world', from 'Burnt Norton'. Eliot has woven these lines into the philosophical discourse or inserted them as lyric 'movements' *where the feeling has demanded it*, not to relieve the reader, as Haydn might insert a *scherzo* in a quartet as contrast to a *largo* movement. The pattern of Eliot's *Quartets* is as rigid and formal as that of a musical quartet, but the internal texture of thought and feeling is quite different from anything we know in music. No one has ever assimilated *Der Zauberberg*, I suspect, the better for knowing Mann's avowed debt to Wagner and interest in reproducing his methods. Whatever Eliot's speculations in 'The Music of Poetry' about musical-verbal analogies, we are really left, in this instance, with no better clue than a recurrent structural pattern of five 'movements' of alternated lyric and discourse and not appreciably nearer enjoyment of the poems than if we had never heard of the string quartet, or the familiar cliché that Beethoven turned to them in his last years to express his ultimate 'wisdom'. It is easier to enjoy the parallel between Rilke and the later Beethoven since the philosophy of the *Duino Elegies* is, on the whole, a vague and undistinguished derivative, rich in sympathy, but short on concentration and exclusion. So much, then, by way of parenthesis, about a stylistic 'difficulty' adduced by some critics who have not been happy about Eliot's philosophical bias.

IV

The first two *Quartets* set the stage, or more exactly, empty the stage to prepare for the transformations of the last two. The poet is concerned with his ambiguous temporal situation, his 'distraction fits' out of time, and 'the waste sad time stretching before and after'. The problem, as in all of Eliot, is how to redeem the time, his definition of salvation. Only the mystical moments which are few and far between are the work of Grace; the rest is more or less in our hands. The suggested answer at the end of

'East Coker' points the way to the magnificent sea-change of
'The Dry Salvages'.

> We must be still and still moving
> In another intensity
> For a further union, a deeper communion
> Through the dark cold and the empty desolation,
> The wave cry, the wind cry, the vast waters
> Of the petrel and the porpoise.

In 'The Dry Salvages' Eliot exploits the sea imagery of his boy-
hood on the New England seacoast, Maine, Gloucester, and
Cape Ann. In earlier poems we had glimpses of the somber
heights he was later to reach with this material when his experience had grown to match his visual imagination – the sea poem
'Marina', the 'Gull against the wind, in the windy straits of Belle
Isle', or 'the lost heart' that 'stiffens and rejoices in the lost lilac
and the lost sea-voices'. Now, all stops are pulled out to a degree
that suggests his hoarding these riches for just such an opportunity. He is occupied with two aspects of historical time: its
pattern and its meaning. The pattern is to be completed by a
return on itself, a return which takes place on several symbolic
levels. He goes back to his beginnings to elucidate his end and
complete the pattern, but he also goes back to a place, a profound
experience, and a natural emotional relationship to his material.
There are few conceits, hidden allusions, or cross-references in
this sea-poetry. It stands by itself in a direct lyric and dramatic
self-sufficiency. The metaphor is so massive and prolonged that
it becomes psychological allegory of the most effective and inoffensive sort. The sea, or external world-time, is contrasted
with the river which stands for the stream of personal impulse,
Freud's Id, roughly speaking.

There is a sureness of touch and of values in the last two *Quartets* which shows how far Eliot has come from the constrictions
of *Ash Wednesday*, beautiful as that poem is. After the shock of
his famous declaration of principles that for a long time seemed
to have set a gulf of reaction between him and any genuinely
progressive spiritual impulses, he was put sharply on the defen-

sive. We heard about 'the vanished power of the usual reign'; the renunciation had a pleading unhappy quality as if his sense of justice had let him in for more stringency than he really wanted. 'The Dry Salvages' is proof that in gaining detachment he was able to achieve a poetic vision free of an overburdened and constricted aestheticism. He is closer in this poem to Dante than he has been before; he can now present a detailed and impassioned picture of the natural world that is correlative with a closely reasoned philosophical discourse.

With crushing understatement, the poem begins, 'I do not know much about gods . . .'. This is the poet who wrote in his Norton lectures that his mind was 'too heavy and concrete for any flight of abstract reasoning'. Like Socrates he knows what he wants to know. The river, the Id, 'destroyer, reminder of what men choose to forget', reminds us of the other rivers in Eliot, especially the savage refrain 'Weialala leia / Wallala leialala' from the river lyric in *The Waste Land*. The sea makes its appearance, not to absorb the tensions of the personal as one might expect from a conventional mystic, but further to objectify and intensify them. 'Where is the end of them, the fishermen sailing / Into the wind's tail, where the fog cowers?' It is a seascape after Aeschylus, Paul, Conrad, or Melville, not Debussy; a moral extrapolation of the internal world in which the final boundaries of futility are explored. The past has ceased to be 'mere sequence – / Or even development:' – but Eliot never thought it was. 'Gerontion' disposed of any theory of cumulative or successive meaning in history.

(You cannot argue the ethics of the prosy philosophical interstices of these poems because it is not really a question of ethics. In a less thoughtful poet they would be inexcusable. In the *Quartets* they represent the urgency of Eliot's religious wisdom demanding a clearer expression than his 'poetic' style allows. It is a grave mistake to think of them as merely filler to set off the lyrics just as the reverse is equally untrue. The whole cycle fulfills its gnomic and prophetic purpose by being poetic in its total effect.) The lesson of the second and third part of 'The Dry Salvages' is a familiar answer to the poor benighted Hegelians:

history *in itself* is meaningless. There are two consequences of
this discovery; the psychological observation of the reality of
certain moments in time that exist outside of time 'beyond any
meaning we can assign to happiness', moments of illumination or
agony which are permanent 'with such permanence as time has':
and the moral consequence, make perfect your will.

> 'On whatever sphere of being
> The mind of man may be intent
> At the time of death' – that is the one action
> (And the time of death is every moment)
> Which shall fructify in the lives of others.

This is the sum-total of Eliot's 'message' in moral and psychological terms; rightly understood it should clarify his real pre-
occupation with the social consequences of his faith, if *The Rock*
had not made that sufficiently clear already. The prescription for
fruitfulness, again, has the Jamesian ring. He omits any reference
here to the Catholic conception of the Will of God which moved
him so much in Dante. It is a moral command in psychological
terms. 'Not fare well, / But fare forward, voyagers.'

We would cloud the issue by trying to make any more of the
doctrine of the Incarnation than Eliot makes of it in the poem. It
is not at all, as Professor Matthiessen seems to imply, the
Catholic Incarnation which Eliot is opposing to nineteenth-
century romantic heresies of deification, but merely the constant
ingression of spiritual reality into time, and it defines an indefinite series of such moments rather than a specific moment in
history. Much of the difficulty of these poems for some readers
arises from a yen to damn or defend Eliot as an orthodox Anglo-
Catholic, and read more into them than is there. We have
recently had several studies that proved Hopkins to be no better
a Christian than his time would allow, and the same is certainly
true of Eliot especially in the last two *Quartets*. Professor
Matthiessen refers to their complexity in his article, comparing
them with the *Duino Elegies*. Actually, Rilke, Blake, Auden, or
any highly idiosyncratic poet of their stamp is considerably more
complex than the later Eliot, who, by a process of exclusion and

concentration, has developed a taste for essentials, so much so
that he plays on a few key words, rearranging them endlessly in
new combinations like a child with his first handful of phrases.
Eliot's discussion of time, although perhaps hard for an un-
speculative mind to grasp, is on a relatively simple level, as any
student of the subject can testify.

V

There is a progressive richness, a steady broadening of reference
and expansion of feeling in the last *Quartets* that finally belies any
analogy with the musical form. 'Little Gidding', far from being
a decorative coda, moves on to further resolution of the social
tensions implicit in Eliot's rejection of history as a self-sufficient
realm of being. It relates the poet to his time, and to the past,
that 'familiar compound ghost', in terms of the doctrine of love
and self-sacrifice arrived at previously. Love is given its widest
and yet closest definition in that extraordinarily effective lyric
which links the fire of Heraclitus to the fire of the German *Taube*
bomber, the dove that descends. This love is cousin to the curse
pursued in *The Family Reunion*, of equally inscrutable genealogy.
Here, finally and decisively, Eliot repudiates any theory of love
as 'practical' benevolence. Eliot is not a liberal Christian nor yet
a strict disciple of Paul. He has not yet, to my knowledge,
identified the Incarnation with the ingression of a specific redeeming love into history at a definite moment in time.

As Professor Matthiessen observes, the shadow of war lies
over this poem and we find more prophetic sympathy and less
prophetic scorn than in the choruses from *The Rock*. Eliot seems
willing to step down from the pulpit for a while, to forgive and
be a part of the common suffering of his time – after one last
grand oracle:

You are not here to verify,
Instruct yourself, or inform curiosity
Or carry report. You are here to kneel
Where prayer has been valid.

The dead leave us only a symbol. 'History may be servitude, History may be freedom.' In other words, history is whatever one makes of it at the moment. It is not (as he had once heard Santayana insist) determined by any dialectic, but it can be a realm of meaning if it is 'renewed, transfigured, in another pattern'. Traditionalism, an indefinite sin which Eliot is most commonly and irresponsibly accused of committing, is denounced. 'We cannot revive old factions . . .'

'History is now and England.' If I were asked to choose the most moving line in Eliot, this would probably be it. This is the poet who had prayed, not long before, to be taught how to care and not to care, and how to sit still. Sitting still, caring and not caring, he did move into another intensity, one of the very few poets to whom the war years seem to have taught any final lessons, or whose poetry reached a level of fused eloquence, love, and understanding where war experience was transformed into great art. The quiet beauty of the last 'movement' of 'Little Gidding' is inaccessible to anyone unable to grasp the depths of thought and experience out of which it speaks. Many will make a brave effort to pretend to enjoy it, just as there must, I suppose, always be people whose enjoyment of Dante is largely pretense. Many others, like the good Dr Johnson, may prefer to kick the stone and leave it at that.

SOURCE: *Sewanee Review* (1948)

Helen   Gardner

THE MUSIC OF
FOUR QUARTETS (1949)

> And thou, sweet Music, Dancing's only life,
> The ear's sole happiness, the Air's best speech,
> Loadstone of fellowship, Charming rod of strife,
> The soft mind's Paradise, the sick mind's Leech.
> SIR JOHN DAVIES, 'Orchestra'.

BY calling his poem *Four Quartets*, Mr Eliot has made it necessary for any critic, even though as ignorant as he confesses himself to be of 'a technical knowledge of musical form', to discuss
the debt he owes to the art of music in his solution of the problem of finding a form for the long poem. He has given some
indications of what that debt is in his lecture on 'The Music of
Poetry'.

I think that a poet may gain much from the study of music:
how much technical knowledge of musical form is desirable I do
not know, for I have not that technical knowledge myself. But I
believe that the properties in which music concerns the poet
most nearly are the sense of rhythm and the sense of structure. I
think that it might be possible for a poet to work too closely to
musical analogies: the result might be an effect of artificiality; but
I know that a poem, or a passage of a poem, may tend to realize
itself first as a particular rhythm before it reaches expression in
words, and that this rhythm may bring to birth the idea and the
image; and I do not believe that this is an experience peculiar to
myself. The use of recurrent themes is as natural to poetry as to
music. There are possibilities for verse which bear some analogy
to the development of a theme by different groups of instruments; there are possibilities of transitions in a poem comparable
to the different movements of a symphony or a quartet; there
are possibilities of contrapuntal arrangement of subject-matter.
It is in the concert room, rather than in the opera house, that the
germ of a poem may be quickened.

As the title shows, each poem is structurally a poetic equivalent of the classical symphony, or quartet, or sonata, as distinct from the suite. This structure is clear when all four poems are read, as they are intended to be, together, and is essentially the same as the structure of *The Waste Land*. It is far more rigid than would be suspected from reading any one of the poems separately, but it is sufficiently flexible to allow of various arrangements and modifications of its essential features. It is capable of the symphonic richness of *The Waste Land* or the chamber-music beauty of 'Burnt Norton'. The form seems perfectly adapted to its creator's way of thinking and feeling: to his desire to submit to the discipline of strict poetic laws, and at the same time to have liberty in the development of a verse capable of extremes of variation, and in the bringing together of ideas and experiences often divorced. The combination of apparent licence with actual strictness corresponds to the necessities of his temperament.

Each poem contains what are best described as five 'movements', each with its own inner necessary structure. The first movement suggests at once a musical analogy. In each poem it contains statement and counter-statement, or two contrasted but related themes, like the first and second subjects of a movement in strict sonata form. The analogy must not be taken too literally. Mr Eliot is not imitating 'sonata form', and in each poem the treatment or development of the two subjects is slightly different. The simplest is the treatment of the river and sea images in 'The Dry Salvages', the symbols for two different kinds of time: the time we feel in our pulses, in our personal lives, and the time we become aware of through our imagination, stretching behind us, beyond the record of the historian, and continuing after we have gone. The two subjects are presented successively, in contrast. The first movement of 'Burnt Norton' shows a similar division into two statements. Here the contrast is between abstract speculation and an experience in a garden, a meditation on consciousness and a presentation of consciousness. But in 'East Coker' the first movement falls into four parts. The first theme of the time of the years and the seasons, the rhythm of birth, growth and death, is resumed in the third paragraph, and the second theme, the experience of being outside time, of time having stopped, is briefly restated at the close. While in 'Little Gidding', the most brilliantly musical of the four poems, the third paragraph is a development of the first two, weaving together phrases taken up from both in a kind of counterpointing. In general, however, it is true to say that the first movement is built on contradictions which the poem is to reconcile.

The second movement is constructed on the opposite principle of a single subject handled in two boldly contrasted ways. The effect is like that of hearing the same melody played on a different group of instruments, or differently harmonized, or hearing it syncopated, or elaborated in variations, which cannot disguise the fact that it is the same. The movement opens with a highly poetical lyric passage, in a traditional metrical form: irregularly rhyming octosyllabics in 'Burnt Norton' and 'East Coker', a simplified sestina[1] in 'The Dry Salvages' and three lyric stanzas in 'Little Gidding'. This is followed immediately by an extremely colloquial passage, in which the idea which had been treated in metaphor and symbol in the first half of the movement is expanded and developed in a conversational manner. In the first three poems the metre used is the same as the metre of the first movement, though in each case here the passage begins with the long line; in 'Little Gidding' a modification of *terza rima* is employed. In 'Burnt Norton', the highly obscure, richly symbolic presentation of the 'flux of life' perceived as a unity in the consciousness, turns to a bare statement in philosophic language of the relation of stillness and movement, past, present and future. At the close there is a return to imagery, when after the abstract discussion three concrete moments are mentioned:

> the moment in the rose-garden,
> The moment in the arbour where the rain beat,
> The moment in the draughty church at smokefall.

In 'East Coker' we have first a confusion in the seasons and the constellations. This turns to a flat statement of the same confusion in the lives of individual men, where the settled wisdom of old age is dismissed as a deception. Imagery returns here also, in the expansion of Dante's 'selva oscura':

> In the middle, not only in the middle of the way
> But all the way, in a dark wood, in a bramble,
> On the edge of a grimpen, where is no secure foothold,
> And menaced by monsters, fancy lights,
> Risking enchantment.

Again in the last two lines

> The houses are all gone under the sea.

> The dancers are all gone under the hill,

we have a faint recalling of the whole of the first movement, the briefest possible evocation of what was there said. In 'The Dry Salvages' the beautiful lament for the anonymous, the endless sum of whose lives adds up to no figure we can name, and leaves little trace but wrecks and wastage on time's ocean, hints in its last stanza where meaning can be found, and the hint is then developed directly, at first with little metaphor, but at the close with a full and splendid return to the original images of the river and the sea. This return to imagery in 'The Dry Salvages' comes with wonderful power and force after the purging of our minds by the colloquial and discursive passage in which the poet has deliberately deprived himself of the assistance of imagery. It is a poetic effect comparable to the moment when, after a long and difficult passage of musical development, the original melody returns with all its beauty. The particular treatment of the second movement in 'The Dry Salvages' is the poetic expression of its subject:

> We had the experience but missed the meaning,
> And approach to the meaning restores the experience.

The effort to find meaning restores the original imaginative vision of the river and the sea; the images return with power. In 'Little Gidding' the exquisite lyric on the decay of our mortal world changes to the colloquy with the 'dead master', after the air-raid, when human fame and the achievement of the poet are likewise shown to be vanity. The second part of the movement, though metrically distinct from the first, is metrically formal,[2] and imagery runs through it. This is in keeping with the whole tenor of 'Little Gidding' in which the stylistic contrasts are less violent than in the two middle poems and one is more conscious of the counterpointing of themes. As in the first movement then, the relation between the two parts varies with the character of each poem. We can say generally that the first part is traditional in its metre, symbolic, romantic in its imagery, and lyrical; and the second part discursive, colloquial, meditative. But in 'Burnt Norton' the second part is philosophic and abstract, in 'East Coker' and 'The Dry Salvages' it is personal and reflective – more immediately personal in 'East Coker' and more generally reflective in 'The Dry Salvages' – and in 'Little Gidding' it is particular, and the reflection arises out of a firmly established situation.

In the third movement one is less conscious of musical analogies. The third movement is the core of each poem, out of which reconcilement grows: it is an exploration with a twist of the ideas of the first two movements. At the close of these centre movements, particularly in 'East Coker' and 'Little Gidding', the ear is prepared for the lyric fourth movement. The repetitive circling passage in 'East Coker', in particular, where we seem to be standing still, waiting for something to happen, for a rhythm to break out, reminds one of the bridge passages and leading passages between two movements which Beethoven loved. The effect of suspense here is comparable to the sensation with which we listen to the second movement of Beethoven's Violin Concerto finding its way towards the rhythm of the Rondo. But the organization of the movement itself is not fixed. In 'Burnt Norton' it falls into two equal parts, divided by a change of mind, with no change of metre. In 'East Coker' the change of feeling is not represented by a break. The break in the metre occurs after the change the movement records has occurred. The change is one that 'comes upon' the mind: 'the darkness shall be the light, and the stillness the dancing'. There is a change in the rhythm, not a break, from the six-stress line to the four-stress. Then after a pause there comes the 'bridge passage', in which we wait for the moment when its 'requiring' is answered by the firm rhythm of the great Passion lyric. In 'The Dry Salvages' there is no real break; but there is a change in temper from the reflective to the hortatory, represented by a similar change of rhythm from the tentative six-stress line to the firm handling of the line of four stresses. In 'Little Gidding' there is a very definite break as the poet changes from the personal to the historic. The poet here turns to the beautiful three-stress line which before this was reserved for the close of the last movement.

After the brief lyrical movement, the fifth recapitulates the themes of the poem with personal and topical applications and makes a resolution of the contradictions of the first. It falls into two parts in each poem, but the change is slighter than in the second movement, and it is reversed. Here the colloquial passage comes first, and then, without a feeling of sharp break, for the metre remains fundamentally the same, the base of the line contracts and images return in quick succession. In various ways the last lines echo the beginning of the whole poem or employ images from the other poems in a conclusion of tender gravity, touched at times by a lyric sweetness.

The Waste Land, if one allows for its much wider scope, its essentially dramatic method of presentation, and its hosts of characters, follows the same main pattern. 'The Burial of the Dead' contains far more than two statements, but formally it is a series of contrasts of feeling towards persons and experiences, which are related by a common note of fear. 'The Game of Chess' opens with the elaborate, highly poetic description of the lady at her dressing table, a passage like a set-piece of description in a late Elizabethan play. This contrasts with the talk of Lou and her friends in the public-house at closing time. But the violence of the stylistic contrast only makes clearer the underlying similarity of emotion: boredom and panic, and the common theme of sterility. There is something comparable to the return of images at the close of this section in the Quartets in the use made of Ophelia's words: 'Good night, sweet ladies, good night', though here the effect is ironical. 'The Fire Sermon', the poem's heart, has moments when the oppression lifts, and a feeling of release and purification floods in. This twist is given by the evocations of another world than the appalling world of the twining serpents which Tiresias sees. The reference to the Buddha, the 'collocation of western and eastern asceticism', to which attention is drawn in the notes, anticipates the use of the *Bhagavad-Gita* in the same movement of 'The Dry Salvages'. 'Death by Water', the fourth movement, is again a brief lyric, and the fifth section, 'What the Thunder Said', while being naturally far more complex than the final movements of the Quartets, performs the same function of resolution. It returns also to many of the themes of the first movement, recalling its crowds, as well as the separate figures of the second and third movements, and treating again of its theme of birth and death.

It is obvious, however, that, in spite of the basic similarity of structure, the form is far more highly developed in *Four Quartets*, and that both the whole poem and the separate poems depend upon the form in a way that *The Waste Land* does not. In *The Waste Land* Mr Eliot took the Grail myth, as interpreted by Miss Weston, for his ostensible subject, or starting point. *The Waste Land* is given coherence not by its form, but by this underlying myth, to which constant reference can be made, and of which all the varied incidents and the many personages are illustrative. But in *Four Quartets* the title of the whole poem tells us nothing of its subject, and the titles of the separate poems tell us very little. The poems are not 'about places' though their subjects are bound up with particular places.[3] There are no books to which we can direct an inquirer. The works of St John of the Cross, though relevant, will not help a reader in the same way as *The Golden Bough* or *From Ritual to Romance* will in Mr Eliot's own words 'elucidate the difficulties' of *The Waste Land*. We might begin a description of *Four Quartets* by saying it presents a series of meditations upon existence in time, which, beginning from a place and a point in time, and coming back to

another place and another point, attempts to discover in these
points and places what is the meaning and content of an experience, what leads to it, and what follows from it, what we bring
to it and what it brings to us, but any such description will be
brief and abstract; we have to use words like 'time' 'memory',
'consciousness', words whose meaning we do not really grasp,
abstractions from sensation. We shall find we are leaving out
all that makes the poem memorable, whereas if we told the story
of the Fisher King we should be leading a reader towards the
poetry of *The Waste Land*. It is better to abandon these abstractions and return to a consideration of the form, to which the
meditation owes its coherence. The form is inspired by the com-
poser's power to explore and define, by continual departures
from, and returns to, very simple thematic material. The 'thematic material' of the poem is not an idea or a myth, but partly
certain common symbols. The basic symbols are the four elements, taken as the material of mortal life, and another way of
describing *Four Quartets* and a less misleading one, would be to
say that 'Burnt Norton' is a poem about air, on which whispers
are borne, intangible itself, but the medium of communication;[4]
'East Coker' is a poem about earth, the dust of which we are
made and into which we shall return; it tells of 'dung and death',
and the sickness of the flesh; 'The Dry Salvages' is a poem about
water which some Greek thinkers thought was the primitive
material out of which the world arose, and which man has
always thought of as surrounding and embracing the land,
limiting the land and encroaching on it, itself illimitable;[5] 'Little
Gidding' is a poem about fire, the purest of the elements, by
which some have thought the world would end, fire which con-
sumes and purifies. We could then say that the whole poem is
about the four elements whose mysterious union makes life,
pointing out that in each of the separate poems all four are
present; and perhaps adding that some have thought that there is
a fifth element, unnamed but latent in all things: the quintessence,
the true principle of life, and that this unnamed principle is the
subject of the whole poem.

By relying on form and these simply underlying symbols, Mr

Eliot has found not only a personal solution of his personal problems as a poet, but a solution, which may greatly influence later writers, of the problem of the long poem. He has freed it from its dependence on a subject that can be expressed in non-poetic terms. In lyric poetry, particularly in brief lyrics and songs, it is often true to say that the subject cannot be separated from the poem; but the longer meditative poem has usually to find a subject which is separable from the poetry, though often of little interest in itself when so separated. One can, for instance, 'summarize the argument' of the *De Rerum Natura*; one can give a factual account of Wordsworth's life from *The Prelude*; one can 'trace the development of the thought' in *In Memoriam*. But with *Four Quartets* we cannot summarize the argument, nor can we say 'what happens'. Mr Eliot has not given us a poem of philosophic argument, though his poem includes philosophic argument. He would probably assent to Keats's confession: 'I have never yet been able to perceive how anything can be known for truth by consequitive reasoning'. He has not related to us in autobiographical narrative 'the growth of a poet's mind', though this would be one possible sub-title for *Four Quartets*. The difficulty of employing an autobiographical framework is that the present is always ahead. The Red Queen and *Tristram Shandy* both show us how hard one has to run to keep in the same place. The poet who sets out to tell us what brought him 'to this place and hour' has passed on to another place and hour by the time he comes to finish. There cannot be a true conclusion. By rejecting autobiography, Mr Eliot has been able to include without difficulty, and with perfect relevance, experience that was in the future when the poem was planned. The poem has grown with the poet and changed with changing circumstances, without out-growing its original plan. 'Burnt Norton' was published in the *Collected Poems* (1936) and it was announced then that it was the first of a series of four Quartets.[6] The scheme appears to have been laid aside while *The Family Reunion* was written. 'East Coker' was not published until Good Friday 1940, and came with extraordinary appropriateness. Its words 'And that, to be restored, our sickness must grow worse',

seemed prophetic at that time of waiting, the period of war
that was not war. When 'The Dry Salvages' appeared the war at
sea was at its height, and 'Little Gidding' includes without any
distortion of its original purpose a fire-raid on London and a
warden's patrol in Kensington. But while *Four Quartets* shares
with a spiritual diary such as *In Memoriam* the power to include
present experience without irrelevance, it escapes the diary's
defect of diffuseness and lack of concentration. The diary can
give us a sense of progress and development, but not the sense
of the end implicit in the beginning, of necessary development;
it has the interest of narrative, not the deeper delight of plot. In
the long poem that depends on the day-to-day development of a
mind, the parts will seem greater than the whole, and even
Tennyson's powers of variation can hardly save *In Memoriam*
as a whole from the monotony of life and give it the coherence
of art. The form of *Four Quartets* transforms living into art, not
thought, gives us a sense of beginning and ending, of the theme
having been fully worked out, which is rare in the long poem.
The separate parts combine in a way that the sonnets of a sonnet
sequence, or a series of repeated stanzas cannot. The strict limitations of the form make possible the freedom of the treatment.
The poet can say what he wishes because he must say it in this
way. The nearest analogy I can suggest is the Greek Pindaric
Ode, and Mr Eliot might be said to have succeeded in finding
what earlier English poets had tried to find, a proper English
equivalent for the formal ode. Here again, as in his metrical
experiments, he has found a way suited to the genius of the
English language, which has formed, and been formed by, the
English ear, impatient of the kind of elaborate pattern that the
Greeks and Italians enjoyed. He has not in any sense imitated
the Pindaric Ode, but he has found a kind of equivalent: an
original form supplying the same need, and giving something of
the same delight. The strict Pindaric has never seemed more than
a feat of virtuosity in English, while the loose Pindaric has too
little formal organization to give pleasure; it arouses no expec-
tancy, and so cannot delight by satisfying or surprising. The
Quartet form, though capable of almost unlimited variations,

has a secure formal basis by which we recognize the variations as variations.

The more familiar we become with *Four Quartets*, however, the more we realize that the analogy with music goes much deeper than a comparison of the sections with the movements of a quartet, or than an identification of the four elements as 'thematic material'. One is constantly reminded of music by the treatment of images, which recur with constant modifications, from their context, or from their combination with other recurring images, as a phrase recurs with modifications in music. These recurring images, like the basic symbols, are common, obvious and familiar, when we first meet them. As they recur they alter, as a phrase does when we hear it on a different instrument, or in another key, or when it is blended and combined with another phrase, or in some way turned round, or inverted. A simple example is the phrase 'a shaft of sunlight' at the close of 'Burnt Norton'. This image occurs in a rudimentary form in 'The Hollow Men', along with a moving tree and voices heard in the wind:

> There, the eyes are
> Sunlight on a broken column
> There, is a tree swinging
> And voices are
> In the wind's singing
> More distant and more solemn
> Than a fading star.

At the close of 'Burnt Norton' a 'moment of happiness', defined in 'The Dry Salvages' as a 'sudden illumination' is made concrete by the image of a shaft of sunlight which transfigures the world:

> Sudden in a shaft of sunlight
> Even while the dust moves
> There rises the hidden laughter
> Of children in the foliage
> Quick now, here, now, always –
> Ridiculous the waste sad time
> Stretching before and after.

This is the final concrete statement of what 'Burnt Norton' is about; but it recalls the experience we have been given in a different rhythm and with different descriptive accompaniments in the second half of the first movement, as the sun for a moment shines from the cloud, and the whole deserted garden seems to become alive:

> Dry the pool, dry concrete, brown edged,
> And the pool was filled with water out of sunlight,
> And the lotos rose, quietly, quietly,
> The surface glittered out of heart of light,
> And they were behind us, reflected in the pool.
> Then a cloud passed, and the pool was empty.

The image repeated, but with such a difference, at the close establishes the validity of the first experience. Brief and illusory as it appears in the first movement, it has not been dismissed. It has remained in thought and it returns. Though

> Time and the bell have buried the day,
> The black cloud carries the sun away

when the 'sudden shaft' falls, it is time that seems the illusion.

But this image of 'a shaft of sunlight' seems to have a rather different meaning when we meet it at the close of 'The Dry Salvages', united with the images of 'East Coker': the 'wild thyme unseen' and 'winter lightning', and deprived of 'suddenness'.

> For most of us, there is only the unattended
> Moment, the moment in and out of time,
> The distraction fit, lost in a shaft of sunlight,
> The wild thyme unseen, or the winter lightning
> Or the waterfall, or music heard so deeply
> That it is not heard at all, but you are the music
> While the music lasts. These are only hints and guesses,
> Hints followed by guesses; and the rest
> Is prayer, observance, discipline, thought and
>   action.

Here the poet seems to suggest by his tone, and by the natural images which he associates with his 'shaft of sunlight', and by the phrase 'distraction fit', and by the whole slow, rather dreamy rhythm, that these moments must not be relied on or indeed hoped for very much, but received in thankfulness as gifts when they occur. 'The Dry Salvages' is a poem about ordinary people; its annunciations are the common annunciations of danger, calamity and death. It is not about special people with special gifts; it mentions the saint, only to turn back to 'most of us' who are given no special revelation, but the one Annunciation which is for all men. The image occurs here lightly and beautifully; no weight of meaning is put on to it.[7]

At the opening of 'Little Gidding' this image of sunlight is totally transformed; it is made highly particular, linked with a particular season, and worked out with great descriptive detail. It is also made impersonal. The flash of winter sunlight which creates 'midwinter spring' is not a hint or a guess, or a hint followed by guesses, nor is it an almost indefinable moment of happiness, so brief that it seems perhaps an illusion; it is a revelation, apocalyptic in its intensity and brilliance:

> The brief sun flames the ice, on ponds and ditches,
> In windless cold that is the heart's heat,
> Reflecting in a watery mirror
> A glare that is blindness in the early afternoon.
> And glow more intense than blaze of branch, or brazier,
> Stirs the dumb spirit: no wind, but pentecostal fire
> In the dark time of the year.

The sunlight of the earlier poems has become 'frost and fire' and turns to 'flame of incandescent terror'.

The more one reads *Four Quartets* the more these recurring images fix themselves in the mind, and through them and the changes in them we can apprehend the changing, developing subject. The yew-tree, for instance, used many times in the last three poems of *Ash Wednesday*, occurs only three times in *Four Quartets*, but each time with great and different significance. In the second verse of the lyric in 'Burnt Norton', the 'chill fingers of yew' – the touch of death hardly brushing the cheek – give us a vague sense of foreboding; at the close of 'The Dry Salvages', on the other hand, the phrase 'not too far from the yew-tree' gives a sense of security. This is the familiar yew of the church-yard, symbol both of mortality and immortality, beneath whose shade we may rest in peace. While at the end of 'Little Gidding', 'the moment of the rose and the moment of the yew-tree', the apprehension of love and the apprehension of death, are linked together, so that each seems of equal validity, an apprehension of life.

In the same way as images and symbols recur, certain words are used again and again, their meaning deepened or expanded by each fresh use. Indeed, another way of describing *Four Quartets* would be to say that the poem is an exploration of the meaning of certain words. Like the images and symbols just referred to, they are common words, words we take for granted. Perhaps the words that first strike us in this way as recurring with a special and changing emphasis are the pair 'end' and 'beginning', sometimes occurring together, sometimes apart from each other. The word 'end' occurs first, by itself, in the opening lines of 'Burnt Norton':

> What might have been and what has been
> Point to one end, which is always present.

Here 'end' has plainly some meaning beyond that of 'termina-tion', but we are not quite certain how much meaning to give it. Even when these two lines are repeated at the end of the first movement, the word 'end' remains vague. It is only in the fifth movement – when the word is linked with 'beginning', in the context of ideas about form and pattern and we have apparently paradoxical statements – that we begin to think of end as meaning 'completion' 'purpose' or even 'final cause':

> Or say that the end precedes the beginning,
> And the end and the beginning were always there
> Before the beginning and after the end.
> And all is always now.

In 'East Coker', the opening inversion of Mary Stuart's motto throws the stress on the word 'beginning' and the whole poem

ends with the word. If in 'Burnt Norton' it is 'end' we are thinking of, and the word 'beginning' seems used mainly to give
meaning to 'end', in 'East Coker' the opposite is true. It is a
poem about 'beginning'. On the other hand in 'The Dry Salvages' the word 'beginning' does not occur at all, and the word
'end' is only used to be negated. At the close of the first movement we hear of women lying awake

> Between midnight and dawn, when the past is all deception,
> The future futureless, before the morning watch
> When time stops and time is never ending.

To stop is not to 'end'; there is no more meaning in time stop-
ping than in time going on. For there to be an 'end' there must
be a 'beginning', and there is no beginning without an end. In
the *sestina* the word 'end' is repeated again and again, but only
in questions and negative replies: 'Where is there an end of it?'
and 'There is no end'; until the last line points us to where both
Beginning and End are to be sought. 'Little Gidding' not merely
uses the words again and again, but is full of synonyms for both,
picking up one or other of the various meanings, and it constantly translates the words into images. The refusal to speak of
'beginning' and the consequent denial of 'end' in 'The Dry
Salvages' make the restoration of both words to us in the last
poem particularly moving. The tentative paradoxes of 'Burnt
Norton' return with confident certainty:

> What we call the beginning is often the end
> And to make an end is to make a beginning.
> The end is where we start from.

Read in this way, with a mind alert to recognize recurrences –
not only of words like 'end' and 'beginning', 'movement' and
'stillness', 'past', 'present' and 'future', but recurrences of the
common prepositions and adverbs: 'before' and 'after', 'here',
'there', 'now' – the poem seems to have for its 'thematic material'
not only symbols and images, but certain words in common use,
which bring with them no images, though they can be associated
with various images. These words receive the same kind of

development as the images do. The line from the close of 'Burnt Norton' – 'Quick now, here, now, always' – is as meaningless and unpoetic by itself, on a page, without any context as Shakespeare's 'Never, never, never, never, never'. When it is repeated right at the close of 'Little Gidding', it gives us one of the most intense poetic experiences of the whole poem. After all the variation and turning, the discussion and development, the subject is once more, for the last time, given us. It is given in the briefest possible way, with all adornment stripped away. For a moment, it is just as simple as that, and we knew it all the time. It is the end, and we are back at the beginning; we have had this answer before, and we recognize it as the only answer.

This musical treatment of the image, the phrase and the word, to bring out latent meanings and different significances, should prevent any reader from trying to fix the symbols in *Four Quartets*. The poem must not be read as if it were allegory, in which one 'finds values for x, y and z' and then can make the whole work out. Here one must not hunt for meanings and precise correspondencies, and because an image seems to mean something definite in one context force the same meaning on it whenever it occurs. It is obvious that the sea of 'East Coker' holds a different meaning from the sea of 'The Dry Salvages'. It is better in reading poetry of this kind to trouble too little about the 'meaning' than to trouble too much. If there are passages whose meaning seems elusive, where we feel we 'are missing the point', we should read on, preferably aloud; for the music and the meaning arise at 'a point of intersection', in the changes and movement of the whole. We must find meaning in the reading, rather than in any key which tells us what the rose or the yew 'stands for', or in any summary of systems of thought, whether pre-Socratic or Christian. Reading in this way we may miss detailed significances, but the whole rhythm of the poems will not be lost, and gradually the parts will become easier for us to understand. In fact to read *Four Quartets* one must have some sense of the whole before one attempts to make very much of the parts. The sources are completely unimportant. No knowledge of the original context is required to give force to the new context. In *The Waste Land* the poet showed it was necessary to pay some regard to his sources by himself directing us to them. But we do not need to remember Tennyson's 'Mariana' when we read in 'East Coker' of

> a time for the wind to break the loosened pane
> And to shake the wainscot where the field-mouse trots
> And to shake the tattered arras woven with a silent motto.

If we recognize that Mr Eliot is drawing on this favourite poem, we have pleasure in the recognition; we are not helped towards understanding what a house falling into ruin and decay is going to mean within the poem. Again, in 'Little Gidding', the initial capital and the archaic form in 'Behovely' tell us that the words 'Sin is Behovely, but all shall be well, and all manner of thing shall be well' are a quotation, and we need to realize that they have the authority of a maxim. The poet is speaking in words that are not his own, because these words are more expressive than anything he could say. We do not gain any particular help in the understanding of 'Little Gidding' from knowing that the sentence comes from Juliana of Norwich.

When we read *Four Quartets* in this way, attentive to this 'music of meaning', which arises at 'the point of intersection', where word relates to word, phrase to phrase, and image to image, we realize that though Mr Eliot may have given to other poets a form they can use for their own purposes, and though his treatment of the image and the word may suggest to his successors methods of developing poetic themes, *Four Quartets* is unique and essentially inimitable. In it the form is the perfect expression of the subject; so much so that one can hardly in the end distinguish subject from form. The whole poem in its unity declares more eloquently than any single line or passage that truth is not the final answer to a calculation, nor the last stage of an argument, nor something told us once and for all, which we spend the rest of our life proving by examples. The subject of *Four Quartets* is the truth which is inseparable from the way and the life in which we find it.

SOURCE: *The Art of T. S. Eliot* (1949).

NOTES

1. The *sestina* is a poem of six six-line stanzas, each stanza repeating the rhyme words of the first but rearranging them. There is often a coda of three lines with the rhyme words in their original order in the middle and end of each line. Spenser adopted a simpler form of rearrangement of the rhymes than the Italian *sestina* shows in his August Eclogue, no doubt to suit our duller ears. Mr Eliot does not rearrange his rhymes, as he wishes to give the effect of repetition without progression, a wave-like rise and fall. He also does not confine himself to the repetition of the six rhyme words of the first stanza, employing other rhymes and sometimes assonance, and only returning to the original rhyme words in his last stanza.

2. The metre is an original modification of *terza rima*. The 'want of like terminations' in an uninflected language such as English involves most translators and imitators of Dante in a loss of his colloquial terseness and austere nobility in an effort to preserve the rhyme. Mr Eliot has sacrificed rhyme, and by substituting for it alternate masculine and feminine endings, he has preserved the essential forward movement of the metre, without loss of directness of speech and naturalness.

3. When a resident of East Coker, justly enthusiastic over its beauty, said to me: 'Personally, I don't think Eliot has done justice to the village', it was difficult to do anything but agree, without wounding local pride by the suggestion that he had not really tried to.

On the other hand failure to recognize that the titles are place-names may mislead. 'Je suppose que le quatrième quatuor, "Little Gidding", porte le nom d'un petit garçon cher à T. S. Eliot', writes a Belgian critic, Pierre Messiaen, in *Etudes* (Dec 1948). But his summary of the poem's 'message' does not suggest that a mere understanding of the title would have helped him very much: 'A ce petit garçon, l'auteur veut léguer trois pensées: que la vie est dure, qu'elle est composée d'echecs et qu'elle est sans cesse un recommencement. Ce qui compte, c'est que le feu brûle et la rose fleurisse.'

4. Donne speaks of air in this way, as a necessary medium, in 'The Extasie':

> On man heavens influence workes not so,
> But that it first imprints the ayre.

In Sir John Davies's 'Orchestra', in the passage from which I have taken the epigraph for this chapter, there is a disquisition on Air also:

> For what are breath, speech, echoes, music, winds
> But Dancings of the Air, in sundry kinds?

5. A glance at a collection of early maps shows how man instinctively conceives the sea as 'the land's edge'.

6. [Editor's note.] Professor Gardner has subsequently acknowledged that she was mistaken here.

7. When Walter Hilton, at the end of the fourteenth century, a time of much mystical enthusiasm, wrote his tract *Of Angels' Song*, he did not deny that some men might truly hear wonderful sounds, though he plainly thought that a good many more thought they did and were deceived; but he concluded with some words which have the same humility as this closing section of 'The Dry Salvages': 'it sufficeth me for to live in truth principally and not in feeling'.

Morris Weitz

T. S. ELIOT: TIME AS A MODE OF
SALVATION (1952)

I

THE relation between philosophy and the study of poetry is still
in a confused state. I. A. Richards and the New Criticism have
taught us that the traditional mode of philosophical analysis of
poetry, which consisted in reducing the total poetic communication to a paraphrased prose statement, that was then to be
evaluated on the basis of its truth or falsity, was a gross injustice
to the intrinsic nature of poetry.

But the counter-position of this new approach has never been
unanimous as to the place of philosophical exegesis in the reading of the poetry which happened to contain philosophical ideas.
Richards proclaimed that it never matters what a poem *says* but
what it *is*; and it was inferred from this that what a poem is
somehow *excludes* what it says: that is, that it would be wrong to
accept as any part of the poem's reality its philosophical 'say-
ings'. Thus, some of the members of this group have tried to
make out that the big ideas of a poem were mere 'scaffoldings',
existing only outside of the poem, serving as an aid to the
reader's scaling its heights, but to be discarded once he got there.

That this is an insupportable position, I think, can be seen
from a simple example. In Eliot's 'The Love Song of J. Alfred
Prufrock', Prufrock says, 'I have measured out my life with
coffee spoons.' This implies, 'My life has been trivial.' The latter
is not printed but it would be wrong to say that it does not exist
within the poem.

In the same way many philosophical ideas can be said to exist
within the poem, either as printed meanings or as implied depth
meanings. This is not to say that the whole poem can be reduced

to these ideas, only that they are in the poem as certain elements among others, as part of a total poetic complex.

In one sense, then, if in no other, the discipline of philosophy can be of service to the study of poetry. It can probe the total meaning of a poem and offer clarifications of its basic ideas or doctrines. These clarifications illumine the printed meanings and are themselves part of the entire poem. In what follows, we shall present a partial reading of some of Eliot's poetry, especially his *Four Quartets*; and we shall try to make explicit his doctrine of time, in terms of which his poetry becomes more intelligible and richer than it now is to most readers. The question of the truth or falsity of the doctrine shall not be raised, on grounds, suggested by Richards, that such an enterprise shifts one's interest from an aesthetic to a non-aesthetic reading. Our own conviction is that Eliot's theory of time is incorrect but to the well-wrought reader this will make no difference, since the fullest appreciation of poetry ought not to depend in any way on agreement or disagreement with the doctrines within the poem, even when these happen to be philosophical ones.

II

It is often said that Eliot's conception of time is derived from Heraclitus, and is consequently similar to Bergson's. The second of the two epigraphs of the *Four Quartets* may be offered as evidence for this view, especially since Eliot has incorporated it into the body of the work: in 'The Dry Salvages', for example, he writes; 'And the way up is the way down, the way forward is the way back.'

It is part of the intention of this essay to deny this interpretation and to argue that Eliot's conception of time is rather a repudiation of the Heraclitean with its insistence upon the ultimate character of time as flux (or pure *durée*).

There are elements from Heraclitus' philosophy in Eliot, especially in the *Four Quartets*, but these do not relate to Eliot's own positive theory of time. They are rather the notion of the Logos in the flux: the contrast of wisdom and learning: the ulti-

mate reality of fire: and the generative-destructive character of
the four elements; earth, water, air and fire. What Eliot does
with these ideas is to transform them into his own Christian
philosophy. The first epigraph of the *Four Quartets*, a quotation
from Heraclitus, reads; 'Although the Logos is common to all,
the majority of people live as though they had an understanding
of their own.' In Eliot, this fragment becomes the distinction
between those who accept what is true for all men, namely, the
reality of the Incarnation, 'the gift half-understood', and those
who deny it.

This same transformation occurs in 'Little Gidding', where
Eliot changes Heraclitus' 'Much learning does not teach one to
have understanding: else it would have taught Hesiod and
Pythagoras, and again Xenophanes, and Hekataios', to 'You are
not here to verify, / Instruct yourself, or inform curiosity / Or
carry a report. You are here to kneel / Where prayer has been
valid'. Understanding, that is to say, comes through faith and
belief, not by means of the accumulation of facts or through
science.

Again, Heraclitus states; 'This order, the same for all things,
no one of gods or men has made, but it always was, and is, and
ever shall be, an ever-living fire, kindling according to fixed
measure, and extinguished according to fixed measure.' In 'Little
Gidding' this naturalistic fire becomes the Christian fire of
purification and damnation:

> The dove descending breaks the air
> With flame of incandescent terror
> Of which the tongues declare
> The one discharge from sin and error.
> The only hope, or else despair
>   Lies in the choice of pyre or pyre –
>   To be redeemed from fire by fire.
>
> Who then devised the torment? Love.
> Love is the unfamiliar Name
> Behind the hands that wove
> The intolerable shirt of flame

> Which human power cannot remove.
> We only live, only suspire
> Consumed by either fire or fire.

Finally, Heraclitus writes; 'Fire lives in the death of air, and air lives in the death of fire; water lives in the death of earth, earth in that of water.' In the first three stanzas of the second movement of 'Little Gidding', Eliot omits the generative power of these four elements and stresses their totally destructive character because he wishes to emphasize the ultimacy of death in the flux, if we regard the flux as ultimate:

> Ash on an old man's sleeve
> Is all the ash the burnt roses leave.
> Dust in the air suspended
> Marks the place where a story ended.
> Dust inbreathed was a house –
> The wall, the wainscot and the mouse.
> The death of hope and despair,
>   This is the death of air.

> There are flood and drouth
> Over the eyes and in the mouth,
> Dead water and dead sand
> Contending for the upper hand.
> The parched eviscerate soil
> Gapes at the vanity of toil,
> Laughs without mirth.
>   This is the death of earth.

> Water and fire succeed
> The town, the pasture and the weed.
> Water and fire deride
> The sacrifice that we denied.
> Water and fire shall rot
> The marred foundations we forgot,
> Of sanctuary and choir.
>   This is the death of water and fire.

What, then, is the meaning of Heraclitus' 'The way up is the way down, the way forward is the way back', as Eliot conceives it? Eliot does not mean that time (or space) is relative, or that the temporal is the ultimate reality. Rather: that within the flux the choice is always the same, either death or God; and that, if we deny God, Who is the Timeless, the Eternal, all experiences are the same in their value, that is, they are all worth nothing. Living and dying, action and cessation, murder and creation – without any fixed reference to God – are of equal insignificance. It is in this way that Eliot changes the Heraclitean theory of time into a Christian theory of value: that, within the flux, if nothing else is recognized as more real than it, no experience is any different from any other, so far as its value character is concerned.

III

Eliot's theory of time is neo-Platonic, not Heraclitean. It is essentially an Immanence doctrine according to which the Eternal or Timeless is regarded as the creative source of the flux or temporal. This is not to say that Eliot denies the reality of the flux, in some Parmenidean fashion. He is no dualist, pitting the reality of the Eternal against the illusion of the flux. Instead, the flux, with all of its many ordinary experiences, is taken as real but its reality is derived from and sustained by the more ultimate reality of the Eternal. The flux is not an illusion, but it is an illusion to regard it as the only reality.

This immanence doctrine of time is no novelty in Eliot's work which he developed late in his creative life. In fact, it is already present in his first important poem, 'The Love Song of J. Alfred Prufrock'. And, in so far as the concept of time is a major one in the whole of Eliot's poetry, which I think it is, we may say that the unity of his poetry is now intact; and that the contention that Eliot's work somehow divides itself into the two periods of before and after *The Waste Land* will have to be rejected. Both Eliot and Matthiessen have repudiated the notion, advanced by I. A. Richards, that Eliot became a religious poet after *The Waste Land*; and it is our contention that the fundamental idea of his latest major poetic work, the *Four Quartets*, namely, the immanence doctrine of time, is already worked out in 'Prufrock'.

There are two sorts of time in 'Prufrock', which we may call true time and false time. False time has to do with those experiences that get nowhere, like the aimless streets of Prufrock's wanderings. This is the time of the third stanza, a time which seems to allow for everything but actually for nothing since all the events turn back on themselves:

> And indeed there will be time
> For the yellow smoke that slides along the street,
> Rubbing its back upon the window-panes;
> There will be time, there will be time
> To prepare a face to meet the faces that you meet;
> There will be time to murder and create,
> And time for all the works and days of hands
> That lift and drop a question on your plate;
> Time for you and time for me,
> And time yet for a hundred indecisions,
> And for a hundred visions and revisions,
> Before the taking of a toast and tea.

We must not construe this stanza as entirely negative. Actually, Eliot conceives the conflict within human experience in terms of immanence. The real or the true is already present in the false or lesser reality; the significant already part of the insignificant, waiting to be understood by us. Just as the streets of the first stanza do lead to the overwhelming question, so the insignificant in human experience does embody, as one of its dimensions, the significant, Thus, real or true time, which is time that encompasses significant experiences – those having purpose and direction – is immanent in false time, the time which returns unto itself. This is the meaning of the lines: 'And time for all the works and days of hands / That lift and drop a question on your plate.' All experiences, from creation to murder (death), contain as their ultimate dimension the overwhelming question. It is also the meaning of the difficult last stanza:

> We have lingered in the chambers of the sea
> By sea-girls wreathed with seaweed red and brown
> Till human voices wake us, and we drown.

Many interpret these lines as meaning; All of us, who are like Prufrock, have remained indecisive in the midst of the possibilities of salvation; and we will continue there until we die. But such a reading leaves out too much of what is in the poem as a whole. A more plausible interpretation is offered through the concept of immanence: We etherized patients, who live in our limbo-like trance of doing nothing, have been near the sources of salvation: we will remain there until we cease our state of mere physical existence, of 'death-in-life', and attain our spiritual rebirth, our 'life-in-death'. The key phrase of the latter interpretation is 'lingering in the chambers of the sea', which is tied organically to the questions that are dropped on our plate and the streets that lead to the overwhelming question. The possibilities of salvation are *within* our ordinary temporal experiences; we need only reach out to secure them.

The whole of 'Prufrock' is the struggle to emancipate ourselves from the acceptance of the ultimate character of false time and to recognize instead that which is *within* our temporal experiences as their ultimate moment, the overwhelming question. It is in this sense that 'Prufrock' is a deeply religious poem.

The doctrine of immanence makes its appearance at various places in the later writings of Eliot. We find it in one of its forms in Eliot's famous essay, 'Tradition and the Individual Talent':

The historical sense involves a perception, not only of the pastness of the past, but of its presence; the historical sense compels a man to write not merely with his own generation in his bones, but with a feeling that the whole of the literature of Europe from Homer and within it the whole of the literature of his own country has a simultaneous existence and composes a simultaneously order. This historical sense, which is a sense of the timeless and of the temporal together, is what makes a writer traditional.

It appears also in his poetry. In 'Choruses from *The Rock*', VII, Eliot writes:

Then came, at a predetermined moment, a moment in time and of time,

A moment not out of time, but in time, in what we call history:
transecting, bisecting the world of time, a moment in time
but not like a moment of time,
A moment in time but time was made through that moment: for
without the meaning there is no time, and that moment of
time gave the meaning.

And, in *Murder in the Cathedral*, Archbishop Becket proclaims:

It is not in time that my death shall be known;
It is out of time that my decision is taken.

However, it is in the *Four Quartets* that the immanence theory
of time is worked out fully in poetic terms. The first lines open
on what seems to be the classical Augustinian conception of
time, with its placing of the sense of the past and the future in
the present; but the poem soon shifts to an orthodox neo-
Platonic theory;

Time present and time past
Are both perhaps present in time future,
And time future contained in time past.
If all time is eternally present
All time is unredeemable.
What might have been is an abstraction
Remaining a perpetual possibility
Only in a world of speculation.
What might have been and what has been
Point to one end, which is always present.

The present and the past are perhaps already part of the
future but the future is determined by the past. In this sense, all
temporal experiences are in the present, at every moment, and we
cannot redeem the temporal because it is never away from us to
be redeemed. Also, and this becomes clear in the total context,
'All time is unredeemable' has another meaning: There is no
redemption if we recognize only the flux. Further, even the
realm of pure possibilities, of things that might have happened,
is no different from the temporal: Past, present, future and
possibility point to one end which is always with us; that is,

which end, as the Eternal or Timeless, immanent in the flux, is the ultimate source of explanation of it.

This notion of the Eternal or ultimate reality being immanent in the flux as the Logos which anyone can discern, but which only a few do discern, clarifies most of 'Burnt Norton'. Consider the following lines;

> Footfalls echo in the memory
> Down the passage which we did not take
> Towards the door we never opened
> Into the rose-garden. My words echo
> Thus, in your mind.

The rose-garden is the key idea in this passage. Eliot has used this image in much of his poetry and there is cogent conflicting opinion about its meaning. Whatever the general meaning may be, if there is one, at least here it seems to function in a double sense, as an actual place – a rose-garden; and as a symbol of those temporal experiences which reveal most poignantly the immanent character of the ultimately real. Like the Christian 'Kairos', the rose-garden symbolizes those moments that show, more than any others, the meeting of the Eternal and the temporal.

Besides the echo of the Logos, which is the meaning of the temporal, there are other echoes in the garden. There is, first, the deception of the thrush, calling us to a world of mere temporality. But such a world is one of indolence and desiccation, a reiteration of the waste land and the land of the hollow men:

> There they were, dignified, invisible,
> Moving without pressure, over the dead leaves,
> In the autumn heat, through the vibrant air. . . .

> There they were as our guests, accepted and accepting,
> So we moved, and they, in a formal pattern,
> Along the empty alley, into the box circle,
> To look down into the drained pool.

There is also the echo of the undeceiving bird, who leads us to other, more alive voices, to those who are less dignified and patterned: to those who can *see* the reality of the roses, for the roses do have 'the look of flowers that are looked at'. These are the voices of the children, hidden excitedly in the apple tree, who are laughing and singing; but who are, as we realize in 'Little Gidding', 'Not known, because not looked for / But heard, half-heard, in the stillness / Between two waves of the sea.'

The bird is the messenger of Truth, telling us that the rose-garden echoes with life: and that this life itself is a manifestation of something which is more than the mere flux. But the bird also knows that man will not acquiesce to that which is true:

> Go, go, go, said the bird: human kind
> Cannot bear very much reality.

The second movement of 'Burnt Norton' sharpens the immanence conception of time: that the Eternal or Timeless is the ultimate dimension of the flux and gives it whatever reality and meaning it has. After an introductory passage, in which physical movement, 'The trilling wire in the blood', epitomized in the struggle between the boarhound and the boar that ends in death, is falsified as the only movement there is, we come to true, non-physical movement:

> At the still point of the turning world. Neither flesh nor fleshless;
> Neither from nor towards; at the still point, there the dance is,
> But neither arrest nor movement. And do not call it fixity,
> Where past and future are gathered. Neither movement from nor
> towards,
> Neither ascent nor decline. Except for the point, the still point,
> There would be no dance, and there is only the dance.

The still point, of course, is the symbol of the Logos, but it is also the symbol of the Christian God. In God is the source of movement and the temporal. Not that God is movement; rather from Him emanates movement, to utilize a neo-Platonic idea. There is the temporal, the flux; but without God, the Timeless, there would be no temporal.

To experience the Eternal, the 'still point', is to transcend the temporal; it is to give up desire, action and suffering; to rise up to God, but with no physical action; and to understand both the Timeless and the temporal for the first time:

I can only say, *there* we have been: but I cannot say where.
And I cannot say, how long, for that is to place it in time.
The inner freedom from the practical desire,
The release from action and suffering, release from the inner
And the outer compulsion, yet surrounded
By a grace of sense, a white light still and moving,
Erhebung without motion, concentration
Without elimination, both a new world
And the old made explicit, understood
In the completion of its partial ecstasy,
The resolution of its partial horror.

We must start with the temporal, the ever-changing experience; and come to see its dependence upon the Timeless:

                              Time past and time future
Allow but a little consciousness.
To be conscious is not to be in time
But only in time can the moment in the rose-garden,
The moment in the arbour where the rain beat,
The moment in the draughty church at smokefall
Be remembered; involved with past and future.
Only through time time is conquered.

In the final movement of 'Burnt Norton', the distinction between the Timeless and the temporal becomes the distinction between The Word and words. Words lie, but it is only through words that we can conquer them, to express the truth which is The Word. And what we want to say we cannot say because words are always changing, being in the flux; but even with words we can suggest The Word: That God, Who is the Final Cause, did initiate the first event and does determine the last event:

Desire itself is movement
Not in itself desirable;
Love is itself unmoving,
Only the cause and end of movement,
Timeless, and undesiring

> Except in the aspect of time
> Caught in the form of limitation
> Between un-being and being.

The movement and the poem end with a concrete and visual
return to the rose-garden with their contrast between the inadequate affirmation of the sole reality of the flux and the true
recognition that there is something more, the Eternal, echoing in
the laughter of the children. How ridiculous, then, the sole
acceptance of 'the waste sad time / Stretching before and after'.

The remaining three parts of the *Four Quartets* rest, in great
measure, upon the immanence theory of 'Burnt Norton', and
constitute either expansions, modulations or recapitulations of it.
In 'East Coker', for example, we shift from the relation between
the temporal and the Eternal to an emphasis upon the active and
passive ways of salvation of St John of the Cross, the sixteenth-
century Spanish mystic. But there is implicit throughout the
recognition of the reality of both the temporal and the Eternal.
The poem opens with an affirmation of the reality of the flux in
human life and nature;

> In my beginning is my end. In succession
> Houses rise and fall, crumble, are extended,
> Are removed, destroyed, restored, or in their place
> Is an open field, or a factory, or a by-pass.
> Old stone to new building, old timber to new fires,
> Old fires to ashes, and ashes to the earth
> Which is already flesh, fur and faeces,
> Bone of man and beast, cornstalk and leaf.

Within the present, there is, as a part of it, the presence of the
past, in the form of Eliot's sixteenth-century Somerset ancestors,
whom he visualizes 'in that open field', as 'dancing around the
bonfire'; and participating in the various natural activities
governed by the passing of the seasons.

But his past is larger than his family ancestry, for it includes
the whole of creation:

> Dawn points, and another day
> Prepares for heat and silence. Out at sea the dawn wind

Wrinkles and slides. I am here
Or there, or elsewhere. In my beginning.

The past and the present are real but, by themselves, they offer
no understanding. The knowledge we derive *from* our temporal
experiences – empirical knowledge – is untrustworthy since it
imposes patterns on that which is always changing. Thus, we
cannot hope to learn from the past and present in preparation for
the future, because the future will bring its own modes of deception, being new at every moment. There is but one lesson we
can hope to learn from our living in the flux, the wisdom of
humility; 'humility is endless'.

In 'The Dry Salvages', Eliot follows his family ancestry from
England to America – to New England, the Mississippi, and St.
Louis, where he was born. The first movement of the poem is
the contrast between both the river, 'sullen, untamed and intractable', and the sea, vast and incomprehensible, on the one
hand, and the mechanized artifices of man, on the other hand.
His mechanical accomplishments have allowed man to forget the
river which is within him and the sea that is all about him: but
the river remains, 'waiting, watching and waiting'; and the sea,
with its 'many gods and many voices', is a perpetual reminder of
the ultimate destiny of man and his fancy creations.

We can regulate our watches, we can measure the time of our
ordinary experiences, but we can never control the intractable,
inevitable character of destruction, which is the real meaning of
the flux if we take it as the ultimate. This is the time that is
measured by the tolling bell of the ground swell, 'that is and
was from the beginning', which is Death:

And under the oppression of the silent fog
The tolling bell
Measures time not our time, rung by the unhurried
Ground swell, a time
Older than the time of chronometers, older
Than time counted by anxious worried women.

The second movement is a series of annunciations which
resolves into either the annunciation of death, if we take the tem-

poral as ultimate, or the Annunciation of rebirth, if we accept God as ultimate. Accept the flux and

> There is no end of it, the voiceless wailing,
> No end to the withering of withered flowers,
> To the movement of pain that is painless and motionless,
> To the drift of the sea and the drifting wreckage,
> The bone's prayer to Death its God. Only the hardly,
>> barely prayable
> Prayer of the one Annunciation.

The temporal preserves its own destruction. Ironically, this is its timeless character, with its burden of sin and death:

> Time the destroyer is time the preserver,
> Like the river with its cargo of dead negroes, cows and
>> chicken coops,
> The bitter apple and the bite in the apple.

But the temporal includes *within* it also the manifestation of God in the form of His Church – the Rock:

> And the ragged rock in the restless waters,
> Waves wash over it, fogs conceal it;
> On a halcyon day it is merely a monument,
> In navigable weather it is always a seamark
> To lay a course by: but in the sombre season
> Or the sudden fury, is what it always was.

It is in the fifth movement of 'The Dry Salvages', however, that the penultimate character of the relation of immanence between the temporal and the Eternal is fully revealed, in a kind of Spinozistic rhapsody:

> Men's curiosity searches past and future
> And clings to that dimension. But to apprehend
> The point of intersection of the timeless
> With time, is an occupation for the saint –
> No occupation either, but something given
> And taken, in a lifetime's death in love,
> Ardour and selflessness and self-surrender.

Like Spinoza, Eliot believes that the highest moment of

human achievement is reached when one understands everything *sub specie aeternitatis*; but, unlike Spinoza, he does not surrender the reality of the flux as a result of this understanding. To apprehend the immanence of God in the temporal is not to deny the reality of the temporal or to proclaim its illusory character; but to comprehend its mode of reality for the first time as a creation of God, with its own characteristics of individuality. It is in this sense that Eliot is neither Bergsonian nor a Spinozist in his philosophy of time, but essentially a Christian neo-Platonist.

'Little Gidding' is the grand recapitulation of the whole of the *Quartets*, so far as time is concerned, although the emphasis is now on the active or positive way of salvation. Detachment from things, persons and places is the right goal of man. It is the condition which arises through reflection on the nature of history, for 'history is a pattern of timeless moments'; and no people can deny its ultimate significance and meaning which is God and His benevolent relation to the world. We need not know the whole (sum) of history but only any one of its moments, for that moment will contain the whole (meaning) within it:

> We shall not cease from exploration
> And the end of all our exploring
> Will be to arrive where we started
> And know the place for the first time.

And, finally, it is in any of these moments that man can find his unity with God through the identification of his human love with the love of the Divine:

> Quick now, here, now, always –
> A condition of complete simplicity
> (Costing not less than everything)
> And all shall be well and
> All manner of thing shall be well
> When the tongues of flame are in-folded
> Into the crowned knot of fire
> And the fire and the rose are one.

SOURCE: *Sewanee Review* (1952).

Donald Davie

T. S. ELIOT: THE END OF AN ERA (1956)

I

I FIND it very surprising that all readers seem to either accept or reject the *Four Quartets* as a whole – and yet not really surprising, since the cleavage comes plainly not along any line of literary fact, but is flagrantly ideological; the religiously inclined applaud the *Quartets*, the more or less militantly secular and 'humanist' decry them. As simple as that.

At any rate, I find it still surprising (and depressing) that no one should yet have remarked to my knowledge how the third quartet, 'The Dry Salvages', sticks out among the rest like a sore thumb. At first sight it is not only incongruous with the others, strikingly different in conception and procedure, but different unaccountably and disastrously. One could take it by itself and prove convincingly that it is quite simply *rather a bad poem*. It amazes me that, so far as I know, no one has yet done this; and until very lately I thought I was the person to do it. In fact, I aim to do it here and now – but now with the proviso that all I can say against it is true only so far as it goes, that from another point of view all the vices become virtues and fall into place. It is possible, of course, that all other readers have been clever enough to see the thing aright from the start. But it goes without saying that I don't think so. Here at any rate, to begin with, is my case against 'The Dry Salvages'.

II

Leavis and Rajan have both applauded the opening lines of the poem, and Helen Gardner was so misguided as to choose them

for the basis of her claims for Eliot specifically as a manipulator
of language:

> I do not know much about gods; but I think that the river
> Is a strong brown god – sullen, untamed and intractable,
> Patient to some degree, at first recognized as a frontier;

Miss Gardner says that the 'strong brown god' is 'a personifica-
tion which the poet's tone makes no more than a suggestion, a
piece of only half-serious myth-making'. But the first line has not
sufficiently defined the tone (a single line hardly could) for this
to be true; and indeed it is to my ear still too uncertain, eight
lines later, to carry the journalistic cliché, 'worshippers of the
machine', by giving it the invisible quote-marks which, as Miss
Gardner allows, such an inert and faded locution requires. What
in any case, we may well ask, is the tone in which we could hear
without embarrassment the first line spoken? 'I do not know
much about gods' – who could conceivably start a conversation
like that without condemning himself from the start as an
uncomfortable poseur? Is it not rather like

> Poems are made by fools like me
> But only God can make a tree?

What is it but a gaucherie? And yet there *is* a tone in which we
have been addressed, which hovers here in the offing, a tone
familiar enough but still far from acceptable, a tone which has
indeed become a byword as a type of strident uncertainty in the
speaker and of correspondingly acute embarrassment in the
hearer – it is the tone of Whitman.

But what is Eliot thinking of, that he should talk like Whitman? And our bewilderment deepens:

> Unhonoured, unpropitiated
> By worshippers of the machine, but waiting, watching and wait-
>   ing.
> His rhythm was present in the nursery bedroom,
> In the rank ailanthus of the April dooryard,
> In the smell of grapes on the autumn table,
> And the evening circle in the winter gaslight.

'Worshippers of the machine'; then the incredibly limp 'watching and waiting'; and finally, limpest of all, 'his rhythm was
present'. 'His rhythm was present in the nursery bedroom' –
could anything be more vague and woolly? After this statement
has been issued, we know not a tittle more about the relation
between river and bedroom than we did before. And the poetry
is not just bad, but unaccountably so. For 'His rhythm was
present in' represents just that bridgework, that filling in and
faking of transitions, which Eliot as a post-symbolist poet has
always contrived to do without. From first to last his procedure
has been the symbolist procedure of 'juxtaposition without
copula', the setting down of images side by side with a space
between them, a space that does not need to be bridged. There
is an example just over the page in 'The Dry Salvages':

> The salt is on the briar rose,
> The fog is in the fir trees.

For now, from 'The river is within us' through to the end of the
first section, the poetry picks up, the diction becomes distinc-
tively Eliotic and fine; and only an unwonted straightforward-
ness, the vulnerable stance face to face with the subject, the
overtness of the evocation, are there to trouble us with something pre-symbolist and old-fashioned.

But, then, what shall be said of the famous sestina of the second
section, which Rajan calls 'as intricately organized as anything
Eliot has written'? Shall I be thought laughably naïve for calling
attention to the rhymes? In the first sestine comes an extremely
beautiful perception;

> The silent withering of autumn flowers
> Dropping their petals and remaining motionless;

The rhymes found to correspond to these in the later sestines are
as follows, in order:

> . . . the trailing
> Consequence of further days and hours,
> While emotion takes to itself the emotionless
> Years of living among the breakage . . .
> . . . the failing

Pride or resentment at failing powers,
The unattached devotion which might pass for devotionless . . .
   Where is the end of them, the fishermen sailing
Into the wind's tail, where the fog cowers?
We cannot think of a time that is oceanless . . .
Setting and hauling, while the North East lowers
Over shallow banks unchanging and erosionless . . .
No end to the withering of withered flowers,
To the movement of pain that is painless and motionless . . .

Should we not be justified in seeing here a case of sheer incompetence? Is it not plain that the *trouvaille* at the head of the page, 'Dropping their petals and remaining motionless', gets the poet into more and more patent difficulties (and dishonesties) once the rhyme on it has been taken up as a determining feature of his stanza-form? 'Emotionless' – how? 'Oceanless' – grotesque! 'Erosionless' – does he mean 'uneroded'? And 'movement . . . pain . . . painless . . . motionless' – our confidence in the poet has by this time been so undermined that we cannot, in justice to ourselves, take this as anything but incantatory gibberish. Faced with this, we have to feel a momentary sympathy with the rancour even of a Robert Graves – who, whatever his limitations, would never allow such slapdash inefficiency into his own verses.
   The next passage reads:

   It seems, as one becomes older,
That the past has another pattern, and ceases to be a mere
   sequence –
Or even development: the latter a partial fallacy
Encouraged by superficial notions of evolution
Which becomes, in the popular mind, a means of disowning
   the past.

Is this the poet who wove to and fro the close and lively syntax at the beginning of 'East Coker', or the passage from 'Burnt Norton' beginning 'The inner freedom from the practical desire'? How can we explain that the same poet should now proffer, in such stumbling trundling rhythms, these inarticulate ejaculations of reach-me-down phrases, the debased currency of the study circle? And worse is to come – Possum's little joke:

> The moments of happiness – not the sense of well-being,
> Fruition, fulfilment, security or affection,
> Or even a very good dinner . . .

At the dismal jocularity of that 'very good dinner', we throw in our hands. The tone that Miss Gardner thought established in the very first line can now, we realize, never be established at all. Or else, if we prefer to put it this way – it has been very thoroughly established, as excruciatingly unsettled, off-key. To be sure, the diction now picks up again for a while, though still liable to such upsets as the lame gabble, 'not forgetting / Something that is probably quite ineffable . . .' But section III begins with *Krishna*, which sticks in the throat even of Dr Rajan (who for the most part seems to be reading a different poem): 'Mr Eliot is never happy in "the maze of Oriental metaphysics" and his wanderings this time are uncomfortably sinuous.' And there is, as Rajan further notes, a self-advertising virtuosity, almost Euphuistic, about 'the future is a faded song, a Royal Rose or a lavender spray . . .'

At this point re-enter Whitman, conspicuously. S. Musgrove, author of *T. S. Eliot and Walt Whitman*, compares with this passage turning on 'Fare forward, travellers', Whitman's *Song of the Open Road*; and he comments (p. 55):

> Once again, Eliot has employed Whitman's material and manner in order to reject his philosophy. For Whitman, time stretches away in one infinite linear direction, towards a positive and perfect future, in which the possession of something actual, something better than the present, awaits the growing spirit of man. For Eliot, the sense of a direction is illusory; time is an eternal present which can never yield more than is now known, in which the only kind of possession conceivable is one alike in kind to dispossession from the demands of the self. . . .

This is a good deal less than fair to Whitman, who is at pains in *Song of the Open Road* to make it clear that there is no destination to the voyaging, no end to it, no perfection to be aimed at or

achieved except in the process of still and still going on. Thus
Eliot, with his 'Fare neither well nor ill, so it be forward' (my
words, of course, but a fair summary of Eliot's drift), has
dropped from Whitman only his optimism, substituting for it
the Chekhovian compassion which strips its objects of all dignity: 'Fare forward, you who think that you are voyaging . . .'
And to be sure, Musgrove talks as if the one unforgiveable thing
about Whitman, what proves his vulgarity, is precisely his optimism – a good example of that rigid neo-Augustinian temper
among Eliot's adherents which very properly enrages a secular
liberal like Kathleen Nott. For Whitman's optimism is not by
any means the worst thing about him. There is beneath and
beside it what Lawrence pointed to – 'Always wanting to merge
himself into the womb of something or other': that is, the drive
to 'transcend' the self by losing it in identification with some inhuman process, of which, as Wyndham Lewis pointed out long
ago, the process of time is perhaps the most obvious and popular. Moreover, as Lawrence and, following him, Yvor Winters
have shown, this drive is especially marked in the American
literary tradition, from Emerson and Melville to Hart Crane* –
its obsessive symbol very frequently, as here in 'The Dry Salvages', the sea. And, sure enough, Rajan comes aptly in once
more with the suggestion that section IV, 'Lady, whose shrine
stands on the promontory', 'perhaps owes something to the
sermon in *Moby Dick*'. Even the Hinduism fits in, if one recalls
Yeats's remark about 'those translations of the Upanishads,
which it is so much harder to study by the sinking flame of
Indian tradition than by the serviceable lamp of Emerson and
Walt Whitman'. And yet, when one recalls also Yeats's verdict
on Emerson and Whitman, 'writers who have come to seem
superficial precisely because they lack the Vision of Evil', one
finds it unaccountable that Eliot, the author of the essay on
Baudelaire, however American, should have fallen into this trap
of ecstatic merging with the process.

The last section begins with an admirable new departure, in

* One traces it as far afield as Berenson, in his remarks on Umbrian
space-composition and 'the religious emotion'.

the vigour of 'To communicate with Mars, converse with
spirits . . .', but then it modulates, through a very beautiful yet
again strangely uncritical treatment of the Bergsonian *durée* in
music ('but you are the music / While the music lasts'), into the
inhuman conclusion that human life for all but the saints is mere
purposeless *movement*, scurrying activity, only at fleeting uncon-
trollable moments elevated into the meaning and dignity of true
action. We realize that the poet indeed meant the shocking
'emotionless' of the sestina; and if that helps to validate the
poetry of that passage, it only makes the poet seem even less
humane.

III

If we are to turn the force of these numerous objections we have
to go a long way round – and yet in a way we need to go no
further than Hugh Kenner's essay on 'Eliot's Moral Dialectic'
(*Hudson Review*, 1949),[1] which relegates to the status of curio
every other piece of criticism on the *Quartets*. Kenner there distinguishes the predominant structural principle of this poetry as
a diagram in which two terms (life and death, beginning and
end) are first opposed, then falsely reconciled in a third term, and
then truly reconciled in a fourth term, a metaphysical conception.
His examples are section III of 'Burnt Norton', where the opposed
terms light and darkness are combined in the parody-reconciliation of the 'flicker' in the twilit murk of London, only to be truly
reconciled paradoxically in the metaphysical Dark Night of the
Soul; and section III of 'Little Gidding', where the opposing
terms attachment and detachment are reconciled in parody in
'indifference', only to be truly reconciled in Love.
Section III of 'East Coker' yields up the same pattern:

So the darkness shall be the light, and the stillness the dancing.
Whisper of running streams, and winter lightning,
The wild thyme unseen and the wild strawberry,
The laughter in the garden, echoed ecstasy
Not lost, but requiring, pointing to the agony
Of death and birth.

> You say I am repeating
> Something I have said before. I shall say it again.
> Shall I say it again? In order to arrive there,
> To arrive where you are, to get from where you are not,
> You must go by a way wherein there is no ecstasy.
> In order to arrive at what you do not know
> You must go by a way which is the way of ignorance.

Darkness and light, stillness and dancing, are two pairs of opposed terms. They are reconciled in 'the agony / Of death and birth'. Birth, coming from the dark to the light, is a sort of death, for as soon as we are born we begin to die; and death, going from the light to the dark, is a sort of birth – into eternal life. And the stillness of a seizure, the dance of pain, are reconciled in agony. But this is a false reconciliation which is at once abandoned for the true one carried in the borrowings from St John of the Cross. Thus, 'I shall say it again / Shall I say it again?' is an ironical trap. Musgrove suggests an allusion to Whitman's 'Do I contradict myself? Very well, I contradict myself.' This points it up even more; for the point is that Eliot *is* contradicting himself even as he *seems* to repeat himself – inevitably, because it is characteristic of the terms he is thinking in that the false reconciliation, being a parody of the true one, is very hard – all but impossible – to distinguish from it in words, even in words charged to the utmost, as in poetry.

Since the third sections of 'Burnt Norton', 'East Coker' and 'Little Gidding' are thus broadly parallel in structure, one would expect to discern the same structure in section III of 'The Dry Salvages', which is the Whitmanesque passage I have just discussed. But 'The Dry Salvages', as we noted at the start, is the odd one out in all sorts of ways; and though the pattern is there, it is there only with a difference, and is hard to discern. 'And the way up is the way down, the way forward is the way back' – here are the terms opposed, right enough. But we look in vain for the false reconciliation, though the image of the traveller is obviously apt for it – since travelling is the same state whether one travels from here to there, or there to here. But this parody-reconciliation is ruled out of court when the poet jumps at once to his insight (a restatement, as Kenner has noted, of the insight of 'Tradition and the Individual Talent'):

> You cannot face it steadily, but this thing is sure,
> That time is no healer: the patient is no longer here.

Yet the parody-reconciliation *is* present in the lines that follow, though never overtly offered – it is there precisely in the shade of Whitman that haunts the passage, the Whitmanesque tone that hovers here as an overtone.

But we can, and must, go further. This diagram that Kenner has brilliantly extricated he does not offer to us merely as the structural principle informing these passages and others like them. He hints that the same diagram informs the *Four Quartets* as a whole. If this is so, then 'The Dry Salvages', the third of them, should appear as the false reconciliation, the parody. And here it seems we may at last be coming near to understanding, and forgiving, its peculiarities.

It is generally recognized that parody is to be found in the *Four Quartets*, that in 'East Coker', for instance, when the poet says, of the lyric at the start of section II, 'That was a way of putting it – not very satisfactory: / A periphrastic study in a worn-out poetical fashion', we are meant to take this at its face value and to agree that the passage referred to is, therefore, a parody. But when Kenner asks us to compare 'Down the passage which we did not take' at the start of 'Burnt Norton' with the 'cunning passages, contrived corridors' of Gerontion (himself, as Kenner argues, a living parody of the true self-surrender that we find in Simeon), we are advised that we must look for parody elsewhere in the *Four Quartets*, where it is not explicitly pointed out to us by the poet. For instance, the false reconciliation which I have pointed out in 'East Coker', 'the agony / Of death and birth', while it looks back to the significantly theatrical image, 'With a hollow rumble of wings, with a movement of darkness on darkness', looks forward surely to 'The wounded surgeon plies the steel' and the much-elaborated skull-and-crossbones conceit which occupies the whole of section IV of the poem. Several readers have objected to this as strained and laboured;

and since the necrophily which informs it has already been
shown as a parody of the true reconciliation between dark
and light, should we not take it that the strain and the labouring
are deliberate, a conscious forcing of the tone, a *conscious* movement towards self-parody? What is it in fact but what we were
warned of in the typically opalescent lines from 'Burnt Norton' –

> The crying shadow in the funeral dance,
> The loud lament of the disconsolate chimera?

It is my argument, then, that in the sense and to the degree in
which section IV of 'East Coker' is a parody the whole of 'The
Dry Salvages' is a parody. It is hardly too much to say that the
whole of this third quartet is spoken by a nameless persona; certainly it is spoken through a mask, spoken *in character*, spoken in
character as the American. This, and nothing else, can explain the
approximations to Whitmanesque and other pre-symbolist
American verse-procedures; and the insistent Americanism, of
course, as all the commentators have noted, is a quality also of
the locale persistently evoked by the images – of the Mississippi
and the New England coast for instance. It is thus that the incompetence turns out to be dazzling virtuosity; and the in-
humanity of the conclusion reached turns out to be only a parody
of the true conclusion reached in 'Little Gidding', which is
thoroughly humane in its insistence that all varieties of human
folly and imperfection are the conditions for apprehending
perfection, that the world is therefore necessary and to that
extent – even the worst of it – good.

IV

There remains only one question. Admitting, as we have had to
admit, that the *Four Quartets* – and 'The Dry Salvages' no less
than every other part – represent a superbly controlled achievement of its kind, what are we to say of that kind? What kind of
poetry is this, in which loose and woolly incoherent language
can be seen to be – in its place and for special purposes – better
than clear and closely articulated language? This is a question

raised not just by the *Quartets* but by Eliot's work as a whole. The opening paragraph of the fifth section of *Ash Wednesday* is what Leavis says it is – a magnificent acting out in verse-movement and word-play of 'both the agonized effort to seize the unseizable, and the elusive equivocations of the thing grasped'. But it is also, from another point of view, what Max Eastman says it is – an 'oily puddle of emotional noises'. It is easy to say that Leavis's point of view is right, and Eastman's wrong – that any poetic effect can be seen and judged only as it plays its part in the economy of a whole poem, and that any amount of violence done to language, any amount of sheer ugliness, can be justified as means to a justifiable poetic end. But this is to assert that Eastman's pang of angry discomfort, which I suppose is shared by every sensitive reader at least at a first reading, is not a protest against ugliness on behalf of beauty, but only a protest against the functional in favour of the pretty. Are we in fact prepared to waive the claim 'beautiful' which we make for those lines of poetry which move us to applause as surely as the lines from *Ash Wednesday* move us to rebellion? And are we, moreover (for this too is implied), prepared to waive the claim 'poetry' for those lines we applaud – unless, that is, their engagingness can be seen as functional?

Well, we – you and I, dear reader – may be prepared to waive these claims. What is quite certain is that not only that legendary figure, the common reader, but the enthusiast and the specialist – a person like Dr Rajan – is not prepared to do so; not prepared because he has not realized it is what is required. More, the poet himself – a poet like Robert Graves – is not prepared to do so. And (what perhaps should make us pause) younger poets than either Graves or Eliot *have* realized what is required of them by poetry like Eliot's and have refused – at least where their own writing is concerned – to waive their claims to poetry and to beauty in the old-fashioned pre-symbolist sense.

'Pre-symbolist', yes. For it is pre-eminently symbolist and post-symbolist poetry that waives these claims and insists that the reader waive them also. Eliot waives them when he says, in 'East Coker', 'The poetry does not matter.' The exegetes cushion the shock of this by taking it to mean '*That sort* of poetry doesn't . . .', the sort which we have just heard called 'a periphrastic study in a worn-out poetical fashion', which we have agreed to consider as parody. Well, that interpretation can be allowed to stand for classroom consumption. But it isn't what Eliot means, or it isn't all that he means. He means what he says: the poetry doesn't matter, and beauty doesn't matter – for no verse can be judged either poetic or beautiful except in so far as it is seen to be expressive; and what it has to express may demand, as it does in 'The Dry Salvages', rather the false note than the true one, the faded and shop-soiled locution rather than the phrase new-minted, the trundling rhythm rather than the cut, woolliness rather than clarity –

> See now they vanish,
> The faces and places, with the self which, as it could, loved
>   them.

Woolliness becomes the only sort of clarity, the wrong note is the right note, and nothing is so beautiful as what is hideous – in certain (not uncommon) poetic circumstances.

If it is true that Kenner's essay has made everything else on the *Quartets* (and not on them only but on Eliot's work in general) seem like literary curiosities, none of these curios is so appealing to me as Anthony Thorlby's essay, 'The Poetry of *Four Quartets*', which was published after Kenner's (in the *Cambridge Journal*, 1952) but was obviously not written in the light of that. Thorlby is seriously wrong about the *Quartets*; nothing could be further from the truth than his assertion, 'What is remarkable in Mr Eliot's use of imagery is not that it is symbolic or capable of interpretation, but that the interpretation is essential to its poetic coherence.' Or rather, if this is true in one sense, if we take 'interpretation' to mean 'seeing the place of any part in relation to the whole', it is certainly untrue if we take it to mean, as Thorlby does, that each image as we come to it must be construed, like the images of allegory. What is appealing and important about Thorlby's essay is that it represents a man recognizing that the symbolist revolution in poetry has happened, and trying to come to grips with it. To be sure, Thorlby does not acknowledge that the revolution he perceives is the symbolist revolution; indeed, he writes as if it were inaugurated specifically by *Four Quartets*, seemingly unaware that the revolution was over, and successfully over, long before Eliot began to write, and that all Eliot's poems, the earliest as well as the latest, are constructed on that assumption – that the symbolist procedures have arrived and supplanted all others. Then, again, Thorlby's objections to the procedure as he detects it could be easily countered by anyone versed even a little in symbolist theory; for his argument rests upon a hard and fast distinction between 'having an experience' and 'seeing the significance of that experience' – a distinction made untenable by Bergson. Nevertheless, Thorlby at least perceives the essentially post-symbolist nature of the poetry of the *Quartets* – which is more than can be said for most of the commentators – even if he hasn't the label to tie on to it. And he grasps quite a lot of the implications of the symbolist revolution in terms of the revised expectations that the reader must now entertain – a matter of crucial importance which is hardly ever touched upon.

Thus it is very nearly correct – it is entirely correct from most points of view – to say with Thorlby: 'Mr Eliot's poetry is *about* the many forms in which the life of poetry has flourished; which is a very different thing from simply accepting one form and creating within it a poetry of life.' And it is entirely correct to say, as he does: 'Mr Eliot, then, is not standing outside his material looking in upon the experience he is writing about, composing it into one form; he is himself at the centre . . . looking around him upon so many of the problems of to-day which he hopes to illumine by its light.' This last point is the vital one. If no one has made it before Thorlby, that was (I suspect) for fear of falling foul of the master's own propaganda for impersonality in poetry, on the gap between the man who suffers and the poet who creates. Eliot was playing perfectly fair in this, and one can hardly resent his insistence when one finds critics, deaf to all his warnings, reading 'Gerontion' as a *cri de coeur* rather than what it is – the rendering of the state of mind of an ima-

gined persona, from which the poet is wholly detached. From
this point of view Eliot is indeed impersonal, standing quite
aside and apart from his creation – my diagnosis of 'The Dry
Salvages' as parody makes the point all over again. And yet
Thorlby is right too; in another sense Eliot is never outside and
apart from his poems. No post-symbolist poet can be outside his
poem as Milton was outside 'Lycidas': and no post-symbolist
poem can ever be as impersonal as 'Lycidas' was for John Crowe
Ransom when he called it 'a poem nearly anonymous'. If Eliot
enters his own poems only disguised as a persona, wearing a
mask, at least he enters them. Reading a parody, we are inevitably aware (though as it were at one remove) of the parodist.
Perhaps no other kind of poet is so much in evidence in his own
poems as the parodist is, the histrionic virtuoso, always tipping
the wink. And if Eliot thus enters into his own poems, his
reader must do likewise, changing his focus as the poem changes
focus, knowing when to give almost full credence to what the
poetry says, when to make reservations according as he detects
the voice of now one persona, now another parodying the first.

I share Thorlby's preference for a kind of poetry which stands
on its own feet, without my help, as an independent creation, a
thing to be walked around, and as satisfying from one standpoint
as from another. And so I hope I shall not be thought lacking in
gratitude to Eliot for the *Four Quartets*, nor lacking in respect for
the prodigious achievement of that poem, if I say that I hope for
quite a different sort of poem in the future, a sort of poem more
in harmony with what was written in Europe before symbolism
was thought of, even (since symbolist procedures are only the
logical development of Romantic procedures) before Romanti-
cism was thought of. I am not forgetting the lesson of 'Tradition
and the Individual Talent'. I know that history cannot be un-
written that there can be no question of putting the clock back;
the post-symbolist poetry I look for may be more in harmony
with pre-Romantic poetry, it can never be the same. There
cannot be a conspiracy to pretend that the symbolist revolution
never happened. (The annoying thing of course is that, because
Eliot has been seen by the influential critics most often in the

perspective of the specifically English tradition rather than in the perspective of Europe as a whole, it is commonly held that he has done just what I seem to ask for, has re-established continuity with the poetry of the seventeenth and eighteenth centuries. And he has really done so – but only in relatively superficial ways.)

If I hope for a different sort of poetry, that hope is reasonably confident – not because I give much weight to the younger poets of today who, when they think in these terms at all (they seldom do), declare that the post-symbolist tradition is 'worked out'; not even because the respectable poetry written in England and America by poets younger than Eliot is plainly not written according to his prescription; but simply because the *Four Quartets* represent a stage of such subtlety and intricacy in the post-symbolist tradition that it is impossible to think of its ever being taken a stage further. Surely no poet, unless it be Eliot himself, can elaborate further this procedure in which the true key is never sounded, but exists in the poem only as the norm by which all the voices that speak are heard as delicately off-key, as the voices of parody. It is, at any rate, in this hope and this confidence of something quite different in the offing, that I have written the second half of my title: 'T. S. Eliot: *The End of an Era*'.

SOURCE: *Twentieth Century* (1956).

NOTE

1. [Editor's note.] This essay was subsequently incorporated into *The Invisible Poet*: see pp. 168–96.

Hugh Kenner

INTO OUR FIRST WORLD (1959)

I

IN the summer of 1934 Eliot, vacationing at Chipping Campden in Gloucestershire, visited an uninhabited mansion, erected on the site of an earlier country house two hundred years burnt, and wandered in its deserted formal garden.

> Other echoes
> Inhabit the garden. Shall we follow?
> Quick, said the bird, find them, find them,
> Round the corner. Through the first gate,
> Into our first world, shall we follow
> The deception of the thrush? Into our first world.
> There they were, dignified, invisible,
> Moving without pressure, over the dead leaves,
> In the autumn heat, through the vibrant air,
> And the bird called, in response to
> The unheard music hidden in the shrubbery,
> And the unseen eyebeam crossed, for the roses
> Had the look of flowers that are looked at. . . .

This experience catalyzed certain fragments which *Murder in the Cathedral* did not finally incorporate, and provided him with the terminal poem to *Poems: 1909–1935*, where it follows and transfigures the 'Choruses from *The Rock*'.

'Burnt Norton' terminates Eliot's most fluent poetic years. The sinuous easy gravity, the meditative poise, the pellucid certainty of cadence and diction, draw strength from two years' unremitting work with stage verse, which if it permitted diffuseness exacted clarity or the show of clarity, and which brought to his disposal techniques for generating with cool assurance an air of unemphatic meaning.

Many small things draw the mind forward through this verse. The syntax beckons just a little ahead of our attention, never delivering over everything to some resonant line on which we can come to rest.

> And the bird called, in response to
> The unheard music hidden in the shrubbery,
> And the unseen eyebeam crossed, for the roses
> Had the look of flowers that are looked at

which is utterly different from the characteristic movement of *The Waste Land*: 'In this decayed hole among the mountains' an achieved quotable line, followed by 'In the faint moonlight, the grass is singing' another self-sufficient line, after which comes 'Over the tumbled graves, about the chapel' – followed in turn by the next item in this accumulation of strong lines 'There is the empty chapel, only the wind's home'. The sentence in 'Burnt Norton' goes so delicately about its business that we forget to be puzzled by the 'unseen eyebeam'; it takes its place on the plane of half-apprehensible fact where the inhabitants of 'our first world' move without pressure. *The Waste Land*, working by accumulation, cannot afford to relax its mantic intensity. Its obscurities envelop themselves in folds of sound, dogmatically impenetrable: 'Revive for a moment a broken Coriolanus'. 'Broken' is a luminescent enigma, its alternative connotations of moral defeat and a shattered statue not central to the line but by-products of the presence in the line of a word with a suitable open vowel. In 'Burnt Norton' we are not detained in that way. 'Our first world', by not insisting, establishes itself in a pattern of meaning, whether we accept it as the world of childhood and 'they' as departed elder presences, or as the garden of Eden and 'they' as our first parents, or as the garden at the Burnt House in ceremonial use, and 'they' as seventeenth-century spectres whom the imagination conjures into a scene now deserted. These connotations detach themselves, but the words themselves are innocently transparent, untouched by rhetoric:

> Through the first gate
> Into our first world.

'First' twice takes meaningful stress; we cannot be sure what the meaning is, but the structure of discourse is seamless, like that of superb conversation imperfectly heard. In the same way, the otherwise precarious mystery of 'music hidden in the shrubbery' is neutralized by a tactful 'unheard':

> And the bird called, in response to
> The unheard music hidden in the shrubbery.

The responding bird call, again, establishes the reality of 'unheard music' on some plane of consciousness in which we can believe though we do not at the moment share it. And as for the 'unseen eyebeam', invisible presences and unheard music prepare us for it, and the roses, we are told, respond to its crossing:

> for the roses
> Had the look of flowers that are looked at.

That *we* are looking at them seems irrelevant, so tactfully have we by this time been effaced, so substantial have the inapprehensible presences become.

The four-stress line in this passage is manipulated with a new easy authority; admitting as it does four unobtrusive opportunities for emphasis, it selects without insisting just those components of the vision that will sustain one another:

> Móving without préssure, over the déad léaves,
> In the áutumn héat, through the vibrant áir.

Dead leaves and autumn heat the senses can testify to; vibrant air and pressureless movement acquire by association a comparable authority.

Eliot was a long time settling on this characteristic four-beat measure, which can relax toward colloquial intimacy – 'There would be nó dánce, and there is ónly the dánce' or contract in meditative deliberation – 'Tíme pást and tíme fúture'. We first encounter it in 'Journey of the Magi', then find it in the 'Choruses from *The Rock*', accommodating within its hortatory firmness an unexpected wit:

> 'Here were decent godless people:
> Their only monument the asphalt road
> And a thousand lost golf balls.'

– in *Murder in the Cathedral*, spanning a scale from doggerel to exaltation; now in 'Burnt Norton', the unassertive Eliotic measure framing verse that, for the first time, we suppose to be selflessly transparent. The development of this measure, in the course of eight years or so, was Eliot's last feat of technical innovation.

To devise a measure is to devise a voice, and the appropriate range of expressive content the Voice implies. Of this Voice we may remark first of all its selflessness; it is Old Possum's last disappearing-trick. No persona, Prufrock, Gerontion, Tiresias or the Magus, is any longer needed. The words appear to be writing themselves:

> Footfalls echo in the memory
> Down the passage which we did not take
> Towards the door we never opened
> Into the rose-garden.

This is not a troubling Prufrockian 'Let us go'; 'we', like the French *on*, is devoid of specificity, so much so that the first person singular –

> My words echo
> Thus, in your mind.

– intrudes with dry Puritanic mischief, compounded by the gesture of pedagogic despair that follows:

> But to what purpose
> Disturbing the dust on a bowl of rose-leaves
> I do not know.

This mimics a lecture-room trick without personifying the trickster; it serves to locate in the Harvard graduate seminar the dozen lines of speculation concerning Time present and Time past with which 'Burnt Norton' opens, slyly justifying their austere exactness without allowing us to suppose that a didactic poet is on his high horse. Prufrock's 'There will be time, there will be time' is by comparison a forensic toying with syllables.

This mimicry of the dynamics of personal intercession, the Voice moving from exposition through intimacy to reminiscence, passing through lyric, expending itself in overheard meditation, without ever allowing us to intuit the impurities of personal presence, transforms at last into self-sustaining technique the anonymity which Eliot always devised, by one means or another, as the indispensable condition of his poetry. He had employed masks, he had employed styles: he had manipulated ventriloquially the effects of respected poets; in *Ash Wednesday* he had allowed a discontinuous *poésie pure* to imply a moving zone of consciousness. In *Ash Wednesday* the relation between speaker and reader – indeed the speaker's very mode of existence – is made to seem artless by an extreme of artifice, like the perspective in some pastiche of Fra Angelico. In 'Burnt Norton' such problems are not so much solved as caused to vanish, as Euclid or the author of 'Thirty Days hath September' caused them to vanish. The man holding the pen does not bare his soul, but on the other hand we feel no compulsion to posit or pry into some persona. The motifs of the poem simply declare themselves; and when we come upon the line 'I can only say, *there* we have been: but I cannot say where' the first person pronoun prompts no curiosity.

We never know quite where we are in the poem, but all possible relevant experiences are congruent. When

> Footfalls echo in the memory
> Down the passage which we did not take
> Towards the door we never opened
> Into the rose-garden,

we are at liberty to suppose that this is a picturesque evocation of 'what might have been', or to recall the White Rabbit's footfalls and the garden which Alice had to traverse the whole of Wonderland in order to enter. A moment later it is the formal garden of the Burnt House, and when we move

> Along the empty alley, into the box circle,
> To look down into the drained pool

there is no harm in allowing 'the box circle' to remind us of a theatre as well as a hedge. The lotus, sure enough, moves rather like a ballerina of Diaghilev's –

> Dry the pool, dry concrete, brown edged,
> And the pool was filled with water out of sunlight,
> And the lotos rose, quietly, quietly,
> The surface glittered out of heart of light,
> And they were behind us, reflected in the pool.

This is – to complicate matters further – ideal water and an imagined lotus: 'Then a cloud passed, and the pool was empty'. This garden now disenchanted resembles Eden transformed into a place where the soil must be tilled:

> Go, go, go, said the bird: human kind
> Cannot bear very much reality.
> Time past and time future
> What might have been and what has been
> Point to one end, which is always present.

We have very nearly stepped into some world where happenings are simultaneous, the past actual, what might have been really so, our first world still here, 'that vanished mind of which our mind is a continuation' sensibly co-present with our restricted sphere of experience. But this would be reality, of which human kind cannot bear very much, so it is as a concession to our weakness that we are shut up in the present moment. This motif is first announced by Becket, minutes before his death. The Chorus has smelt the death-bringers, and has perceived that

> What is woven on the loom of fate
> What is woven in the councils of princes
> Is woven also in our veins, our brains.

And when it has taken upon itself the guilt for what might have been and what will be, Becket assures it –

> Peace, and be at peace with your thoughts and visions.
> These things had to come to you and you to accept them.
> This is your share of the eternal burden,
> The perpetual glory. This is one moment,
> But know that another

> Shall pierce you with a sudden painful joy
> When the figure of God's purpose is made complete.
> You shall forget these things, toiling in the household,
> You shall remember them, droning by the fire,
> When age and forgetfulness sweeten memory
> Only like a dream that has often been told
> And often been changed in the telling. They will seem
> unreal.
> Human kind cannot bear very much reality.

It is a much quieter revelation in the Burnt Norton garden, that becomes unbearable, but a revelation so rich in its promise that the whole of *Four Quartets* exfoliates from it. The next lines move into a lyric extrapolation from the Women of Canterbury's discovery that what is woven on the loom of fate is woven also in their veins and brains:

> The dance along the artery
> The circulation of the lymph
> Are figured in the drift of stars.

A harmonious circling order comprehends all movement:

> Ascend to summer in the tree
> We move above the moving tree
> In light upon the figured leaf
> And hear upon the sodden floor
> Below, the boarhound and the boar
> Pursue their pattern as before
> But reconciled among the stars.

Since the whole passage unites mundane and celestial phenomena, there is no need for its opening lines,

> Garlic and sapphires in the mud
> Clot the bedded axle-tree,

to occasion puzzlement. The axle-tree appears to be that of the turning heavens, its lower end, like the bole of Yggdrasil, embedded in our soil. A moment later the image of the axle-tree gives place to an abstract equivalent, and the measure expands to accommodate meditation picking its way:

At the still point of the turning world. Neither flesh nor fleshless;
Neither from nor towards; at the still point, there the dance is,
But neither arrest nor movement. And do not call it fixity,
Where past and future are gathered.

This is the philosophers' paradox of the Wheel, the exact centre
of which is precisely motionless, whatever the velocity of the
rim. Though one may imagine the centre as a point of can-
cellation, Aristotle presented it (*De Anima* III 10) as the ener-
gizing point:

> Except for the point, the still point,
> There would be no dance, and there is only the dance.

The still point confers meaning; G. K. Chesterton remarked that
since the time of Chaucer human society had been converted
from a dance into a race. And it is some apprehension of the still
point, where past and future are gathered, that has occurred in
the garden –

> both a new world
> And the old made explicit, understood
>
> In the completion of its partial ecstasy,
> The resolution of its partial horror.

This is consciousness, not the consciousness which philosophers
think about, but a consciousness as enveloping and undiscussible
as the Bradleyan 'immediate experience'; and, 'To be conscious
is not to be in time'.

There is however something that does occur in time, and that
is memory. Memory is to be cherished and resorted to because
one cannot often expect to be conscious. And memory which
occurs in time is our weapon against Time:

> But only in time can the moment in the rose-garden,
> The moment in the arbour where the rain beat,
> The moment in the draughty church at smokefall
> Be remembered; involved with past and future.
> Only through time time is conquered.

These speculations have all grown out of the experience of

déjà vu in the garden. They generalize that strange concurrence of sensations, supply it with meaning not merely eerie, and unite its gravity with that of the meditative life. The third section of 'Burnt Norton' provides a second experience, located not in the Garden but in the City, or rather beneath the City, on an underground platform, no doubt of the Circle Line. The Underground's 'flicker' is a mechanical reconciliation of light and darkness, the two alternately exhibited very rapidly. The traveller's emptiness is 'neither plenitude nor vacancy'. In this 'dim light' we have

> neither daylight
> Investing form with lucid stillness
> Turning shadow into transient beauty
> With slow rotation suggesting permanence
> Nor darkness to purify the soul
> Emptying the sensual with deprivation
> Cleansing affection from the temporal.

There is rotation, but it does not suggest permanence; there is darkness, purifying nothing; there is light, but it invests nothing with lucid stillness; there is a systematic parody of the wheel's movement and the point's fixity –

> Men and bits of paper, whirled by the cold wind
> That blows before and after time,

not like the souls of Paolo and Francesca, who were somewhere in particular throughout eternity for a particular reason known to them, nor even like de Bailhache, Fresca, and Mrs Cammel, who were disintegrated; but simply

> The strained time-ridden faces
> Distracted from distraction by distraction
> Filled with fancies and empty of meaning
> Tumid apathy with no concentration.

Light and darkness are opposites, apparently united by this flicker. Their actual reconciliation is to be achieved by 'descending lower', into an emptier darkness:

> Descend lower, descend only,
> Into the world of perpetual solitude,
> World not world, but that which is not world,
> Internal darkness, deprivation
> And destitution of all property,
> Desiccation of the world of sense,
> Evacuation of the world of fancy,
> Inoperancy of the world of spirit;
> This is the one way . . .

Opposites falsely reconciled, then truly reconciled: in the central section of the poem its central structural principle is displayed. The false reconciliation parodies the true one, as the Hollow Men parody the saints, as Gerontion parodies Simeon, as Becket suicide would have parodied Becket martyr, as the leader's eyes in which there is no interrogation parody that certainty which inheres 'at the still point of the turning world'.

In this Underground scene, curiously enough, the instructed reader may catch a glimpse of the author, sauntering through the crowd as Alfred Hitchcock does in each of his films. For its locale, Eliot noted, sharing a private joke with his brother in Massachusetts, is specifically the Gloucester Road Station, near the poet's South Kensington headquarters, the point of intersection of the Circle Line with the Piccadilly tube to Russell Square. Whoever would leave the endless circle and entrain for the offices of Faber & Faber must 'descend lower', and by spiral stairs if he chooses to walk. 'This is the one way, and the other is the same'; the other, adjacent to the stairs, is a lift, which he negotiates 'not in movement, but abstention from movement'. As Julia Shuttlethwaite observes in *The Cocktail Party*, 'In a lift I can meditate'.

After this whiff of the Possum's whimsy, section IV displays the flash of the kingfisher's wing, to offset an instance of the Light which rests. The sun is the still point around which the earth turns, and light is concentrated there; it subtly becomes (for Eliot does not name it) a type of the still point where every variety of light inheres, which transient phenomena reflect. And section V presents language itself as a transience on which sufficient form may confer endurance. The poem ends with a reassertion of the possibility, and the significance, of timeless moments:

> Sudden in a shaft of sunlight
> Even while the dust moves
> There rises the hidden laughter
> Of children in the foliage
> Quick now, here, now, always –
> Ridiculous the waste sad time
> Stretching before and after.

In this elusive vision the moving dust in sunlight suggests the conditions of human existence, dust sustained and made visible by whatever power emanates from the still point; 'quick' means both instantaneous and alive; here and now acquire momentarily the significance of 'always'; and the 'before and after' which for Shelley contained those distracting glimpses of 'what might have been', cease to tantalize: they are merely aspects of 'the waste sad time' which the timeless moment has power to render irrelevant.

This remarkable poem, which no one, however well acquainted with Eliot's earlier work, could have foreseen, brings the generalizing style of the author of 'Prufrock' and the austere intuitions of the disciple of Bradley for the first time into intimate harmony. Suggestion does not outrun thought, nor design impose itself on what word and cadence are capable of suggesting. It was a precarious unobtrusive masterpiece, which had for some years no successor. Having recovered 'Burnt Norton' from the chaos of one play, Eliot concerned himself not with a successor to 'Burnt Norton' but with another play, which ought to have been a securer achievement that it is. In 1939 he published *The Family Reunion.*

II

Approaching *The Family Reunion* not as Eliot's first play for the commercial stage, but rather as his next poem after 'Burnt Norton', we discover a woman who has attempted for eight

years to enforce, at a country house named Wishwood, a pro-
tracted artificial timeless moment ('Nothing has been changed.
I have seen to that'); a man who is more dogmatically convinced than the musing voice at the 'Burnt Norton' opening that

> all past is present, all degradation
> Is unredeemable,

but who has nonetheless returned to his first world to seek out
the presences that move without pressure over its dead leaves;
and a chorus of strained, time-ridden faces, distracted from distraction. The man who has come back recalls a life transacted in
a more lurid facsimile of the 'Burnt Norton' underground

> The sudden solitude in a crowded desert
> In a thick smoke, many creatures moving
> Without direction, for no direction
> Leads anywhere but round and round in that vapour –
> Without purpose, without principle of conduct
> In flickering intervals of light and darkness. . . .

In this subterranean void he has willed a deed of violence, which
he has incurred the obligation of expiating; for he has discovered that he cannot simply leave the past behind, just as his
mother needs to discover that she cannot simply keep it with her.

Through time, however, time is conquered. He gains the
means of liberation from his nightmare past by acquiring, in
Wishwood, insight into a still earlier past which he had never
comprehended. His father, a presence out of his first world,
becomes intelligible to him, 'dignified, invisible', and his own
crime, which he had been concerned to expiate in isolation, turns
out to be simply the present cross-section of a family crime
projected through generations. As he has willed to kill his wife,
so his father, it turns out, had once willed to kill his.

> The trilling wire in the blood
> Sings below inveterate scars
> Appeasing long forgotten wars;

and Harry, the purpose of his visit to the great house with its
garden now accomplished, takes his departure.

It is easy to see the application to Harry's plight of the enig-
matic epigraphs from Heraclitus which Eliot affixed to 'Burnt
Norton': 'Though the law of things is universal in scope, most
men act as though they had insight of their own'; and 'The way
up and the way down are one and the same', 'Whether in Argos
or England'. The *Family Reunion* Chorus proclaims,

> There are certain inflexible laws
> Unalterable, in the nature of music.

Harry has supposed himself the centre of a totally sick world
which has arranged itself around his unique malaise. When he
tells his impercipient uncles and aunts that they have gone
through life in sleep, never woken to the nightmare, and that life
would be unendurable if they were wide awake, it is because he
supposes himself a privileged person, habituated to 'the noxious
smell and the sorrow before morning'. But though it is true that

> the enchainment of past and future
> Woven in the weakness of the changing body,
> Protects mankind from heaven and damnation
> Which flesh cannot endure,

nevertheless the 'inflexible laws, unalterable, in the nature of
music', are not the iron chains Harry supposes them to be; like
the laws of music, they define the conditions of freedom.

> Only by the form, the pattern,
> Can words or music reach
> The stillness, as a Chinese jar still
> Moves perpetually in its stillness.

By approaching it from 'Burnt Norton', we see the intelligible
play Eliot was attempting to write. Looking at it as a first-night
audience, we are more likely to behold an impenetrable screen
of symbols that do not declare themselves and events that do
not occur. The ending is particularly troublesome. Harry goes,

> the consciousness of [his] unhappy family,
> Its bird sent flying through the purgatorial flame,

and where he is going and what he proposes to do, what will be
the nature of his liberated existence, these are of obvious drama-

tic importance. But 'Burnt Norton' does not carry things that far, and the fundamental thinking for the play is what is contained in 'Burnt Norton'. The problem is in fact a pseudo-problem, forced upon the play by the exigencies of dramatic construction; for, as we learn from subsequent poems, the state promised in the garden at 'Burnt Norton' is, like the reorientation of Becket's will, not reducible to terms of exhibited action, but rather an invisible inflection of whatever action one performs. If this consideration spoils *The Family Reunion*, it lends itself intimately to further meditative poems; and in 1940, the year after the performance of the play, Eliot published 'East Coker'. While working on it, he conceived the sequence of four poems to which 'Burnt Norton' was ultimately transferred, and by 1942 had completed *Four Quartets*.

III

The series title suggests a further insight into the language developed in 'Burnt Norton'; it is string music, more closely analogous to the human voice than any other instrumentation, but still not to be confused with either quotidian discourse or with a particular person speaking. The *Quartets* muse, they traverse and exploit a diversity of timbres and intonations, interchange themes, set going a repetitive but developing minuet of motifs. *The Waste Land* is by comparison a piece of eloquence. Like the voices of a string quartet, the lyric, didactic, colloquial, and deliberative modes of these poems pursue in an enclosed world the for: is of intent *conversation*; the occasional voice that rises above the consort does so tentatively, mindful of the decorum in which there is no audience to address, but only the other voices. We are not addressed, we overhear.

Like instruments, the voices have stable identities. 'East Coker' introduces them in turn: the inhabitant of England, with a family, a past, and a penchant for visiting significant landscapes; the lyric poet; the sombre moralist, intermittently Christian; and the man of letters, 'trying to learn to use words'. We may enumerate them in this way without implicating the now wholly effaced Invisible Poet, who composed the score, but is only figuratively present in the performance.

There is an empty custom of referring here to the 'late' quartets of Beethoven, a parallel which impedes understanding by suggesting that the *Quartets* offer to be an Olympian's transfinite testament. Eliot is reported to have said that he was paying attention chiefly to Bartok's Quartets, numbers 2–6. (I owe this information to Mr M. J. C. Hodgart of Pembroke College, Cambridge.)

The title also implies that the deliverances of the poem will be as formal and as elusive as music, which they are; and that something resembling a strict form is going to be observed, as it is. The five-parted dialectic of 'Burnt Norton' is exactly paralleled three times over, and so raised by iteration to the dignity of a form.

Or so one would say, were not 'Burnt Norton', surprisingly enough, the exact structural counterpart of *The Waste Land*. That form, originally an accident produced by Pound's cutting, Eliot would seem by tenacious determination to have analyzed, mastered, and made into an organic thing. 'Burnt Norton', terminating the 1935 *Collected Poems*, appears meant to bear the same relation to *The Waste Land* as Simeon to Gerontion. Its rose-garden, for instance, with the passing cloud and the empty pool, corresponds to the Hyacinth garden and the despondent '*Oed' und leer das Meer*', while 'the heart of light, the silence' that was glimpsed in the presence of the hyacinth girl is the tainted simulacrum of that light which 'is still at the still point of the turning world'.

Each *Quartet* carries on this structural parallel. The first movement, like 'The Burial of the Dead', introduces a diversity of themes; the second, like 'A Game of Chess', presents first 'poetically' and then with less traditional circumscription the same area of experience; the third, like 'The Fire Sermon', gathers up the central vision of the poem while meditating dispersedly on themes of death: the fourth is a brief lyric; the fifth, a didactic and lyric culmination, concerning itself partly with language, in emulation of the Indo-European roots exploited in 'What the Thunder said'.

Numerous other formalities resemble in function those conventions of musical structure that distinguish a Quartet from an improvization. The poems concern themselves in turn with early summer, late summer, autumn, and winter; with air, earth, water, and fire, the four elements of Heraclitus' flux; their brief fourth movements celebrate successively the Unmoved Mover, the redeeming Son, the Virgin, and the Holy Ghost; and each poem is named after some obscure place where the poet's personal history or that of his family makes contact with a more general Past.

East Coker is the village in Somerset where Eliots or Elyots lived for some two centuries, before the poet's ancestor Andrew Eliot emigrated in 1667 to found the American branch of the family. On that act depends T. S. Eliot's status, an almost assimilated Englishman, nowhere at home, whose first twenty-five years were spent in 'a large flat country'. Whether, on the other hand, if Andrew Eliot had remained in England, his family would have boasted an eminent man of letters must remain

> a perpetual possibility
> Only in a world of speculation.

This poem deals with the pastness, beyond significant recall, of the irrevocable past, and with its irrevocability. Andrew and various other ancestors have done what they have done, and 'In my beginning is my end'.

Like 'Burnt Norton', the poem begins by leading us from a meditation of sombre principles, through a landscape into a vision. The landscape is ominously static:

> And the deep lane insists on the direction
> Into the village, in the electric heat
> Hypnotised. In a warm haze the sultry light
> Is absorbed, not refracted, by grey stone.
> The dahlias sleep in the empty silence.
> Wait for the early owl.

The vision presents not a polysemous 'first-world', but a dancing of sixteenth-century peasants around a midsummer fire,

> Leaping through the flames, or joined in circles,
> Rustically solemn or in rustic laughter
> Lifting heavy feet in clumsy shoes,
> Earth feet, loam feet, lifted in country mirth
> Mirth of those long since under earth
> Nourishing the corn.

A native of East Coker, Sir Thomas Elyot, had discussed in *The Boke named The Gouvernour* (1531) 'wherefore in the good ordre of daunsinge a man and a woman daunseth to gether', and four centuries later his collateral descendant weaves phrases from *The Boke* onto his poem:

> Two and two, necessarye coniunction,
> Holding eche other by the hand or the arm
> Whiche betokeneth concorde.

As the spelling indicates, that past lives but quaintly; and the emphasis falls on the decay of so many transient bodies,

>   ashes to the earth
> Which is already flesh, fur and faeces,
> Bone of man and beast, cornstalk and leaf.

If 'daunsinge' has signified 'matrimonie – A dignified and commodious sacrament', matrimony in the universe of 'flesh, fur and faeces' is governed by

> The time of milking and the time of harvest
> The time of the coupling of man and woman
> And that of beasts. Feet rising and falling.
> Eating and drinking. Dung and death.

This dance, though it comes to us in a vision, is not the one containing 'neither arrest nor movement' which is located 'at the still point of the turning world'. It is merely a Tudor festival of fire, now superseded: an incident in the unecstatic rhythm of peasant life.

In succeeding passages 'Burnt Norton's' perpetual possibilities

are refuted by 'what has been'. The intimate identity between
'the dance along the artery' and 'the drift of stars' gives place to
a universe which is all of a piece only in being pointed towards
destruction. The presences in the rose-garden become 'the quiet-
voiced elders' who have nothing to tell us,

> The serenity only a deliberate hebetude,
> The wisdom only the knowledge of dead secrets
> Useless in the darkness into which they peered
> Or from which they turned their eyes.

Indeed not only traditional wisdom but one's own past seems
of limited value;

> The knowledge imposes a pattern, and falsifies,
> For the pattern is new in every moment
> And every moment is a new and shocking
> Valuation of all we have been.

Section III, like the third section of 'Burnt Norton', invites us to
'descend lower':

> be still, and wait without hope
> For hope would be hope for the wrong thing. . . .

Section IV introduces Christ the Wounded Surgeon; section V,
under His aegis, a reconsideration of apparent personal failure.
The 'twenty years largely wasted' were

> perhaps neither gain nor loss.
> For us, there is only the trying. The rest is not our business.

Hence it is relevant to continue trying, and not to count on

> the long looked forward to,
> Long hoped for calm, the autumnal serenity
> And the wisdom of age.

The cemetery of East Coker takes its place in the pattern which
is new in every moment; for it is of the nature of human life to
complicate endlessly its relations with the dead and the living:

> a lifetime burning in every moment
> And not the lifetime of one man only
> But of old stones that cannot be deciphered.

Hence 'old men ought to be explorers', and Andrew Eliot's enterprise becomes both a justification and a precedent, itself justified.

> We must be still and still moving
> Into another intensity
> For a further union, a deeper communion
> Through the dark cold and the empty desolation,
> The wave cry, the wind cry, the vast waters
> Of the petrel and the porpoise.

The 'wounded surgeon' enters this communion, and so does the dead ancestor; the poem ends by reversing its initial despairing motto, and aligning it with the words which Mary, Queen of Scots had embroidered on her Chair of State: 'In my end is my beginning.'

There is no faking in this reversal; 'East Coker' stays within its own dark ambit, not Eliot's least animated poem, but the one least touched by possibilities of animation. In its presence even 'The Hollow Men' seems to an imponderable degree satiric, the circuit round the prickly pear positively facetious. It is not a depressed poem, though depression has entered it ('twenty years largely wasted'). The presence of Ecclesiastes within ten lines of the opening serves to remind us that the pervasive sombreness is more than personal, that it is a view of the world that has seemed tenable to men in every generation. It weights, moreover, the redeeming elements when they enter. We hear of Good Friday, not of the Love that moves the sun and the other stars; the concluding forward journey passes 'through the dark cold and the empty desolation' to a 'further union' not specified;* the very 'laughter in the garden', when it makes its brief appearance, simply points 'to the agony of death and birth'.

Moods change, but a man's stable moods correspond to the things he chooses to regard as important. Unless the disparity of emotion between 'Burnt Norton' and 'East Coker' can be resolved, they become alternative ways in which the mind responsible for their existence deceives itself. As the next phase

* But compare 'Marina'.

in the programme of the *Quartets*, a reconciliation of opposites seems in order.

But Eliotic opposites may be resolved in contrary ways. Of certain opposites presented in 'Burnt Norton' itself, the Underground world in section III is a parody-reconciliation, its dominating natural force Gerontion's wind. Its 'flicker' combines darkness and light, plenitude and vacancy, in a barrenly mechanical way; the mechanically ordered movement of the pasengers, restless but predictable on its 'metalled ways', combines stillness and dancing. But this relationship of three terms, the third falsely combining the first and second, is the poet's means of localizing a fourth: the darkness which is still further from natural darkness than is the eternal half-light of the tube, and which is hence introduced by a spatial gesture:

> Descend lower, descend only
> Into the world of perpetual solitude,
> World not world, but that which is not world.

And this 'world not world', described always positively yet always with circumstantial tact in terms of what it is not, really does, we are given to understand, perform the function which the place of the flicker only pretends to perform. The light and darkness with which it has affinity are the opposites it reconciles.

This is diagrammatic; in 'Burnt Norton' it is diagrammatically presented. The diagram, however, points up the manner in which, from first to last, *Four Quartets* deals with opposites first falsely, then truly, reconciled, exactly as suicide and martyrdom, superficially identical, were the false and true modes by which Becket's plight could be resolved. It should not surprise us, therefore, that 'The Dry Salvages' moves off from the first two Quartets in a direction not wholly commendable, dwelling on the poet's merely personal past by the Mississippi and the Atlantic seaboard, and plucking its conciliating formulae from those mazes of Hindu metaphysics in which, he once remarked, he spent some years at Harvard 'in a state of enlightened mystification'. 'The Dry Salvages' is a poem of *opinion*: 'I do not know much about gods; but . . . ', or 'I sometimes wonder if that is what Krishna meant. . . .' In section v we hear the voice of Eliot playing one of his public roles, the anxious social commentator; haruspication on the Edgware Road is filtered through this medium, not allowed to establish its own melancholy identity. And in section II he nearly expostulates with us, urges us to follow an argument which he is having difficulty in formulating satisfactorily.

> I have said before
> That the past experience revived in the meaning
> Is not the experience of one life only
> But of many generations –

He has *not* said this before: it has said itself, with unselfconscious authority:

> a lifetime burning in every moment
> And not the lifetime of one man only
> But of old stones that cannot be deciphered.

But the voice we hear in 'The Dry Salvages' is using this poetic illumination, or his own leaden paraphrase of it, as a datum in a laboured construction. The rhythms are cumbrous, the phrase-ology has neither grace nor pith –

> the latter a partial fallacy,
> Encouraged by superficial notions of evolution;

the instances lack sureness –

> Fruition, fulfilment, security or affection,
> Or even a very good dinner;

the second sentence in the passage loses its direction and its syntactic identity entirely; and the laboured 'I have said before' has none of the ironic grace of the comparable detail in section III of 'East Coker'. 'The Dry Salvages' contains enough detach-able mannerisms to have permitted the only successful parody of an Eliot manner, Henry Reed's 'Chard Whitlow':

> I think you will find this put,
> Far better than I could ever hope to express it,
> In the words of Kharma: 'It is, we believe,
> Idle to hope that the simple stirrup-pump

Can extinguish hell.'
                    Oh, listeners,
And you especially who have switched off the wireless. . . .

It is the necessary false truce in the economy of the *Quartets*, the
necessary phase of satisfaction with what our own capacity for
insight can deliver, from which the taut revelations of 'Little
Gidding' are later distinguished.

Not that he has deliberately written a second-rate poem; 'The
Dry Salvages' not only contains the most powerfully articulated
passage he has ever published, the twenty-three-line sentence
that enumerates the sea's voices

> The menace and caress of wave that breaks on water,
> The distant rote in the granite teeth. . . .

but it also provides, in the course of its attempts to mediate
between recurrent illumination and pervasive failure, several
formulae of both structural and exegetical utility:

> We had the experience but missed the meaning,
> And approach to the meaning restores the experience,
> In a different form, beyond any meaning
> We can assign to happiness.

Or,

> do not think of the fruit of action.
> Fare forward.

Or,

> time is no healer: the patient is no longer here.

These it can provide by virtue of its persistent inquiry within the
sphere where such formulations are arrived at. There is nothing
in the last three-quarters of 'The Dry Salvages', not the materials
handled, the mode of ideation, nor the process by which instance
yields formulation, that is beyond the scope of a sensitive prose
essayist. The function of the verse is not to leap gaps, but simply
to establish and sustain the meditative tone, sufficiently remote
from the idiom in which you address other people to obviate the
lengthy and distracting ceremonial by which the prose writer

assures his readers that he isn't leaving them behind. The poem leads us *out of* 'poetry' – the river and the sea – down into small dry air in which to consider in an orderly fashion what 'most of us' are capable of. The saints are capable of more:

> to apprehend
> The point of intersection of the timeless
> With time, is an occupation for the saint –
> No occupation either, but something given
> And taken, in a lifetime's death in love,
> Ardour and selflessness and self-surrender.

We who are not saints may from time to time enjoy hints of that apprehension –

> the unattended
> Moment, the moment in and out of time,
> The distraction fit, lost in a shaft of sunlight,
> The wild thyme unseen, or the winter lightning
> Or the waterfall, or music heard so deeply
> That it is not heard at all, but you are the music
> While the music lasts.

If these seem familiar experiences, that is the point of the passage. For 'These are only hints and guesses, hints followed by guesses': and 'The hint half guessed, the gift half understood, is Incarnation'.

This is literally meant; such a 'moment in and out of time' as occurred in the 'Burnt Norton' garden is not the saint's beatitude, but the temporary translation of that beatitude into a more familiar medium, into a mode of experience available to human kind. This is what our least time-ridden moments can give us, not timelessness but a glimpse of it; hence to decide that we live for those moments is to be content with the parody of the real. 'The Dry Salvages', similarly, is what our capacity for orderly generalization from experience can give us, not the continual apprehension of the still point but an account of how our experience would be related to such an apprehension if we could have it. To repose in such an account is to be free from irrelevant desires; but it may also be to wonder, with the student of Francis Herbert Bradley, what it was we wanted and why we ever supposed we wanted anything. The poem's last formulation is one from which no agnostic propounder of a free man's worship would dissent. No one succeeds, the thing is to try; our efforts 'fructify in the lives of others', and we ourselves enrich the ground. This is very close to the social gospel of ants; and the final line empties of inconsistent optimism a Ruskin-like cliché about 'significant toil':

> For most of us, this is the aim
> Never here to be realized;
> Who are only undefeated
> Because we have gone on trying;
> We, content at the last
> If our temporal reversion nourish
> (Not too far from the yew-tree)
> The life of significant soil.

Thus the parody-reconciliation, the collective voice of the late nineteenth century, urging us to strive without personal hope, to consider how we are placed in a cosmos whose dimensions dwarf us on an earth whose soil at least knows how to make use of us, seeking our fulfilment in a collective endeavour, and our religious support in 'religious experiences' which are likely to be experiences of nature – 'the winter lightning / Or the waterfall' – or of music, and not really distinguishable from the fulfilment of 'a very good dinner'. It is some ideal Matthew Arnold's road out of East Coker.

IV

Upon this decent self-abnegation bursts the 'midwinter spring' of 'Little Gidding', a poem of paradox, metamorphosis, and climax. Snow on the hedgerow,

> a bloom more sudden
> Than that of summer, neither budding nor fading,
> Not in the scheme of generation,

asserts in the midst of death ('no earth smell / Or smell of living thing') not the wistful apprehension of invisible presences in a rose-garden but the possibility of

>   the unimaginable
>   Zero summer.

This time suspended in time, 'zero' because heat is cancelled, though not by cold, and because movement is ended, though not in immobility, this actuality toward which we are admonished by 'pentecostal fire' flaming on ice, comes shockingly against our senses to subsume many tedious abstractions, 'neither from nor towards', 'concentration without elimination', and the rest of it. Our next surprise is to discover that the place associated with this vision is a place accessible to anyone, distinguished, at the end of a rough road, by a pig-sty, a dull façade, and a tombstone. It is a place where intentions alter:

>   what you thought you came for
> Is only a shell, a husk of meaning
> From which the purpose breaks only when it is fulfilled
> If at all,

thus rendering irrelevant the curiosity which 'searches past and future and clings to that dimension'; a place which is in many senses 'the world's end', though similar to other such places,

>   some at the sea jaws,
> Or over a dark lake, in a desert or a city –

These were all zones of combat in 1942, where many men encountered the world's end. They are also places associated with saints; in a note for his brother, Henry Ware Eliot, the author cited the isles of Iona and Lindisfarne, associated with St Columba and St Cuthbert; St Kevin's lake of Glendalough; the Thebaid of St Anthony (who is also the tempted 'word in the desert' of 'Burnt Norton'); and the Padua of the other St Anthony. But this place has been celebrated neither by canonized saints nor by topical warriors. It is a place 'where prayer has been valid', and as to what may happen there,

>   what the dead had no speech for, when living,
> They can tell you, being dead: the communication

Of the dead is tongued with fire beyond the language of the living.

This place is Little Gidding in Huntingdonshire. Like the Burnt House, the Little Gidding chapel is a restoration of an earlier place destroyed. Cromwell's soldiers sacked it in 1647, and scattered the saintly community. Charles I took refuge there after Naseby, 'very privately, in the darkness of night'.

If 'East Coker' brings the Eliot family from England to America, and 'The Dry Salvages' brings T. S. Eliot from the 'nursery bedroom' to the phase in which he was a student of Bradley's and a disciple of Irving Babbitt's, 'Little Gidding' returns him to England, and the Church of England, and brings the temporal cycle round from the sixteenth century to a disastrous Now. In 'Burnt Norton' a formal garden centuries old, in 'East Coker' a village life centuries gone, briefly allow the present to participate; in 'Little Gidding', similarly, the loop in time incorporates into an England menaced by Stuka bombers

> (The dove descending breaks the air
> With flame of incandescent terror)

the achievement of a place where 'prayer has been valid' for three centuries.

This place arose from the ashes of the Civil War; so when in the litany of the Four Elements that initiates section II we encounter a reference to its destruction,

> Water and fire shall rot
> The marred foundations we forgot,
> Of sanctuary and choir,

we may take it that all the modes of death in that Litany are likewise redeemable. These deaths –

> Dust in the air suspended
> Marks the place where a story ended

– prompt instances from the bombing of London; no other Quartet is so explicitly located in time as this one in which time is conquered. The ghost is encountered on a London street, by

a fire-spotter dazed after an air-raid, 'at the recurrent end of the
unending', and the horn on whose blowing he fades (by analogy
with the dawn which removed the ghost of Hamlet's father) is
the 'all-clear'.

This ghost (whom Eliot is said to have more or less identified
with W. B. Yeats,[1]) foretells as Yeats did in *Purgatory*, a play
Eliot has greatly admired,

> the rending pain of re-enactment
> Of all that you have done, and been.

His utterance indeed is 'tongued with fire beyond the language
of the living'; no other Voice in Eliot's repertoire articulates
with such authority. That he is the first apparition in the *Quartets* who comes close and speaks is a fact that underlines his
authority; he is no such 'dignified, invisible' presence as moved
in the rose-garden, nor a member of the dance you can see 'if
you do not come too close'. He is 'compound': Yeats, Mallarmé,
Hamlet's father, Ezra Pound, Dante, Swift, Milton, 'some dead
master', 'both one and many'. He embodies also that simul-
taneity of the *literary* past which has been Eliot's theme since
1917; the 'passage' that now

> presents no hindrance
> To the spirit unappeased and peregrine
> Between two worlds become much like each other,

can be a passage of verse as well as the facile transition between
Purgatory and a London ringed with fire:

> So I find words I never thought to speak
> In streets I never thought I should revisit
> When I left my body on a distant shore.[2]

He discloses a Gerontion's future: anaesthesia, acrimony, shame:
these are

> the gifts reserved for age
> To set a crown upon your lifetime's effort,

and the 'fruit of action' becomes indeed 'shadow fruit'. But he
hints at the alternative to such a future:

> From wrong to wrong the exasperated spirit
> Proceeds, unless restored by that refining fire
> Where you must move in measure, like a dancer.

The third section of the poem absorbs such revenants into a 'renewed, transfigured' pattern:

> These men, and those who opposed them
> And those whom they opposed
> Accept the constitution of silence
> And are folded in a single party.

To think of them

> is not to ring the bell backward
> Nor is it an incantation
> To summon the spectre of a Rose:

it is to bring them alive into our present consciousness: if we know more than they, they are that which we know, 'united in the strife which divided them', like the community at Little Gidding and the Roundheads who scattered them. The fourth section celebrates the 'refining fire', incendiary or pentecostal according to the use we make of it. The fifth, having united 'East Coker's' 'beginning' and 'end', affirmed the possibility of words that do not

> strain
> Crack and sometimes break, under the burden,
> Under the tension,

and set to an easy rhythm our comings and goings and those of the dead, returns us for a moment to 'a winter's afternoon, in a secluded chapel', before bringing us back with assurance to the 'first world' 'Burnt Norton' brushed against. The poet, totally effaced, can afford without distraction formally erotic images of fulfilment ('through the unknown, remembered gate'; 'the crowned knot of fire'); can prevent the first world from sounding regressive and the laughter of the hidden children from appearing to complete a personal yearning, 'the source of the longest river' from sounding trite, and 'the voice of the hidden waterfall' from irritating us with 'symbolic' vagueness.

> Quick now, here, now, always –
> A condition of complete simplicity
> (Costing not less than everything)
> And all shall be well and
> All manner of thing shall be well
> When the tongues of flame are in-folded
> Into the crowned knot of fire
> And the fire and the rose are one.

Any of these phrases, escaped from that masterly control, would be merely silly; but Eliot can even insert 'all shall be well' into the climactic passage of his most extensive and demanding poem. The language, unprotected by formalities of diction, maintains commerce with deliquescent cliché, the speech of an age whose speech when sedate is commonly vapid, and these clichés not only never menace its decorum, they even seem transparent coinages. No one will say, 'That is not what I meant at all', and no unnatural vices are fathered by this poetic heroism. 'The poetry does not matter.' These are the qualities that assure us of the new first world's durability. When it was glimpsed in 'Burnt Norton' it was a precarious special thing, prompting contrast with

> the waste sad time
> Stretching before and after.

The finale of 'Little Gidding' fends off nothing. It is a nearly unprecedented triumph of style.

SOURCE: *The Invisible Poet* (1959)

NOTES

1. This information comes from Mr Horace Gregory, who adds to it Eliot's emphasis on the fact that the ghost was also partly himself. [Editor's note.] See also Richard Ellman, *Eminent Domain* (New York, 1967) pp. 94–5.
2. There was a tradition that Dante visited Oxford about 1308. Swift, Yeats, and Pound of course were often in London.

C. K. Stead

THE IMPOSED STRUCTURE OF
THE *FOUR QUARTETS* (1964)

IT is not until *Four Quartets* that we find what seems an important change in Eliot's methods of composition; and the change is exhibited principally in a considerable increase in structural ordering, both of the poem as a whole and of its parts. Our principal observation about *Four Quartets* can be put at its simplest, then, if we say that the poem would be seriously damaged by any large-scale cutting or reshuffling of the kind applied to Eliot's earlier poetry. It is a poem constructed piece by piece into a pattern, the coherence of which contributes to what it has to communicate. The poem has been directed, however gently, by the conscious will. It exhibits progression of a kind lacking in all of Eliot's earlier (non-dramatic) poetry. There is still very little in it that is argued or rhetorically affirmed. But one would never find in his earlier work such lecture-room pronouncements as:

> There is, it seems to us,
> At best, only a limited value
> In the knowledge derived from experience.

Four Quartets is a series of variations on themes which are 'traditional', 'orthodox', in a sense unarguable. Thus 'inspiration' is possible, but only *within* the framework which is fixed as it is not in *The Waste Land*. 'Texture' can only flow into a structure whose inception has preceded it.

Since it is this structure that distinguishes the poem from Eliot's other poetry (and there is, so far as I know, no discussion of *Four Quartets* which sets the structure out with any exactness), it will be as well to sketch it in outline before proceeding to discuss the poetry.

In each Quartet the five sections follow patterns which are sufficiently alike for the following general descriptions to apply in each case.

   I. The movement of time, in which brief moments of eternity are caught.

  II. Worldly experience, leading only to dissatisfaction.

 III. Purgation in the world – divesting the soul of the love of created things – expressed mainly in terms of present movement, a journey which is freedom from past and future.

 IV. A lyric prayer for, or affirmation of the need of, Intercession.

  V. The problems of attaining artistic wholeness which become analogues for, and merge in to, the problems of achieving spiritual health.

I shall try to make clearer this basic similarity of each group of parallel sections; but it should be noted that to set the pattern out as I have done below is to suggest a more rigorous mould than the poem in fact displays. My intention is only to indicate that the pattern is there, not to press my descriptions too far.

Section I of each Quartet
The attainment, in time, of brief moments of eternity.
(1) 'Burnt Norton' I (basic element – air)
The passage leading to an open door (time).
The garden (innocence) briefly transformed in time.

Out of the air the voices of innocence	{ 'echoes' 'the lotus' the laughter of children	} These are images of the permanence of innocence in time.

(2) 'East Coker' I (basic element – earth)
Houses, roads, factories – rising and falling, changing (time).
The field (fertility) briefly transformed in time.

Out of the earth the music of propagation	{ the dancing figures – 'signifying matrimonie'	} These are images of the permanence of 'experience', of the flesh, in time.

(3) 'The Dry Salvages' I (basic element – water)
The river and the sea as erosive forces (time)
The sea (as an image of original chaos) throws up evidence of death.

Out of the sea the voices of death	{	sea howl, yelp, rote of granite teeth, groaner, bell	}	These are images of the permanence of death in time.

(4) 'Little Gidding' I (basic element – fire)
The changes of the seasons (time).
Midwinter ice briefly transformed to fire in the seasonal paradoxes.

Out of the fires the voices of eternity	{	'the communication of the dead is tongued with fire'	}	This is an image of the permanence of eternity in time.

Section II of each Quartet
The world offers no enduring satisfaction; in these sections all attempt to escape from it seems vain.

(1) 'Burnt Norton' II
Formal lyric: an attempt to establish links which ought to exist between the worlds of flesh and spirit.
Discursive passage which looks towards a point at which the tensions of the world are resolved. The lines circle about this point as a concept, but fail to achieve it.
(2) 'East Coker' II
Formal lyric: an attempt to link the events of the earthly seasons with the more spectacular revolutions of the heavens.
Discursive passage on the subject of old age. Age offers no special knowledge, no solution to the problems of living. The only wisdom is humility.
(3) 'The Dry Salvages' II
Formal lyric: telling over the endless destructive force of time, specifically in terms of sailing and the sea.

Discursive passage on the subject of time seen in old age as the destroyer of moments of illumination and the preserver of remembered agony.

(4) 'Little Gidding' II

Formal lyric: the destruction of the physical world by a resolution to its basic elements – air, earth, fire, and water.

Discursive passage (though much less casual, more carefully and finely wrought than any of its equivalent passages) in which the 'dead master' outlines the empty honours offered by the world to its ageing great men.

Section III of each Quartet

Escape from the world is discovered in the present – in a freeing of the self from past and future, from memory and desire. Concentration on the journey which in the present offers the only area in which the world may be transcended.

(1) 'Burnt Norton' III

Experience of travelling in the London Underground, used as an image of the purgation of worldly love. This is achieved by a concentration in the present which looks neither forward nor back.

> Here is a place of disaffection
> Time before and time after
> In a dim light.

(2) 'East Coker' III

The great men of the world travel into the darkness of the future, aware of the darkness of the past recorded in almanacs and directories. Again this section affirms a concentration in the present, vacating the mind of its worldly desires – as in

> the darkened theatre
> the tube train stopped between stations
> the mind under ether.

This process is then seen in a different way as a journey of the mind between opposing sets of abstractions (last 12 lines).

(3) 'The Dry Salvages' III
The images of a journey are explicit here. The travellers should
'fare forward', conscious of neither the point of departure
nor the destination:

> Here between the hither and the farther shore
> While time is withdrawn.

(4) 'Little Gidding' III
Looks to the achievement of a correct 'indifference', which grows
between 'attachment' and 'detachment' –

> and so liberation
> From future as well as past.

This liberation through 'indifference' should also occur in the
journey which is history.

Section IV of each Quartet

The lyric prayer for, or affirmation of the need of, Intercession.
(1) 'Burnt Norton' IV
A lyric questioning the possibility of Intercession in the natural
world.
(2) 'East Coker' IV
Formal lyric affirming the Intercession of Christ as 'the wounded
surgeon', operating in his 'hospital', the world, which was
'endowed' by 'the ruined millionaire' Adam.
(3) 'The Dry Salvages' IV
Lyric prayer to the Virgin for Intercession.
(4) 'Little Gidding' IV
Formal lyric affirming the Intercession of God as Love.

Section V of each Quartet

The specific problems of achieving good art merge, in each case,
into the problems of achieving the good life. Goodness, health,
in both the particular ('art') and the general ('life') depend
largely upon various kinds of precision.

In each of these fifth sections the artistic effort serves as an
analogue for the spiritual effort.

(1) 'Burnt Norton' v

The work of art as movement in which stillness is attained.

The difficulties of precision in art ('Words strain / Crack, and
   sometimes break . . .').

The problems of art merge into the problems of life: the attainment of a 'still centre' is the object in both.

(2) 'East Coker' v

The practice of an art seen as a continual exploration of the means
   of communication.

The difficulties of precision in art ('With shabby equipment always
   deteriorating . . .').

The problems of art merge into the problems of life – life is a
   continual exploration of the means of communication ('communion') with God. In both the desire is to achieve greater
   intensity.

(3) 'The Dry Salvages' v

The false arts, which draw on false traditions, are inevitable
   wrong attempts to apprehend 'the point of intersection of the
   timeless / With time . . .'

But precision in such experience is attained only by the discipline
   of the Saint, not by false agents.

The object of these false arts – a momentary release from time –
   is achieved in life (if at all) only by 'hints and guesses'.

(4) 'Little Gidding' v

The work of art seen as a perfect unity, a poem capable of both
   development in time and the attainment of timeless moments.

Precision is again emphasized ('And every phrase / And sentence that is right . . .').

The achievement of art merges into the achievement of life – the
   discovery of a *form* in life capable, like the forms of art, both
   of development in time and of timeless moments.

These descriptions of each group of parallel sections emphasize
common themes. But within the general theme set for each section there is considerable freedom, and hence a considerable
range of thought and feeling. Nevertheless the change from
Eliot's earlier methods of composition is a radical one. The plan

must have been drafted before the writing began, or at least was fixed by the time 'Burnt Norton' was finished.[1] 'Inspiration', the unwilled creative moment, is still possible within the general framework, but only if it can be used to further one or another relevant theme.

Four Quartets is an attempt to bring into a more exact balance the will and the creative imagination; it attempts to harness the creative imagination which in all Eliot's earlier poetry ran its own course, edited but not consciously directed. The achievement is of a high order, but the best qualities of *Four Quartets* are inevitably different from those of *The Waste Land*.

The place of *The Waste Land* in the piece of literary history which is the concern of this essay has already been defined.[2] The poem is the final realization of an impulse directed against poetic discourse. It is a poem which refuses to be anything else but poetry. This is not to say that it fulfils simple doctrines of 'Art for Art's Sake', but that it is in no sense an agent or instrument of the will. Its virtue resides in its completeness as an entity uniting 'aesthetic' and 'moral' qualities into a fusion which, transcending both, acquires life. The poem *is*; it has a being. Or, to put the matter differently, it has a quality which calls forth organic metaphors when we attempt to describe it. It achieves 'impersonality' of a kind which *Four Quartets*, with its many discursive passages and its consciously controlled plan, does not attempt.

The English poetic tradition has always occupied middle-ground between pure discourse and pure Image. At times it has striven hard towards the Image; at others it has been content to be scarcely distinguished from prose except by its metrical form. At any point where it became *pure* discourse it ceased to be poetry. On the other hand the number of occasions on which it has become pure Image are so few that no generalization can safely be made about them. Two points at which this purity has been significantly achieved are *The Waste Land* and *Ash Wednesday*. But Eliot's development since 1935 suggests that the achievement left him dissatisfied, or left him feeling that he was, as a poet, 'helpless before the contents of his own mind' – a feeling he was not willing to tolerate. In these two poems Eliot achieves his mature style, but it is a style dependent to a large extent on moments he can only in a general way predict or control. In *Four Quartets* he sets out to undo that style, and to achieve another – one in which there would be more of his conscious self, his personality, his wisdom. Yeats's explanation of the change observed in his style after 1909 is not altogether irrelevant here: 'I have tried to make my work convincing, with a speech so natural and dramatic that the hearer would feel the presence of a man thinking and feeling.' There are values the poet wants, not simply incorporated into the texture of his lines, but *affirmed*. By means of his theory of the dramatic mask, Yeats found his way from the passive music of his early poems to the affirming energy of his later work, without any serious intrusion of 'personality'. In *Four Quartets* there is, I think, the same impulse to take up a more usual middle-ground position between the extremes of discourse and the Image. 'Wisdom', an ordered construction upon 'felt life', enters Eliot's later poetry as it enters Yeats's. The question which remains to be answered – or at least put – is whether the style of *Four Quartets* carries the burden satisfactorily. In the view of this essay it does not.

In his early poetry Eliot perfected the non-discursive medium – as Yeats failed to perfect it in the 1890s – to such a degree that he turns to his new task with no ready method for making poetry of the personal voice:

So here I am, in the middle way, having had twenty years –
Twenty years largely wasted, the years of *l'entre deux guerres* –
Trying to learn to use words, and every attempt
Is a wholly new start, and a different kind of failure
Because one has only learnt to get the better of words
For the thing one no longer has to say, or the way in which
One is no longer disposed to say it.

(East Coker v)

There is truth in this, but not imaginative truth: it remains *pure* discourse. If the feeling of failure is truly there, it is there unused; it has not been transmuted by imagination into something larger than itself.

Four Quartets alternates between, on the one hand the 'first voice' of poetry, the voice of *The Waste Land*, less perfect now because directed into a conscious mould; and on the other the 'second voice', the voice of the man 'addressing an audience' in verse barely distinguished from prose. The poem is the expression of a personality so fine, so mature, and so supremely intelligent, that to question the achievement may seem only to quibble. But however wise and admirable the man it displays, the poem remains, in this view, imperfectly achieved, with large portions of abstraction untransmuted into the living matter of poetry.

The discourse of *Four Quartets* points constantly towards 'the unattended moment' –

> the moment in and out of time,
> The distraction fit, lost in a shaft of sunlight. . . .
> (The Dry Salvages v)

In these timeless moments, communion with the Infinite has been achieved: but they lie *outside* the poem and can only be indicated, not entered, and hardly described:

I can only say *there* we have been, but I cannot say where.
(Burnt Norton II)

These are assurances that Eliot the man has achieved such moments; there is no longer a "sensuous re-creation' of the moment itself. Formerly these timeless moments were the moments of literary creation. Now they are private moments between the man and the Infinite, and only discourse can assure us of their occurrence. The poet's concentration is now beyond the world. He has (in the words of St John of the Cross quoted as epigraph to 'Sweeney Agonistes') attempted to divest his soul of the love of created things in order that it may be possessed of the Divine Union. But it is *in* the world, *in* the love of created things, that poetry is generated and takes life. So one is left feeling, after many passages of the poem, that Eliot is saying in a more

elaborate way what Orestes says in the other epigraph to the
Sweeney poems:

> You don't see them, you don't – but *I* see them:
> they are hunting me down. I must move on.

We believe in the poet's experience. The voice is intense and
convincing, but too often intensely personal, the voice of one
man, not of humanity. And when an attempt is made to broaden
the significance of this personal experience, the poem comes to
grief among abstractions:

> You say I am repeating
> Something I have said before. I shall say it again.
> Shall I say it again? In order to arrive there,
> To arrive where you are, to get from where you are not,
>   You must go by a way wherein there is no ecstasy.
> In order to arrive at what you do not know
>   You must go by a way which is the way of ignorance.
> In order to possess what you do not possess
>   You must go by the way of dispossession.
> In order to arrive at what you are not
>   You must go through the way in which you are not.
> And what you do not know is the only thing you know
> And what you own is what you do not own
> And where you are is where you are not.
>   (East Coker III)

What this means is the only thing it means; and what it strives
to be is what it is not.

It is not surprising then that the finest passages in *Four
Quartets* (that there *are* fine passages needs, of course, no special
acknowledgement) are passages which run counter to the planned
intention of the poem. The lines take life when they are permitted to rest for a moment in the physical world, permitted to
express 'the love of created things':

> Now the light falls
> Across the open field, leaving the deep lane
> Shuttered with branches, dark in the afternoon,
> Where you lean against a bank while a van passes,

And the deep lane insists on the direction
Into the village, in the electric heat
Hypnotised. In a warm haze the sultry light
Is absorbed, not refracted, by grey stone.
The dahlias sleep in the empty silence.
Wait for the early owl.

(East Coker I)

Here the poet's feeling takes form in experiencing the visible world, where it is content to rest; only the imposed plan, not the feeling, insists that such experience is unsatisfying, and presses towards abstraction.

In 'East Coker' III the deliberate renunciation of the world is again described:

I said to my soul, be still, and wait without hope
For hope would be hope for the wrong thing; wait without
    love
For love would be love of the wrong thing; there is yet faith
But the faith and the love and the hope are all in the waiting.
Wait without thought, for you are not ready for thought:
So the darkness shall be the light, and the stillness the dancing.

This is a description of the vacation of the conscious mind as a preparation for inspiration – in this case divine inspiration. It is a state of mind clearly related to that in which the poet waits for literary inspiration – the state Eliot described twenty years earlier, in a context which confined it to the writing of poetry, as 'a passive attending upon the event'. Now we are offered only a direction *towards* the experience, not the experience itself. Yet against the will of the man the habit of the poet constantly struggles towards concretion. Despite the conscious plan, the poetry appears and reappears, impatient to assume the world:

Dawn points, and another day
Prepares for heat and silence. Out at sea the dawn wind
Wrinkles and slides.

Lines like these do not advance the plan at all: they represent a moment of poetry, a brief, exact crystallization of feeling, which Eliot could not forgo.

It has been argued that one of the commonest mistakes of
contemporary criticism has been to describe Eliot as an 'intellectual' poet, meaning by this a poet entirely conscious and deliberate in writing his poetry. In *Four Quartets* there are many
attempts to write in a style which, if the attempts had succeeded,
would have justified the description; but in these passages
expressing conscious ideas and beliefs poetry is rarely achieved.
Some of the more obvious examples, where Eliot speaks in the
manner of the public lecturer, have already been quoted. These
are only with difficulty described as poetry. On the other hand
they are not, I think, the least successful passages in the poem:

> I have said before
> That the past experience revived in the meaning
> Is not the experience of one life only
> But of many generations – not forgetting
> Something that is probably quite ineffable:
> The backward look behind the assurance
> Of recorded history, the backward half-look
> Over the shoulder, towards the primitive terror.
>   (The Dry Salvages II)

This is, or is very nearly, pure prose discourse. Yet it remains an
honest 'second voice', the voice of the public man whose personality we can recognize, whose intellect we admire, and whose
ideas we have learned to approach at least with the caution
of a bomb-disposal unit. 'I have said before' calls the class to
attention, and we accept the lecture with only a little shuffling
in the back rows. There is, however, another operation of the
'meddling intellect' for which neither his poetic practice nor his
experience as a lecturer have prepared Eliot: the conscious
working up into verse, through a series of intellectual analogies
and paradoxes, of a 'metaphysical' idea. Section IV of 'East
Coker' is an example of this; and the result is one of the few
sections which not merely fail to be good poetry, but succeed in
being thoroughly bad. The lines exploit and enlarge upon a
number of traditional 'paradoxes': we must die in order to live;
our 'disease' is our hope of 'health' (the paradox of the Fortunate

Fall); the flesh and blood of Christ are the means of the spirit's escape from flesh and blood.

> The wounded surgeon plies the steel
> That questions the distempered part;
> Beneath the bleeding hands we feel
> The sharp compassion of the healer's art
> Resolving the enigma of the fever chart.
>
> Our only health is the disease
> If we obey the dying nurse
> Whose constant care is not to please
> But to remind of our, and Adam's curse,
> And that, to be restored, our sickness must grow worse.

Eliot works these paradoxes out, through a demanding verse form, with the rigorous exactness of a compiler of crossword puzzles. The result is a piece of ingenuity, a synthetic poem, quite without feeling or life. Many of Donne's poems exploit analogies and paradoxes of this kind. The difference is that for Donne the 'ideas' are there, not for their own sake, but only to serve the emotion which generates the poem and takes substance in it. If one analogy ceases to be useful, it is dropped and another taken up; Donne's 'logic' is more apparent than real. His intellect, as Eliot has said, is at the tips of his senses; and it is there only in order that the demands of feeling may be served. In 'The wounded surgeon . . .' Eliot expresses only an abstract idea. He has, in short, attempted a style alien to his own development, and remote from the truest impulses of his poetic sensibility.[3]

On the other hand, achievement must be acknowledged. Throughout *Four Quartets* the uneasy alliance of discourse and Image gains strength. 'Little Gidding' comes closest of the four Quartets to achieving completeness and unity. In its opening twenty lines particularly, the divided impulses of the poem come together. Attention is focussed on the physical world; yet the visible scene carries an abstract idea, entirely incorporated into the rich texture of the lines, so that the scene itself is transmuted, the physical world acquiring a strange *meta*physical intensity:

When the short day is brightest, with frost and fire,
The brief sun flames the ice, on pond and ditches,
In windless cold that is the heart's heat,
Reflecting in a watery mirror
A glare that is blindness in the early afternoon.
And glow more intense than blaze of branch, or brazier,
Stirs the dumb spirit: no wind, but pentecostal fire
In the dark time of year. Between melting and freezing
The soul's sap quivers. There is no earth smell
Or smell of living thing.

Paradoxes the poem has already exploited in a number of ways can be found again in these lines. Midwinter is the soul's spring, for it anticipates the 'unimaginable / Zero summer' after death. Its 'windless cold . . . is the heart's heat' which looks beyond 'the scheme of generation'. Yet here the abstractions come to life, because they assume their form in the physical world, in 'the love of created things'.

'Style' is the poet's way of knowing his world; it is a way of re-creating a world of experience. A failure of style, whether the work is simple description or something more complex, is a false report, the creation of an image which misrepresents 'things as they are'. Hence the conclusion reached in chapter 6 [of *The New Poetic*], that Eliot's concept of style, correctly read where it is best expressed, transcends 'aesthetics' as a concern with beauty, and 'morals' as a set of truths which imply imperatives for right action, fusing the two in a poetics from which neither is detachable. It follows that in such a view, a literary heresy is also inevitably and concomitantly a heresy in a wider sense. The poet, for example, who denies the world in favour of his own abstract thought is in danger of becoming a 'personality', imposing *himself* on the world instead of acting as a medium between it and his readers; he is claiming too much for his own point of the 'triangle'. Likewise, in the wider sense of heresy, the man who denies the world in order to perfect his soul may be in danger of the sin of pride. In the more abstract sections of *Four Quartets* both heresies occur, and the two are one:

> Only a flicker
> Over the strained time-ridden faces
> Distracted from distraction by distraction
> Filled with fancies and empty of meaning
> Tumid apathy with no concentration
> Men and bits of paper, whirled by the cold wind
> That blows before and after time,
> Wind in and out of unwholesome lungs
> Time before and time after
> Eructation of unhealthy souls
> Into the faded air. . . .

> (Burnt Norton III)

Here is a piece of 'fine writing'; but it is also a view of the world which is 'personal' or 'subjective' in a dangerous sense. It is, in so far as it claims the authority of generalization, a false report, for it sells the world short in order that the world may be unlovable. One must love created things in order that one may have love to divest. And one enters the world of imagination – or spirit – only by contemplating with love, not be renouncing, the immediate and the particular. The 'unified sensibility' is in itself a kind of 'divine union', and the will-driven intellect may not achieve it alone.

These remarks, if they are meaningful, indicate the shortcomings of much of the poem; and also the particular success of the opening of 'Little Gidding'. In those twenty lines we have almost the only point in the poem at which a perfect balance is achieved between the rightful claims of flesh and spirit.

SOURCE: *The New Poetic* (1964).

NOTES

1. [Editor's note.] Mr Stead is mistaken; see p. 23.
2. [Editor's note.] See C. K. Stead, *The New Poetic* (1964) pp. 161–167.
3. We may perhaps indicate the failure of this poem in another way if we recall Eliot's definition of metaphysical wit, which includes the remark 'It involves, probably, a recognition, implicit in the expression of every experience, of other kinds of experience which are possible'– see 'Andrew Marvell', *Selected Essays* (1932) p. 303.

Denis Donoghue

T. S. ELIOT'S *QUARTETS*: A NEW READING (1965)

T. S. ELIOT died in his own season, mid-winter, a graceful departure without noise. He was a man of words who loved silence. Indeed, in his greatest poems the words are one part sound and three parts silence, the silence in which he pondered, felt, and remembered. If we ask the source of his words, the answer is easy; they came from the other side of silence. I take this phrase from a passage in *Middlemarch* where the narrative voice says: 'If we had a keen vision and feeling of all ordinary human life, it would be like hearing the grass grow and the squirrel's heart beat, and we should die of that roar which lies on the other side of silence.' This is one text. Add another: 'Words, after speech, reach into the silence.'

The heart of Eliot's poetry is in that silence. To reach it we can only take the words as we find them on the page, confronting them in their immediacy and letting them work upon us as they will, either then or later. Part of their work will be demolition; clearing away the rubble of last year's words, the archaic tokens to which we cling. Another part will be the intimation of new cadences to compel the recognition they precede. And the object is a new and deeper silence, a silence of longer memory and deeper scruple.

It seems a good time to read again the *Four Quartets*. In many respects it is his most challenging work; a dogmatic poem in an age hostile to dogma; a Christian poem written in a time which we are admonished to call 'post-Christian'; a poem which sponsors the silence of understanding and belief. 'Words alone are certain good', Yeats said in a self-beguiling moment. For Eliot, the words are never certain and are good only when they direct the listener to the silent meaning: one name for this is humility. 'Humility is endless.'

Introduction

Four poems, each in five parts; clearly an elaborate structure, indicating that the meaning of the work is likely to be disclosed not in any culminating moment but in the organization of the whole, the relation between the parts, the correspondence of one part to its counterpart in the other poems. After 'Burnt Norton' the later poems will exhibit not a development in the plot as beginning presses toward middle and middle toward end, but perhaps at every moment a new beginning, another raid on the inarticulate, as the poems indicate not positions reached but the reaching of positions, the struggle toward an object not promised, not in the contract. Hence while the poems have an unusually high proportion of abstract terms, suggesting that the experience has been brought to an unusually high degree of generalization, the poet will 'take the harm out of' these certitudes by going back over them and discarding those now deemed inadequate. The work will not be 'dramatic', it will not drive itself toward the fulfilment of a form at any moment unrealized. And yet while the leading analogies are musical (like those obtaining between air, earth, water, and fire) rather than logical (as in the parts of a syllogism or a detective story) the poems will be as dogmatic, in their way, as *The Dunciad* or *Night Thoughts*. The dogmas will be declared by making their substitutes illusory or incomplete. For this purpose the poet will use the camouflage of different voices; he will not, like the author of *Night Thoughts*, make everything depend upon the fiat of a single voice. The strategy of *Four Quartets* is to set up several voices, each charged with the evacuation of one area, until nothing is left but 'prayer, observance, discipline, thought and action'. And at that point, presumably, the reader is ready to 'know the place for the first time'.

The Structure of the Quartets

The work begins with two fragments from Heraclitus; untranslated, but now to be translated conservatively as (i)

'Although the Word (*Logos*) is common to all, most people live as if each of them had a private intelligence of his own', and (ii) 'The way up and the way down are one and the same'.[1] The second is a comforting thought, even in the flux, since, if it is true, the choice of direction will not matter. The first admonishes us to give up our private wisdoms, which are almost certainly mere egotistical delusions, the 'fancies' of 'Burnt Norton' III, and to seek the Word which is true precisely because it is not our invention.[2] So a proper humility is launched.

Section I of each poem renders a mode of being in which we impose upon our experience our own meaning and think that it is total; but it is sometimes illusory and, at best, incomplete. In 'Burnt Norton' it is the deception of the thrush, the rose-garden experience. In 'East Coker' it is the 'daunsinge'-scene, handsome but archaic, and Sir Thomas Elyot's couples are led off with half-gentle irony, blessings on their heads. In 'The Dry Salvages' the anxious women try to reckon the sea in their own terms, 'calculating the future', forgetting that 'the sea is all about us', a reality encompassing us for which we are not responsible, incorrigibly real because – like the Word – it is not our invention. And in 'Little Gidding' the pilgrimage is only 'a shell, a husk of meaning' because we, the pilgrims, have chosen our object and (worse still) the choice is in accordance with our own mere 'sense and notion'.

To take one of these sections in some detail: 'Burnt Norton' begins with four statements about Time, each spoken perhaps by a different voice. First, Time as a continuous chain of events:

> Time present and time past
> Are both perhaps present in time future,
> And time future contained in time past.

Second, Time as eternally present and therefore unredeemable because it excludes history, process, and the flux. Third, Time as a continuum of events which might have been different. And lastly, these possibilities are pointed toward a divine purpose not ours and therefore 'the ground of our beseeching':

> What might have been and what has been
> Point to one end, which is always present.

'Burnt Norton' was written as a separate poem, several years before its companions, but it almost seems as if these opening statements embodied a cadence which the poet was to deploy as the musical figure of the entire work; that each of the four statements becomes the ground of meditation for its corresponding poem in the sequence. This would go some distance to meet one of the persistent problems of the *Quartets*, the tone of 'The Dry Salvages', the idea being that the poem has to work out the implications of

> What might have been is an abstraction
> Remaining a perpetual possibility
> Only in a world of speculation

– hence, in the verse, the note of speculation, the feeling of words issuing from a merely speculative universe of discourse. But this problem can wait.

The next lines in 'Burnt Norton' translate 'what might have been' into footfalls which echo in the memory

> Down the passage which we did not take
> Towards the door we never opened
> Into the rose-garden

– a purely linguistic event featuring all the unfulfilled possibilities strewn across our past lives, offering themselves only as a fantasy sound-box in which 'my words echo'. To disturb the fictive past is futile, but it will be disturbed, because we have filled the garden with our own echoes, and nothing is sweeter than our own deception. The rose-garden is each man's fantasy-refuge, the realm of experience which he declares his private property. In the garden what we hear is not sound, Keats's 'heard melodies', but the 'unheard music' which is Absolute Sound, since we will settle for nothing less: when we impose our own meaning we are never satisfied by finite gratifications, we lust for the Absolute. So we arrange the scene to disclose ourselves; the roses are our guests, the dry pool is filled with water out of sunlight

for our benefit because a vital harmony between ourselves and
Nature is our great romantic illusion. But we exaggerate our
control over Reality:

> Then a cloud passed, and the pool was empty.
> Go, said the bird, for the leaves were full of children,
> Hidden excitedly, containing laughter.
> Go, go, go, said the bird: human kind
> Cannot bear very much reality

– even the reality of laughing children. In 'East Coker' III 'the
laughter in the garden' is invoked again as part of our fantasy,
but there it is defined immediately as 'echoed ecstasy', not something that must be abandoned or evacuated but 'requiring, pointing to the agony / Of death and birth'. Here in 'Burnt Norton'
when we have connived with the deception of the thrush, we get
as much as we deserve if the thrush chases us sadly from the
garden; if the illusion is broken we have only ourselves to blame.
Section I ends with the several variants of Time gathered together now and 'pointing' toward one end, 'which is always
present'. In section V when the hidden laughter of children in
the foliage is pointed in this way, the time is redeemed.

Section II of each poem is a statement of the true condition,
set off against the preoccupations which prevent its recognition.
In 'Burnt Norton' it is given as the dance of consciousness,
concentration, the still point, *Erhebung*; against the diverse
impediments of garlic, sapphires, the practical desire, 'the enchainment of past and future'. In 'East Coker' it is the true
wisdom of humility, set off against the vortex, 'the autumnal
serenity / And the wisdom of age', the goodwill of mere Tradition, 'the knowledge derived from experience', and the fear of
old men. In 'The Dry Salvages' it is, quite simply, 'the meaning',
the Annunciation; menaced by the 'currents of action' which
cover our past lives. And in 'Little Gidding' it is the refining
fire of the dancer; obscured by the vanities of spiritless culture,
last year's words, 'the gifts reserved for age'.

In 'East Coker' this second section is particularly vivid. The
true condition is given, as in 'Little Gidding', only at the end of

this section, when the ground has been cleared and the necessary discriminations imposed. The motto for this process is given in the opening lines of the third section of 'Little Gidding':

> There are three conditions which often look alike
> Yet differ completely, flourish in the same hedgerow:

– the discrimination of conditions or modes of being whose signs are often identical. In a secular or neutral context no discrimination is possible; only the vision of spirit can reveal the differences, the difference – to take one example – between the darkness inhabited by 'distinguished civil servants, chairmen of many committees', in 'East Coker' III and that other darkness which is 'the darkness of God'. So the second section of 'East Coker' begins with an experimental jeremiad, an answer to the 'reconciliation' passage in the corresponding section of 'Burnt Norton'. Instead of the still point there is the vortex, which extends to the whole world the fate of three victims in 'Gerontion':

> De Bailhache, Fresca, Mrs Cammel, whirled
> Beyond the circuit of the shuddering Bear
> In fractured atoms.

That was a way of putting it; but the poet now begins again, rejecting the jeremiad, or rather translating it into more urbane terms. Not that the poetry matters: if it must be evacuated along with the rest, well and good; a fresh start is more important. The first obstacle is the dead weight of an unemployed past: this must be cleared away, especially if it comes with the self-righteous panoply of words like 'calm' and 'serenity'. If Tradition is merely an antique drum, we must get rid of it: the past is dead, by definition, unless it is alive. Eliot holds the vaunted terms close to the light of a genuinely live tradition; under this scrutiny the serenity is only 'a deliberate hebetude', the wisdom 'only the knowledge of dead secrets'. The editorial plural of 'it seems to us' is the voice of antiseptic discrimination; its object is 'the knowledge derived from experience', a platitude from whose warmth we must be ejected. The ejecting force is the concept of Tradition as 'a new and shocking / Valuation', every moment, of all

we have been. The tone becomes more astringent as the editorial
'we' focuses in a single rebuking voice:

> Do not let me hear
> Of the wisdom of old men . . .

and the wisdom is given as a self-congratulating fiction, a mere
mockery. In *Ash Wednesday* the speaker prays to be delivered
from this hall of distorting mirrors: 'Suffer us not to mock ourselves with falsehood', meaning our private intelligences. And in
the second section of 'Little Gidding' Eliot will make yet another
attempt, using Yeats's *Purgatory* and the Ghost of Hamlet, now
merging the wisdom of old men with the gifts reserved for the
senile humanist. For 'East Coker' the answer is 'humility is
endless'.

Section III of each poem is a statement of our time-ridden
condition, and a proper admonition to 'wait' without choosing
our object. In 'Burnt Norton' it is the tube-station 'flicker' of
apathy and distraction, followed by the warning, 'Descend
lower'. The descent, if we agree to it, is guided by Heraclitus and
St John of the Cross, and it features the voiding of all claims to
property, sense, fancy, and even – the last surrender – spirit.
This is the 'awful daring of a moment's surrender / Which an
age of prudence can never retract', in the fifth section of *The
Waste Land*. The key-word is Evacuation. But the lines which
will form the starting-point for the corresponding section of
'East Coker' are:

> This is the one way, and the other
> Is the same, not in movement
> But abstention from movement; while the world moves
> In appetency, on its metalled ways
> Of time past and time future.

In section III of 'East Coker' this 'scene' is extended. Some of the
travellers are named, notably those who travel by limousine:

> Industrial lords and petty contractors, all go into the dark,
> And dark the Sun and Moon, and the Almanach de Gotha
> And the Stock Exchange Gazette, the Directory of
>   Directors . . .

And if we gloat upon the discomfiture of the rich, 'we all go with them, into the silent funeral'. Silent because anonymous; since we have obliterated our own identities, 'there is no one to bury'. The proper admonition is: 'Be still'; wait, without choosing even the objects of our faith, hope, or charity. And this admonition, in turn, is intensified in the last lines of this section, and will eventually become Celia's story in *The Cocktail Party*: 'You must go by a way wherein there is no ecstasy.' The last line should probably be read: 'And where you *are* is where *you* are not.' In 'Little Gidding' – to defer the special problems of 'The Dry Salvages' – section III gives our time-ridden condition as indifference, desire, the enchainment of past and future; and the admonition, under Lady Juliana's auspices, is to purify the motive:

> And all shall be well and
> All manner of thing shall be well
> By the purification of the motive
> In the ground of our beseeching.

Lady Juliana's *Shewings* are the Logos common to all, now partially revealed through her but independently of her will: their truth does not depend upon her. She does not suggest that the visions were important because they attended her. There is a reality not ourselves, not our property, not our 'supreme fiction'. This is the transition between sections II and III of 'The Dry Salvages'. When a discursive voice says, 'I sometimes wonder if that is what Krishna meant', the fresh start, the new version of our time-ridden condition, is the facile notion of Time itself as a spatial category in which the self occupies a gratifying secure present tense, looks 'back' to a fixed past and 'forward' to a future rich in anticipated pleasures. The anxious worried women of section I were at least in a more dignified position,

> Between midnight and dawn, when the past is all deception,
> The future futureless . . .

F. H. Bradley had already undermined the cosy assumptions of the travellers in chapter four of *Appearance and Reality*: Eliot's admonition is given in two voices, the nocturnal voice which

WITHDRAWN

snubs the travellers, 'you who think that you are voyaging', and
the voice of Krishna, persuading Arjuna to go with purified
motive into battle. The first voice comes from a reader of
Bradley:

> You are not those who saw the harbour
> Receding, or those who will disembark

and virtually challenges the travellers to declare their 'personal
identity' and prove it. But the travellers can still be saved, if they
heed Krishna. The quoted lines are taken from canto VIII of the
Bhagavad-Gita, with a glance at canto II. The relevant sentences are these:

He who at his last hour, when he casts off the body, goes hence
remembering Me, goes assuredly into My being. Whatsoever
being a man at his end in leaving the body remembers, to that
same he always goes, O son of Kunti, inspired to being therein.
Therefore at all times remember Me, and fight; if thy mind and
understanding are devoted to Me, thou wilt assuredly come to
Me. . . . In Works be thine office; in their fruits must it never be.[3]

Eliot's version is:

> At the moment which is not of action or inaction
> You can receive this: 'on whatever sphere of being
> The mind of a man may be intent
> At the time of death' – that is the one action
> (And the time of death is every moment)
> Which shall fructify in the lives of others:
> And do not think of the fruit of action.
> Fare forward.

This is as close as we are likely to come to the dogmatic centre of
this dogmatic poem. The moment which is not of action or
inaction is presumably the moment of incarnate thought, concentration without elimination, in our own lives hardly more
frequent than Wordsworthian 'spots of time', since human kind
cannot bear very much reality. Krishna's message concerns the
moment of death as his pupil goes into battle, but Eliot's Heraclitean parenthesis gives it a strangely Christian latitude; if we

die every moment and if at every moment we are intent upon the highest sphere of being, then – the Dantean promise runs – this 'intention' will fructify in the lives of others. This is another version of the promise made in section II, after the equation of 'the meaning' with 'the one Annunciation'; that the past experience revived in the meaning 'is not the experience of one life only / But of many generations . . .' And of course it is also, looking back to 'East Coker', the 'lifetime burning in every moment'. If we add, from *Ash Wednesday*, 'Redeem the time', and, from 'Burnt Norton', 'only through time time is conquered', we have a node of Christian emphasis, depending upon the Incarnation, which is as close as the *Quartets* at any one moment will come to 'the meaning'.

Section IV of each poem is a lyric of purgation; not a persuasion toward that act but the act itself. In 'Burnt Norton' when we have renounced the pretentions of action and the black cloud has carried away the sun, we are at the 'ABC of being' – Wallace Stevens's phrase – and in a fit state to ask the appropriately modest questions. 'Will the clematis / Stray down, bend to us' is one of four questions, each a preparation for prayer. Clematis, the Virgin's Bower of blue, Mary's colour, and the fingers of yew point the questions toward death and the Christian hope of immortality. But the last lines are provisional: the harmony between the kingfisher's wing and nature's light is less than a final comfort; these are merely 'notes towards' prayer. In 'East Coker' the lyric of purgation hovers over Adam's curse, Original Sin. The tone is strangely crude; indeed, this is one of the weaker parts of the poem. The analogies of health and disease, surgeons, patients, and hospitals are marginally appropriate, and far too dependent upon our reading 'the wounded surgeon' as Christ, 'the dying nurse' as the Church, the hospital as the earth, 'the ruined millionaire' as God the Father, the briars as the thorns of Christ. When we have effected these translations little remains but the satisfaction of having done so. The corresponding section of 'The Dry Salvages' is much finer, a direct prayer continuous with that of section V of *Ash Wednesday*. And the last version, in 'Little Gidding', is the Pentecostal Fire, the Descent of the Holy

Ghost. The German bomber which was the 'dark dove' of
section III is now transformed:

> The dove descending breaks the air
> With flame of incandescent terror

and if the old dove was deadly the new one is far from being
domesticated. Heraclitus' account of the Death of the Elements
is relevant, but the entire lyric is an extended version of the lines
in the corresponding section of 'East Coker':

> If to be warmed, then I must freeze
> And quake in frigid purgatorial fires
> Of which the flame is roses, and the smoke is briars.

– with a glance at Adam's curse and 'the one discharge from sin
and error'. The first lyric, in 'Burnt Norton', was all question;
the second, in 'East Coker', a sermon of rude reminders; the
third, the prayer of 'The Dry Salvages'; and now the question
can be answered:

> Who then devised the torment? Love
> Love is the unfamiliar Name
> Behind the hands that wove
> The intolerable shirt of flame
> Which human power cannot remove.
> We only live, only suspire
> Consumed by either fire or fire.

In the third section of *Ash Wednesday* the devil of the stairs wore
'the deceitful face of hope and despair'. In 'East Coker' the faith
and the hope and the love were all 'in the waiting'. And now the
tenable hope is specified in 'the choice of pyre or pyre', taking up
where section I left off, 'pentecostal fire / In the dark time of the
year'. The collocation of Fire and Love as the poet remarked of
the ascetic conjunction of the Fire Sermon's 'Burning burning
burning burning' and St Augustine's 'O Lord Thou pluckest
me out', in *The Waste Land*, 'is not an accident'.

Section v of each poem is a meditation on the redemption of
Time. In *Night Thoughts* Young asks, innocently enough,
'Redeem we time?' In *Ash Wednesday* the voice intones:

Redeem

The time. Redeem
The unread vision in the higher dream
While jewelled unicorns draw by the gilded hearse.

Section v of 'Burnt Norton' is the first attempt, a tentative and frustrated figuring of time redeemed in Love. It begins with a Chinese jar which 'still / Moves perpetually in its stillness', but this is merely a slight specification of the 'daylight' of section III,

Investing form with lucid stillness
Turning shadow into transient beauty
With slow rotation suggesting permanence.

But clearly the Chinese jar won't do; nor will the stillness of the violin. And the syntax lurches in dazed considerations of beginning and end. The words strain and crack because they are not the Word, they are one man's fancies, his 'private intelligence', his disconsolate chimeras, the 'merely' human voices which, in 'Prufrock', 'wake us, and we drown'. Or perhaps the 'daemonic, chthonic powers' of 'The Dry Salvages'. The last lines give up the attempt to offer comparisons from a familiar medium and confront the problem head-on, beginning with Aristotle's God as the Unmoved Mover, Dryden's Universal He, 'Unmade, unmov'd; yet making, moving All'. Eliot's version is:

Love is itself unmoving,
Only the cause and end of movement,
Timeless, and undesiring
Except in the aspect of time
Caught in the form of limitation
Between un-being and being

– which I interpret as the Incarnation, a later version of a choric passage in *The Rock* VII:

A moment not out of time, but in time, in what we call history: transecting, bisecting the world of time, a moment in time but not like a moment of time,
A moment in time but time was made through that moment: for without the meaning there is no time, and that moment of time gave the meaning.

'Un-being' is what *The Rock* calls 'negative being': 'being' is the still point. 'Burnt Norton' ends:

> Sudden in a shaft of sunlight
> Even while the dust moves
> There rises the hidden laughter
> Of children in the foliage
> Quick now, here, now, always –
> Ridiculous the waste sad time
> Stretching before and after.

This sounds definitive, the great moment, especially when it is set off against the waste sad time. But each of its terms has already been circumscribed. God as the Timeless is immanent in the temporal, yes, here as in the *Paradiso*. He descended into history and thereby 'made time'. But we have already seen that the rose-garden is each man's fantasy-refuge, not absurd or trivial but incomplete, like the children's laughter. And the proof is in the shaft of sunlight which will flash again across the corresponding section of 'The Dry Salvages', focusing upon an experience declared incomplete. Two conditions are described in this section, and they are distinguished as firmly as in *The Cocktail Party*. In that play the conditions are that of the saint, Celia, and that of the rest of us, Edward and Lavinia at the end of the play, 'a good life' but not sanctity or the refining fire. Critics who were scandalized by this separation in the play did not remark that the same plot is inaugurated in section v of 'The Dry Salvages'. This section begins with an account of 'men's curiosity' which 'searches past and future / And clings to that dimension'. And then there is sanctity:

> But to apprehend
> The point of intersection of the timeless
> With time, is an occupation for the saint –
> No occupation either, but something given
> And taken, in a lifetime's death in love,
> Ardour and selflessness and self-surrender.

Celia, clearly. But most of us are Edwards or Lavinias, and for us

> there is only the unattended
> Moment, the moment in and out of time,

> The distraction fit, lost in a shaft of sunlight,
> The wild thyme unseen, or the winter lightning
> Or the waterfall, or music heard so deeply
> That it is not heard at all, but you are the music
> While the music lasts

– the unheard music in the shrubbery of 'Burnt Norton'. In that poem the words crack and strain before the birth of Celia. When she goes on the 'way of illumination' in section v of 'The Dry Salvages' the rest of us do what we can in the middle style:

> And right action is freedom
> From past and future also.
> For most of us, this is the aim
> Never here to be realised;
> We are only undefeated
> Because we have gone on trying;

– a counsel from which we extract whatever juice we can, perhaps more and perhaps less than Edward when he remarked:

> But Sir Henry has been saying,
> I think, that every moment is a fresh beginning;
> And Julia, that life is only keeping on;
> And somehow, the two ideas seem to fit together.

In section v of 'East Coker' the meditation on Time is carried a little further than in 'Burnt Norton', beginning with a rather damp consideration of life 'in the middle way', where 'For us, there is only the trying'. Eliot seems now to repudiate the rose-garden

> Not the intense moment
> Isolated, with no before or after,

in his rush to define the great mode as

> a lifetime burning in every moment
> And not the lifetime of one man only
> But of old stones that cannot be deciphered

– which is an interim version of 'a lifetime's death in love', prefigured now in 'East Coker' as

> Love is most nearly itself
> When here and now cease to matter.

The last lines seem to imply, even yet, that we can all still make
ourselves Celias:

> We must be still and still moving
> Into another intensity
> For a further union, a deeper communion
> Through the dark cold and the empty desolation,
> The wave cry, the wind cry, the vast waters
> Of the petrel and the porpoise

– an impressive account of Kinkanja, and a reminder that even
the 'way of illumination' leads through the temporal; as Reilly
declared that the Saint in the desert, with spiritual evil always
at his shoulder, also suffered from 'hunger, damp, exposure /
Bowel trouble, and the fear of lions'.

The distinction between the saint and the rest of us occupied
the last moments of 'The Dry Salvages' because it bore down
hard upon the redemption of time, and the same distinction was
to be worked out even more problematically in the plays; but
in section v of 'Little Gidding' the distinction is set aside in a
vision of time redeemed. The hint is picked up from 'East Coker':
'Old men ought to be explorers'. Our words are not the Logos,
but if we resist our self-engrossing fancies and try to apprehend
'the meaning' – and this is what the exploration amounts to –
instead of imposing our own, then 'every phrase and every
sentence is an end and a beginning'. The temporal is the locus of
value, because it is the only locus we have and value must exist;
in the temporal we may still try to apprehend the meaning of the
Incarnation; it is our condition; at its best, a condition of complete simplicity, costing 'not less than everything'. Hence the
poet gathers up, still in time, all the broken images, the hints
and guesses, Dante's scattered leaves ('Nel suo profondo vidi che
s'interna, / legato con amore in un volume, / cio che per l'uni-
verso si squaderna') and folds them into 'one simple flame', the
light of Eternal Love.[4]

A Special Problem: 'The Dry Salvages'
In recent years the critical reception of *Four Quartets* has taken a

curious turn. I shall describe it briefly, especially where it bears upon 'The Dry Salvages'.

The new reading began with Hugh Kenner's essay 'Eliot's Moral Dialectic' (1949) and was pushed to a formidable extreme some years later by Donald Davie. Mr Kenner argued that the structural principle of *Four Quartets* is to be found in the pattern of 'Burnt Norton', two terms, opposed, falsely reconciled, then truly reconciled. Light and Darkness, opposed, are falsely reconciled in the tube-station 'flicker', then truly and paradoxically reconciled in the Dark Night of the Soul. In 'Little Gidding' Attachment and Detachment, opposed, falsely reconciled in Indifference, are truly reconciled in Love. In his recent book *The Invisible Poet* Mr Kenner does not urge us to acknowledge this pattern in each of the four poems. Instead, he suggests that the structural principle of 'Burnt Norton' applies also to the organization of the *Quartets* as a whole. The 'recurrent illumination' of 'Burnt Norton' and the 'pervasive sombreness' of 'East Coker' are to be taken as opposing terms, 'alternative ways in which the mind responsible for their existence deceives itself'; they are then falsely reconciled in the 'conciliating formulae' of 'The Dry Salvages', and truly reconciled in the taut revelations, the 'refining fire' of 'Little Gidding'. This implies, of course, that everything leading up to the last section of 'Little Gidding' from the first words of 'Burnt Norton', is, more or less, parody; the disclosure of moral positions which Eliot – the suggestion runs – has never inhabited or from which he has detached himself. As if the poem were a long 'Gerontion'. This is hard to take. I cannot believe that when the voice of 'East Coker' II says

> The only wisdom we can hope to acquire
> Is the wisdom of humility: humility is endless

we are to interpret this as yet another moment in which the mind responsible for its existence is deceiving itself.

A more modest version of Mr Kenner's case argues that 'The Dry Salvages' becomes the 'flicker' stage in the plot of *Four Quartets*: this follows Mr Davie's suggestion that 'The Dry

Salvages' – he does not include the other three poems – is deliberate parody.

And yet, even this modest version; is it credible? Who is parodying what?

> And on the deck of the drumming liner
> Watching the furrow that widens behind you,
> You shall not think 'the past is finished'
> Or 'the future is before us'.

This does not sound like 'The Hollow Men', but it is clearly not parody; it is a preceptorial voice making our clichés uninhabitable; just as, later, a similar voice performs a similar function in

> Men's curiosity searches past and future
> And clings to that dimension.

There is more in 'The Dry Salvages' than conciliating formulae.

And yet perhaps this is the hint we need. Mr Kenner, if he cared, might have made his structural pattern cover 'The Dry Salvages' by taking Action and Passion as his opposing terms, falsely reconciled in the mere Motion of section II, the 'currents', and truly reconciled in the 'Right Action' of section V which is 'freedom / From past and future also'. This would have acknowledged that the poem is all transit, comings and goings, with the attendant temptation of choosing our direction and the attendant danger of getting lost. But let that be. There is a great deal in 'The Dry Salvages' which requires explanation or apology. My own impression is that after the dark admonitions of 'East Coker' the poet, for a fresh start, sought a new tone, something much more conversational. The new voice should be much more discursive, to begin with; becoming sharper as the decorum changes and the consideration of 'what might have been' becomes more arduous. I think Eliot wanted the voice to begin like Lord Claverton and end like Harry Monchensey. Indeed, the passage beginning

> You cannot face it steadily, but this thing is sure,
> That time is no healer: the patient is no longer here.

> When the train starts, and the passengers are settled
> To fruit, periodicals and business letters.

is taken up again after many years for *The Elder Statesman*:

> It's just like sitting in an empty waiting room
> In a railway station on a branch line,
> After the last train . . .

And the voice which speaks of human questioning as mere curiosity is like Harry Monchensey's, engaged in the demolition of family inquests:

> What you call the normal
> Is merely the unreal and the unimportant.

So there can hardly be any possibility of parody. If 'The Dry Salvages' is bad it is bad because it fails to be good, not because Eliot meant it to sound 'bad' in a sophisticated way.

The Lord Claverton voice begins, 'I do not know much about gods', and speculates about the river as a 'strong brown god'. The river, as I read the passage, is everything in ourselves which we elect to ignore, all the intractable forces within the self which we disregard because they do not lend themselves to our cliché-purposes – conveying commerce, building bridges, dwelling in cities and worshipping machines. Dazzled by the cliché-fancies of our own invention, we ignore the river, but it proceeds, however deviously, to a source alien to our purposes. And yet it was always with us:

> His rhythm was present in the nursery bedroom,
> In the rank ailanthus of the April dooryard.

The syntax is as flabby as Mr Davie says it is. If Eliot wished to suggest a spectral presence in the April dooryard, he would have done better with something like *The Waste Land*'s

> Who is the third who walks always beside you?
> When I count, there are only you and I together
> But when I look ahead up the white road
> There is always another one walking beside you
> Gliding wrapt in a brown mantle, hooded

or the later version of this which he uses in *The Cocktail Party*. 'The river is within us, the sea is all about us'; the sea being, I assume, an omnivorous impersonal reality alien to man and therefore suicidally attractive as a refuge from his consciousness. It has many voices and it measures 'time not our time', but we deceive ourselves like the anxious women and try to take the sea's measure, using our own counters.

But the real embarrassments begin in section II. My guess is that Eliot wanted now to make his anxious women of section I into a choric voice, like the Women of Canterbury in *Murder in the Cathedral*, expressing the usual loud laments in their own terms; and then to bring in a Monchensey voice to evacuate the whole area of plangent cliché and point to the one Meaning. The hint is clear enough in

> The backward look behind the assurance
> Of recorded history, the backward half-look
> Over the shoulder, towards the primitive terror

and in the fact that the notorious rhymes of section II are inaugurated in the last lines of section I with the phrase, 'The future futureless'. The first stanza of section II is very beautiful. But the decision to add five stanzas and to make each line-end rhyme with its counterpart in the other stanzas was disastrous. There is nothing as difficult in the choruses of *The Rock* or *Murder in the Cathedral*. The poet may have been impressed by the air of world-wide plangency which Coleridge evoked from 'measureless' in 'Kubla Khan', or perhaps by Hopkins's efforts with 'motionable' in 'The Wreck of the Deutschland', but for an artist whose vocational concern was speech there is no excusing the coinage of 'oceanless', 'erosionless', and 'devotionless'. The *N.E.D.* gives a certain pale authority for 'emotionless', but when Eliot writes

>   the trailing
> Consequence of further days and hours,
> While emotion takes to itself the emotionless
> Years of living among the breakage
> Of what was believed in as the most reliable –

I do not know what he means. Does he mean that our undiscip-
lined squads of emotion, instead of leaving the symbolic sea of
section I well alone ('emotionless' meaning, if anything, emotionally null) are constantly trying to take possession of it; and
the more successful the emotions in these exploits, the more
impoverished our lives, the more – if we are to 'live' – we shall
have to renounce? The next stanza is an early version of the
'gifts reserved for age' in 'Little Gidding'. 'The unattached
devotion which might pass for devotionless' can hardly mean
much more than 'the capacity for devotion which continues even
when it lacks an object'; but I do not know why it should try to
'pass for' devotionless, playing possum. After the apocalyptic
chorus Eliot returns to the Claverton voice, 'It seems, as one
becomes older . . .' to modulate into the Monchensey voice
which will clear the way for the Meaning. The anxious worried
chorus feared that the whole human scramble was ridiculous;
rather like the fears of the Aunts and Uncles in their trance-
moments in *The Family Reunion*. But the stern voice now says
that 'the meaning' redeems time and because it is the Rock, is
itself:

in the sombre season
Or the sudden fury, is what it always was.

We need not go through the poem: most of its sore thumbs have
been at least noted. I think the defects of 'The Dry Salvages' are
real and serious; where they occur, they are the result of Eliot's
failure to conduct a piece which he scored for an unmanageable
number of voices. It would be easier in the plays, where he
could take whatever time he required to establish his voices. In
the other poems and especially in 'Little Gidding' the voices are
fewer, clearly distinguishable, and under impeccable control.

The Problem

Eliot's problem in *Four Quartets* is a strategic one; how to
evacuate practically all the areas in which his readers live. A pro-
posal of this kind is tolerated only in wartime, and indeed Eliot
wrote most of the poem during a world war and perhaps he
wanted to use the idiom of war in order to enforce a deeper

discrimination of peacetime commitments. The critique is religious, dogmatic, and Christian. Eliot's hope is to clear a space, or if necessary to take over a bombed-out area, and there to build a new life of the spirit; to realize 'the idea of a Christian society'. He will approach the Meaning from several experimental directions, making several fresh starts, because he can hardly hope – the conditions being unpropitious – that one will suffice. And there is a sense in which he himself is the object of his own persuasion. The redemption of time will be his theme, his case, but he will have to resist a Manichean force within himself which is notoriously subversive; it doesn't really believe that time can be redeemed, it fears that the human scale of action is puny, beyond or beneath redemption. This is to give the Manichean force an extreme form, and it will not always be so intransigent; but that it is a complication in Eliot's Christian poetry I have no doubt. Indeed, it is probably inevitable – or an occasional hazard, at the least – in all those 'varieties of religious experience' which are ascetic before they are anything else; taking their bearings from the idiom of cleansing, surgery, and 'voiding'. It is difficult to propose the voiding of all human allegiances without implying that they are in any event meretricious. The idiom of renunciation is more hopeful, since the value of renunciation is all the greater if what is renounced is indisputably fine. And therefore an 'ideal' strategy for a secular age would consist in persuading one's reader to void his allegiances by showing up his daily preoccupations as mere 'fancies'; and then to translate this voiding into renunciation, a positive sacrifice which he is encouraged to make to a God now certified by the quality of the sacrifice itself. This is largely what Eliot tries to do in the *Quartets*.

There is a passage in *The Trembling of the Veil* which throws light upon Eliot's object. Yeats has been discussing 'Unity of Being' in his habitual idiom of Image, Mask, and Anti-Self. But he goes on to say that there are people to whom all this is irrelevant:

I now know that there are men who cannot possess 'Unity of Being', who must not seek it or express it – and who, so far from seeking an anti-self, a Mask that delineates a being in all things the opposite to their natural state, can but seek the suppression of the anti-self, till the natural state alone remains. There are those who must seek no image of desire, but await that which lies beyond their mind – unities not of the mind, but unities of Nature, unities of God – the man of science, the moralist, the humanitarian, the politician, Saint Simeon Stylites upon his pillar, Saint Anthony in his cavern, all whose preoccupation is to seem nothing . . . their imaginations grow more vivid in the expression of something which they have not created.[5]

The great example is George Herbert, a hero, incidentally, in Eliot's mythology. Eliot would probably say, 'all whose pre-occupation is to be nothing', since seeming is not enough – he is not Wallace Stevens. The authority – if he needs one – comes from St John of the Cross, 'To be all things, be willing to be nothing.' These men are the great exemplars, but they are only the most extreme forms of Eliot's ideal reader, his ideal man. In this sense the poetry does not matter: it merely 'points' the reader – and perhaps the writer, too – toward one end.

Our argument, then, is that the course of Eliot's persuasion in *Four Quartets* is to translate voiding into renunciation, negative into its corresponding positive. And some of the rhetoric whistles in the dark, warding off the ghosts. There are certain moments in the *Quartets* when Eliot couldn't quite convince himself of human value, and even the pretty, inoffensive things are voided and cleared away before they can be redeemed. Like the poor dancers of 'East Coker':

> Keeping time,
> Keeping the rhythm in their dancing
> As in their living in the living seasons
> The time of the seasons and the constellations
> The time of milking and the time of harvest
> The time of the coupling of man and woman
> And that of beasts. Feet rising and falling.
> Eating and drinking. Dung and death.

It is a gruff dismissal, when all is said. And it points to the deepest embarrassment – or so I think – in Eliot's poetry; the feeling, in

part, that all the declared values of human life are somehow
illusory and, in part, that nevertheless God so loved the world
that He gave up for its redemption His beloved Son. In *Four
Quartets* when the first part of this feeling is predominant, the
persuasion is all voiding; when the second part asserts itself, the
persuasion is all renunciation. The poems are dogmatic, yes, but
there is often 'the backward half-look / Over the shoulder,
towards the primitive terror'. For many readers, I should guess,
it is this half-look which redeems a poetry otherwise too im-
periously above redemption.

Because of course the readers of *Four Quartets* break apart in
ideological groups; Mr Davie is quite right about this. The
religious believers tend to admire the poem; others don't. So far
as I am a Christian I approve of Eliot's purposes and only wish
that they were charged with an even warmer sense of human
value in all its limitation: I wish it were a more Franciscan poem.
The parts of the poem which I tend to carry in my mind are
those in which the religious feeling is willingly grounded in
place and time, in a human situation of certified value. A passage
like this, for instance, from 'Little Gidding':

> If you came this way in may time, you would find the hedges
> White again, in May, with voluptuary sweetness.
> It would be the same at the end of the journey,
> If you came at night like a broken king,
> If you came by day not knowing what you came for,
> It would be the same, when you leave the rough road
> And turn behind the pig-sty to the dull façade
> And the tombstone.

– where the whiteness of the hedges and the voluptuary sweetness are acknowledged for the civilities they are.

How the non-believer reads this poem, I cannot say. It may be
possible to skim off the poetry, leaving whatever remains,
thereby turning upside-down Eliot's own motto that the poetry
does not matter. But perhaps believer and non-believer can
meet, after all, at another point. There is a passage in *Varieties
of Religious Experience* which offers a possibility. James is discussing the characteristics of saintliness, particularly its ascetic

quality. He remarks·that while it is normal and, seemingly, instinctive to seek 'the easy and the pleasant', at the same time it is also natural, 'in moderate degree' to 'court the arduous':

Some men and women, indeed, there are who can live on smiles and the word 'yes' forever. But for others (indeed for most) this is too tepid and relaxed a moral climate. Passive happiness is slack and insipid, and soon grows mawkish and intolerable. Some austerity and wintry negativity, some roughness, danger, stringency, and effort, some 'no! no!' must be mixed in, to produce the sense of an existence with character and texture and power.[6]

Perhaps this is as far as we should go. *Four Quartets* 'bids' – it is Hopkins's word – in so far as it gives the reader (believing or not) the sense of an existence with character and texture and power. Eliot himself has pointed toward this criterion. It is notoriously difficult to show the coherence of his critical theories; his generalizations are occasional rather than systematic. He is not Yvor Winters. But he has always implied that the poetic satisfactions are disciplinary; the great poem helps to 'purify the dialect of the tribe' largely by making its reader's stupidity unendurable; it renders one's excesses absurd and therefore distasteful. There is a sharp passage, for instance, in Eliot's Introduction to *London* and *The Vanity of Human Wishes* in which he discusses the proper satisfactions of poetry. And then he continues:

Those who demand of poetry a day-dream, or a metamorphosis of their own feeble desires and lusts, or what they believe to be 'intensity' of passion, will not find much in Johnson. He is like Pope and Dryden, Crabbe and Landor, a poet for those who want poetry and not something else, some stay for their own vanity.[7]

Four Quartets, like *The Vanity of Human Wishes*, is offered as a stay for our vanity; this is the condition of its being. When it fails, the poet has dropped his guard, and his own vanity rushes in; as in the second section of 'The Dry Salvages' where the language is self-indulgent and the vanity erupts as bravado, exhibitionism. In the great passages the poet meditates upon the *vanitas vanitatum*, but he is as strict with himself as with us. A proper justice is served. 'Humility is endless.'

SOURCE: *Studies* (1965).

NOTES

1. Fragments 2 and 108, translated by Philip Wheelwright. See his *Heraclitus* (Princeton, 1959) pp. 19, 90.

2. Cf. Dryden's Preface to *Religio Laici*: 'They who wou'd prove Religion by Reason, do but weaken the cause which they endeavour to support: 'tis to take away the Pillars from our Faith, and to prop it onely with a twig: 'tis to design a Tower like that of Babel, which if it were possible (as it is not) to reach Heaven, would come to nothing by the confusion of the Workmen. For every man is Building a several way; impotently conceipted of his own Model, and his own Materials: Reason is always striving, and always at a loss, and of necessity it must so come to pass, while 'tis exercised about that which is not its proper object. Let us be content at last, to know God, by his own Methods; at least so much of him, as he is pleas'd to reveal to us, in the sacred Scriptures; to apprehend them to be the word of God, is all our Reason has to do; for all beyond it is the work of Faith, which is the Seal of Heaven impress'd upon our humane understanding.'

3. Translated by Lionel D. Barnett (1905) p. 123. Cf especially canto II, verses 38 and 47.

4. The most relevant passages of the *Paradiso* are canto XXXI, lines 10–24 and canto XXXIII, lines 85–145.

5. *Autobiographies* (1955 reprint) pp. 247–8.

6. *Varieties of Religious Experience*, The Gifford Lectures, 1901–2 (1960 reprint) p. 295.

7. *Selected Prose* (Penguin Books, 1953) pp. 168–9.

PART FOUR

Briefer Comments

Marshall McLuhan

SYMBOLIC LANDSCAPE

FLAUBERT and Baudelaire had presided over the great city landscape of *Ulysses*. And Mr Eliot's *The Waste Land* in 1922 was a new technical modulation of *Ulysses*, the latter of which had begun to appear in 1917. The *Quartets* owe a great deal to [*Finnegans*] *Wake*, as does *The Cocktail Party*. There is in all these works a vision of the community of men and creatures which is not so much ethical as metaphysical. And it had been, in poetry, due to the technical innovations of Baudelaire, Laforgue and Rimbaud that it was possible to render this vision immediately in verse without the extraneous aids of rhetoric or logical reflection and statement. The principal innovation was that of *le paysage intérieur* or the psychological landscape. This landscape, by means of discontinuity, which was first developed in picturesque painting, effected the apposition of widely diverse objects as a means of establishing what Mr Eliot has called 'an objective correlative' for a state of mind. The openings of 'Prufrock', 'Gerontion' and *The Waste Land* illustrate Mr Eliot's growth in the adaptation of this technique, as he passed from the influence of Laforgue to that of Rimbaud, from personal to impersonal manipulation of experience. Whereas in external landscape diverse things lie side by side, so in psychological landscape the juxtaposition of various things and experiences becomes a precise musical means of orchestrating that which could never be rendered by systematic discourse. Landscape is the means of presenting, without the copula of logical enunciation, experiences which are united in existence but not in conceptual thought. Syntax becomes music, as in Tennyson's 'Mariana'.

In the landscapes of the *Quartets* as in those of the *Wake* everything speaks. There is no single or personal speaker of the *Quartets*, not even the Tiresias of 'Gerontion' and *The Waste Land*. It is the places and things which utter themselves. And this is also a stage of technique and experience achieved by Pound in his *Cantos*, and by St Jean Perse, just as it had earlier been reached by Mallarmé in *Un Coup de Dés*. Browning was groping for it in *The Ring and the Book*. One might say that as the effect of Laforgue had been to open Mr Eliot's mind to the effects of Donne and the Metaphysicals, so the effect of Rimbaud was to make him more fully aware of the means by which Dante achieved a zoning of states of mind through symbolic landscape.

(*Essays in Criticism*, 1951)

A. Alvarez

A MEDITATIVE POET

H E is, in some ways, a meditative poet. But this does not mean a poet who deals in abstractions; Eliot's meditations are meditations on experience, in which the abstractions belong as much as the images; they are all part of his particular cast of mind, the meaning he gives to past experience. But Eliot is, I think, a relatively indifferent, or uninterested, observer of the phenomenal world – though in his earlier poems he was a sharp observer of manners. He is instead a supreme interpreter of meditated experience.

His direct affirmations are always summings-up of this type, concentrations for which all the rest of his verse appears as so many hints. What is, to my mind, one of his finest pieces of writing, section II of 'Little Gidding' is precisely the crystallization of 'the past experience revived in the meaning' with a terrible clarity. The voice has the unpartisan honesty of 'the familiar compound ghost', a man beyond life, like Tiresias in *The Waste Land* and Dante's Vergil:

Let me disclose the gifts reserved for age
　　To set a crown upon your lifetime's effort.
　　First, the cold friction of expiring sense
Without enchantment, offering no promise
　　But bitter tastelessness of shadow fruit
　　As body and soul begin to fall asunder.
Second, the conscious impotence of rage
　　At human folly, and the laceration
　　Of laughter at what ceases to amuse.
And last, the rending pain of re-enactment
　　Of all you have done, and been; the shame
　　Of motives late revealed, and the awareness
Of things ill done and done to others' harm
　　Which once you took for exercise of virtue.
　　Then fools' approval stings, and honour stains.
From wrong to wrong the exasperated spirit
　　Proceeds, unless restored by that refining fire
　　Where you must move in measure, like a dancer.

In the scheme of the poem this section is hardly intended to be final. It is a sort of warning signpost, pointing away from an impasse. But it has more direct power than anything else in the *Four Quartets*. For it seems a subject that Eliot has lived with; he knows it from the inside. It is *The Waste Land* refined, matured and judged with the confidence of standards. But despair and denial in *The Waste Land* were there because of lack of standards, because of the impossibility of finding any solution. Here, dignified as renunciation, they seem in the tissue of life itself. Of course, the positive solution Eliot offers is not one that can be known consistently, still less presented with much directness. He can only suggest and rely on the 'logic of sensibility' to give direction and order to the hints. Yet, in my experience, this passage is one that stays most forcibly with you when the poem is done; much of the rest seems a series of subtle and beautiful hints at something that is just beyond your grasp. It is a sense of the desolation of life which remains. Against the insistence that life attains its meaning in death is the nagging worry that the poetry is dealing with certain states of spiritual refinement in which those two words are interchangeable. And this worry is something more basic than not knowing the states Eliot describes, nor yet believing his beliefs, nor assuming the orthodoxy from which his formality receives its strength. To quote the essay on Dante, which prepared the way for all Eliot's subsequent poetry:

My point is that you cannot afford to *ignore* Dante's philosophical and theological beliefs, or to skip the passages which express them most clearly; but on the other hand you are not called upon to believe them yourself. It is wrong to think that there are parts of the *Divine Comedy* which are of interest only to Catholics or to mediaevalists. For there is a difference . . . between philosophical *belief* and poetic *assent*. . . . In reading Dante you must enter the world of thirteenth-century Catholicism: which is not the world of modern Catholicism. . . . You are not called upon to believe what Dante believed, for your belief will not give you a groat's worth more of understanding and appreciation; but you are called upon more and more to understand it. If you can read poetry as poetry, you will 'believe' in Dante's theology exactly as you believe in the physical reality of his journey; that is, you suspend both belief and disbelief.

There is no difficulty in giving poetic assent to Eliot's world, for it exists by virtue of the purity and control of his writing. But there is a difficulty in accepting the conclusion which is everywhere implied; and that is not the orthodoxy, but the rejection and denial which the orthodoxy honours. (And Eliot's poetry, unlike Dante's, deals more or less entirely, though not always at the same concentration, with those conclusions.)

The development of Eliot's verse, from 'Prufrock' to *The Waste Land*, *Ash Wednesday* and the *Four Quartets*, is not from hesitation to rejection to preparation and arrival; it is of a steadily intensifying withdrawal and denial. The sureness of the *Four Quartets* is in the sureness of their renunciation. It is here that my remarks on the formality of Eliot's verse take their place. The triumphant achievement of the *Four Quartets* is in the peculiar wholeness and isolation of their poetic world, despite the fact that, compared with Dante's or Milton's worlds, Eliot uses only the bare, essential structure; he has created his world

without any of the 'worldly' props of narrative or figures. It is
an inner meditative world that is publicly wedded to dogma
through the offices of a controlled formal poetic language. The
success is well-nigh perfect; you move from meditation to glowing image hardly aware of the remoteness, and still less of the
conclusions to which it is all leading. For little is explicit, still
less didactic. Eliot has always worked obliquely, by suggestion
and by his penetrating personal rhythms. His power is in his sureness and mastery of subject and expression. And this sense of
inviolable purpose seems to remove his verse from the ordinary
realm of human interchange. He has created a world of formal
perfection. It lacks the dimension of human error.

It cannot, for example, stand up to the personal, speaking
voice. Where Eliot himself steps forward without formality, he
steps often into bathos:

> You say I am repeating
> Something I have said before. I shall say it again.
> Shall I say it again? . . .

> It seems, as one becomes older,
> That the past has another pattern, and ceases to be a mere
> sequence –
> Or even development: *the latter a partial fallacy*
> *Encouraged by superficial notions of evolution,*
> Which becomes, *in the popular mind,* a means of disowning
> the past.
> The moments of happiness – not the sense of well-being,
> Fruition, fulfilment, security or affection,
> *Or even a very good dinner,* but the sudden illumination –
>
> (My italics)

Personal lightness of touch is not one of his gifts. It is these
flashes of rather heavy condescension that bring home how much
depends on maintaining the decorum and formality of his poetic
occasions. But the unguarded moments are rare; Eliot hardly
speaks without clearing his throat. When occasionally he falters,
it is usually in the opposite way: the writing evaporates into
words. This verbal element was present in his early work as a

Jamesian self-consciousness: 'That is at least one definite "false note" '. And it has at times led him into an involvement with words almost scholastic in its intensity. Two examples will be enough; the moments are well known:

> You know and do not know, what it is to act and suffer.
> You know and do not know, that acting is suffering,
> And suffering action. Neither does the actor suffer
> Nor the patient act . . .

> And the way up is the way down, the way forward is the
>   way back . . .

The intention and the kind of problem invoked are both clear enough. But the way in which it is stated has been reduced to a gesture; there is a hollowness to the subtlety. Usually a gesture is a weary insistence on personal beliefs already well known to the reader. Eliot's gestures, on the other hand, have almost nothing in them of personal conviction and everything of verbal contrivance. It is the formal world of his poetry emptied of the personal intelligence which gave it life and meaning. It is a sort of verbal vacuum, the intellectual orthodoxy and discipline caricatured, or as though the intellectual will continued when all other personal fullness failed.

Eliot, in short, has created an autonomous poetic world of great power, freshness of expression, intelligence, delicacy, subtlety: but it is a segregated world – equal but separate. Its remoteness is precisely in its orthodoxy. This has nothing to do with the fact that it is a Christian world in a predominantly irreligious society. It is that orthodoxy is a product of discipline, discipline of the emotions, of the intellect, of the will; finally, the discipline of the creative powers into an absolute command of technique. If Eliot is in a tradition, it is, I think, a tradition of what might be called Puritan art, which is never, to use his own word, 'unconscious' when concentrating for action, but always vigilant, critical and aiming always at a sort of superhuman perfection.

(The Shaping Spirit, 1958)

Karl Shapiro

POETIC BANKRUPTCY

THE emergence of Eliot's piety in 'The Hollow Men' and in *Ash Wednesday* takes the form of self-disgust in the one and self-pity in the other. 'The Hollow Men' is in every way a better poem than *The Waste Land*, though the parodistic style again enforces a poverty of statement and language which become the marks of self-imitation in Eliot. *Ash Wednesday* is probably even more laden with gratuitous quotation than *The Waste Land*, but its ecclesiastical imagery and richness of music give the poem a beauty which the poet can finally accept as beauty. Eliot here luxuriates in the emotions of piety and surrender which seemed shameful to his Puritan soul in a purely human situation. The Eliot–God equation, once he has made the daring step, gives him an intellectual–emotional balance for the first time in his career. After the publication of this poem, Eliot's former work seems more of a piece and his future work is all laid out for him, everything from church pageants to Christmas-card poems. The *Ariel Poems* are relatively simple and almost narrative. The rest of the poems are shelved under 'fragments', minor pieces, and unfinished experiments. Eliot's career as a poet virtually comes to a close with *Ash Wednesday*. After that there is criticism, theology, and drama. The *Four Quartets* is the only attempt at what modern criticism calls a 'major' poem – meaning a poem that deals with Culture wholesale. The *Quartets* were hailed by the Eliot critics as his crowning achievement; actually they are evidence of the total dissolution of poetic skill and even a confession of poetic bankruptcy. Eliot is quite open about this in the *Quartets*.

The *Quartets* are Eliot's bid to fame as a 'philosophical poet'. In them he expounds his metaphysics, his poetics, and his own place in the scheme of things. All of this is quite legitimate and not at all surprising; what is disturbing about the poems is their

commonplaceness, their drabness of expression, their convention-
ality, and, worst of all, their reliance on the schoolbook language
of the philosophy class. Eliot has traded poetry for the metaphysical abstraction, as in *The Waste Land* he had traded narrative for 'myth'. This development is psychologically consistent,
a descent from French Symbolism to Metaphysical complexity-
for-the-sake-of-complexity, to pastiche, to the myth-science of
The Golden Bough, to philosophical abstraction without poetic
content. It all ends in the complete abandonment of poetry.
When he comes to the drama in earnest he knows, of course,
that he must use human language and he begins a new ascent into
literature and the voices of poetry. But the *Quartets* lie at the
bottom of the literary heap. All the so-called lyric sections, with
one or two exceptions, are written with such disregard for the
ear that one cannot associate them with the Eliot of 'Prufrock'
or the 'Rhapsody'. 'Garlic and sapphires in the mud / Clot the
bedded axle-tree' is typical of this diction devoid of both image
and music. Eliot, who used to condemn poets like Tennyson for
what he called crudeness of feeling, here shows an insensitivity
toward language which is marvelous. The more prosy passages
are even voided of that kind of poetry which rises from the use
of imagery or sound. As for the philosophical development, it
fails to reach a state of poetry, and it may fail as philosophy – of
this I am no judge. The much-quoted third section of 'East
Coker' about everyone going into the darkness, even people in
the Almanach de Gotha and the Stock Exchange Gazette, is
possibly the best passage of a long, very bad piece of writing;
one feels that here there is an acceptance of the badness of the
writing, as if good writing no longer held any meaning for the
poet. The 'lyric' section that follows contains a stanza ('The
whole earth is our hospital / Endowed by the ruined millionaire
. . .') which in its vulgarity of thought and expression is hardly
superior to 'Only God can make a tree'. For the rest there is a
kind of narcissistic figure of the aging Eliot lolling through the
poem, the climactic Dante imitation in 'Little Gidding', and
finally the magnificent passage 'Sin is Behovely, but / All shall
be well . . .' Unfortunately these glorious lines are not Eliot's

but are one of his borrowings. In general, the *Four Quartets*
appears to be a deliberately bad book, one written as if to convince the reader that poetry is dead and done with. We should
remember Eliot's lifelong interest in the final this and the final
that, and at least entertain the possibility that the *Four Quartets*
were intended to stand as the last poem in the Great Tradition.

(*In Defense of Ignorance*, 1960)

William F. Lynch, S.J.

DISSOCIATION IN TIME

In talking of the *Four Quartets*, let us turn from the problem of
human relations to that of time and human sensibility about it.
The remarkable imagination of Eliot is now dealing with this
very sharp area of trouble. No one is better equipped to reproduce the problem for the bloodstream of the mind through the
resources of poetry. The problem seems to be that we are
immersed in time and are flattened down to its dimensions:

> Time past and time future
> Allow but a little consciousness.
> To be conscious is not to be in time . . .

> Distracted from distraction by distraction.

> Men and bits of paper, whirled by the cold wind
> That blows before and after time,
> Wind in and out of unwholesome lungs
> Time before and time after.
> Eructation of unhealthy souls
> Into the faded air, the torpid
> Driven on the wind that sweeps the gloomy hills of London . . .

> Ridiculous the waste sad time
> Stretching before and after.

> as, when an underground train, in the tube, stops too long
>   between stations
And the conversation rises and slowly fades into silence
And you see behind every face the mental emptiness deepen
Leaving only the growing terror of nothing to think about;
Or when, under ether, the mind is conscious but conscious of
    nothing –

Men's curiosity searches past and future
And clings to that dimension. But to apprehend
The point of intersection of the timeless
With time, is an occupation for the saint —

Or else the poet knows also that men are already swept, in the
temporal sequence of their diseases, into new generations who
have the taste of the abyss of anxiety, who know the terror of a
larger time, the time of the sea and the time of an incredible
history of the race before and after:

> The distant rote in the granite teeth,
> And the wailing warning from the approaching head-
>   land
> Are all sea voices, and the heaving groaner
> Rounded homewards, and the seagull:
> And under the oppression of the silent fog
> The tolling bell
> Measures time not our time, rung by the unhurried
> Ground swell, a time
> Older than the time of chronometers . . .

These are some of the problems of the poem, the flatness of the
small time and the terror of the new; and the question of the
poem, though it is not a conceptual question, seems to be, what
about it, what shall we do, what else is there, what else is there?

If I at all question the answers (they are not conceptual
answers, but come from the refined bloodstream of a great
Christian poet), it is not before considerable hesitation. For the
time of Eliot is most certainly not the time of Baudelaire, of
Proust or Poe. His sense of time is ever so much more subtle. He
knows that only through time is time conquered. He knows that

the moment, as lived by men for good or evil, is more than an
isolated moment; rather, it carries the weight of tradition and
all the past and future,

> Not the intense moment
> Isolated, with no before and after,
> But a lifetime burning in every moment
> And not the lifetime of one man only
> But of old stones that cannot be deciphered.

He knows that time is the preserver, and that if we know more
than the past it is the past we know for all that. Like St Paul
('Leaving behind the things that are past') he also has the sense
that all things are new,

> Fare forward, travellers! ...
> You are not the same people who left that station
> Or who will arrive at any terminus ...

And the nature of language itself, and of poetry, must participate
in the same surge of the same history, so that Dante's figure of
Casella can also be seen in this modern version of a divine
comedy, chasing the poet relentlessly on and away from his
momentary conquest of time:

> Every phrase and every sentence is an end and a beginning,
> Every poem is an epitaph. And any action
> Is a step to the block, to the fire, down the sea's throat
> Or to an illegible stone: and that is where we start.

But here perhaps is the beginning of my difficulty. For it is
hard to say no to the impression, if I may use a mixture of my
own symbols and his, that the Christian imagination is finally
limited to the element of fire, to the day of Pentecost, to the
descent of the Holy Ghost upon the disciples. The revelation of
eternity and time is that of an *intersection*,

> But to apprehend
> The point of intersection of the timeless
> With time, is an occupation for the saint –

It seems not unseemly to suppose that Eliot's imagination

(and is not this a theology?) is alive with points of *intersection* and of *descent*. He seems to place our faith, our hope, and our love, not in the flux of time but in the *points* of time. I am sure his mind is interested in the line and time of Christ, whose Spirit is his total flux. But I am not so sure about his imagination. Is it or is it not an imagination which is saved from time's nausea or terror by points of intersection? There is his concern for

> the hardly, barely prayable
> Prayer of the one Annunciation.

There is the dubiously temporal fascination of the poem for

> ... the still point of the turning world ...

> I can only say, *there* we have been: but I cannot say where.
> And I cannot say, how long, for that is to place it in time.

> To be conscious is not to be in time ...

Everything that is good is annunciation and epiphany (and we may note here the altogether understandable poetic passion for epiphany in our day); there are

> hints and guesses,
> Hints followed by guesses ...

> The moments of happiness – not the sense of well-being
> Fruition, fulfilment, security or affection,
> Or even a very good dinner, but the sudden illumina-
> tion –

> right action is freedom
> From past and future also.

> Here the impossible union
> Of spheres of existence is actual,
> Here the past and future
> Are conquered, and reconciled ...

> For most of us there is only the unattended
> Moment, the moment in and out of time,

The distraction fit, lost in a shaft of sunlight,
The wild thyme unseen, or the winter lightning
Or the waterfall, or music heard so deeply
That it is not heard at all, but you are the music
While the music lasts.

This is the use of memory:
For liberation – not less of love but expanding
Of love beyond desire, and so liberation
From the future as well as the past.

There seems little doubt that Eliot is attracted above all by the image and the goal of immobility, and that in everything he seeks for approximations to this goal in the human order. 'Love is itself unmoving.' There is the violin, and we are the music while the music lasts, and the perpetual stillness of the Chinese jar, and the caught measure of the dance that does not seem to advance as the dance should. There is the detachment, as this poem understands it, of St John of the Cross. Above all, there is this definition of love as 'itself unmoving'. Now this latter definition may be all very true, and capable of sharp substantiation from, let us say, St Thomas. But it is also only partially true, according to the partialities of all human language, and capable of sharp addition, also from St Thomas. For he tells us that God is act, and that everything is perfect in so far as it is in act.

At this point one may very well ask what right we have to impose an abstract metaphysics upon the spontaneous images of the poet. But to this we have already given several answers in passing. For in the first place there is no such thing as an abstract metaphysics; it is composed of images, but these are *composed* according to the metaphysics of the analogy of being; in the second place and more importantly, I do not believe that there is such a thing as a purely spontaneous poetic image, free of the participating creativity of metaphysics and theology. Actually, there is no point in the soul so innocent that it is untouched by metaphysical and theological instincts and conflicts; therefore, our images are always and already going one way or the other.

There is only a doubtful refuge from this fact in the aesthetic of modern poetry.

The readers of Eliot will have to find out what shapes and directions their own imaginations take. One hypothesis I would lay down about this is that, with relation to time and its problems, his own poetic images show a tendency to keep bouncing and leaping off this line in the direction of 'eternity' and all its analogues. It does not evince a native inclination to pursue the possibilities of the line itself. Some possible evidence has been adduced for the validity of this impression. With a little less certainty on the writer's part, one last item will be suggested. Though in another context the poet tells us that here and now does not matter, he tells us even more strongly, and in a more conclusive part of the poem, that our precise place and moment are the precious thing.

> There are other places
> Which also are the world's end, some at the sea jaws,
> Or over a dark lake, in a desert or a city –
> But this is the nearest, in place and time,
> Now and in England.
>
> Here, the intersection of the timeless moment
> Is England and nowhere. Never and always.

It is the word 'nearest' that is interesting here. What does it mean? It could possibly mean that this place and time where we stand are nearest to us. But this would surely be a tautology, pretty much like saying that the nearest is the nearest is the nearest. Very likely what is being said is that it is the nearest to 'eternity'. Whereas, if we accept a dramatic and constructive view of time, it would seem much truer to say that it is nearest to the next moment in time. This is not meant to be subtle or ironic, for the matter is as simple as can be and as simple as that. But, you might very well say, is it not better to leap off the line into any approximation of eternity, or at any rate meet it vertically at the point of the line, than to continue on our horizontal pain with the rest of the 'time-ridden faces'? Perhaps it would be, but actually it is impossible. And here I would recall some of the poem's opening lines,

> What might have been is an abstraction
> Remaining a perpetual possibility
> Only in a world of speculation.

No, what we must do is go along with the time-ridden faces. For they are at least on the right track and dealing with the right fact. We are constitutionally committed to the structures of temporality, and the major reason for most of the pain therein, for the boredom and the terror, is that at the moment we are historically committed to but one level of it. Jumping out of our human facts will not help at all, and will produce nothing but further strains. The only answer, as in every case, would seem to be to deepen the fact and its possible levels, to enter more deeply into it. And that will be done only by adding the dimension of Christic time. . . .

The phases of the life of man are the mysteries of man. The phases of the life of Christ are the mysteries of Christ. But it is the time of man which He re-explored. As St Gregory tells us, the first Adam was constituted in grace and insight *at the point of achievement* of both, but the new Adam takes as his instrument, not the point of achievement, but the whole temporal process. Eliot says that the poetry, the process, does not matter, but the poetry and the process do matter (we have said that poetry is an action) and, like the age of Christ itself over against the first age of man, it must be considered a superior instrument. God is ironic, and He will not be beaten at His own game, and His game is time.

(*Christ and Apollo*, 1960)

David Perkins

ROSE-GARDEN TO MIDWINTER SPRING: ACHIEVED FAITH IN THE *FOUR QUARTETS*

THIS paper contrasts two passages in the *Four Quartets* – the moment in the rose-garden of 'Burnt Norton' and the midwinter scene at the start of 'Little Gidding'. The purpose is to use these texts, one from the beginning and one from the end of the poem, to show what changes have taken place in the protagonist through the course of it. The argument obviously depends on an interpretation of both passages and also on an overall reading of the *Four Quartets*, but I have not attempted to offer a full analysis of either these particular lines or the poem as a whole. It can be taken for granted that both the vision in the rose-garden and the winter landscape offer a brief intimation of transcendent reality, and this is their basic meaning in the poem. Moreover, the *Four Quartets*, like most of Eliot's poetry and drama since *The Waste Land*, dramatizes a process of religious conversion and commitment, with all the hesitation and doubt, the turning and turning again implied in the figure of the winding stairway in *Ash Wednesday*. The difference is, of course, that the protagonist of the *Four Quartets* finally achieves a deeper experience and a fuller understanding of his Christian faith.

The two passages are readily comparable, as several critics have recognized. They both use detail describing a natural scene to suggest supernatural revelation, and within this similarity of method there is also a shared symbolism. For a nexus of water, flower, and light imagery occurs in both passages; and here, as elsewhere in Eliot's poetry (for example, *Waste Land*, lines 35–41, or *Ash Wednesday*, IV), it is this group of images that especially communicates or embodies the brief and partial apprehension of God. The vision is mainly figured in images of light.

In the rose-garden, the protagonist comes to an empty pool in which intense light glancing off the dry concrete creates an illusion of water: 'the pool was filled with water out of sunlight. . . . The surface glittered out of heart of light.' The 'watery mirror' of ice on ponds and ditches in the sun-flooded winter landscape of 'Little Gidding' presents a similar or even stronger 'glare that is blindness'. It is significant that in both passages the light is reflected, and reflected from water or ice, for water in Eliot's poetry usually represents the realm of natural experience in time. Elsewhere in the *Four Quartets* this symbolism is translated into a theological doctrine. Although the 'light is still' or always 'at the still point of the turning world', it can never be known directly, but only in a moment of incarnation when the divine becomes manifest to the senses, 'answers light to light', and so allows man to guess at the final reality.

But though a symbolism of light is central to both passages, it is used to express rather different states of mind. In the first place, the vision in the rose-garden is much less secure. As it is described, it may suggest not a veritable glimpse of the 'heart of light', but an optical illusion, and it is also very fleeting – 'a cloud passed, and the pool was empty'. In the winter scene, however, there is nothing to suggest an illusion, and the visionary brightness is sustained over a longer period of time. Moreover, the light in the rose-garden shines only out of the dry pool, but on the road to Little Gidding the glare surrounds the protagonist, being reflected to him from every object in the landscape. The difference is, perhaps, between gazing at the 'heart of light' and being virtually in it.

The use of flower symbolism in the two passages is as obvious as is the light imagery, but more subtle. In the garden, and, indeed, throughout the *Four Quartets*, roses are associated with love, though that love changes its meaning or object in the course of the poem. The lotus that seems to rise in the pool carries a similar association, perhaps with a more specifically sexual suggestion. (Since the glimpse in the dry pool is a moment 'out of time', there may also be a reminiscence of the fabled lotus whose fruit made the eater forget his native country.) In general, these

flowers suggest an experience of natural sweetness and joy which
becomes impossible for the protagonist as he grows older. But
in 'Little Gidding' the description of the hedgerow blanched
'with transitory blossom / Of snow' recalls and transforms the
flowers in the rose-garden, investing these petals of snow with
all the fragile beauty of actual blossoms and evoking our stock
regret, learned in any number of poems, for transitory flowers.
At the same time, because these are blossoms of a hedgerow and
of snow, they suggest an innocence and a purity beyond even
the flowers in the rose-garden. Moreover, this flowering possesses
a magical or supernatural character. It is

>   a bloom more sudden
> That that of summer, neither budding nor fading,
> Not in the scheme of generation.

Throughout Eliot's poetry, there is a recurring theme that
moments of sudden religious communion may restore a lost
natural sweetness in a different form. In other words, the pro-
tagonists frequently recollect moments of ineffable joy in their
past life, and they have a hope that in the 'new world' of religious
faith they may come to understand such experience, or even
relive it in some way. 'The Dry Salvages' puts the notion
abstractly:

> We had the experience but missed the meaning,
> And approach to the meaning restores the experience
> In a different form.

For a more concrete illustration we can turn to *The Family
Reunion*, where Agatha remarks that 'There are hours when there
seems to be no past or future, / Only a present moment of
pointed light'. Here, of course, she is speaking of what in 'The
Dry Salvages' is described as 'the moment in and out of time'.
The experience in the rose-garden at Burnt Norton is one
example. But Agatha goes on to say, 'They only come once' in
'that kind', and she speculates that 'Perhaps there is another
kind . . . across a whole Thibet of broken stones / That lie, fang
up, a lifetime's march.' It is this notion that particularly inter-
prets the passages we have at hand. In the rose-garden the pro-

tagonist is a child (as I read it); the scene in 'Little Gidding' restores that moment in a different form, across 'the dark cold and the empty desolation', after a lifetime's effort.

With this in mind, we can compare the protagonist in the two scenes. One difference is that 'Burnt Norton' dramatizes a gap between the actor and the narrator, between the child in the garden and the older person imagining and speaking of the incident. This is not true of the parallel occasion in 'Little Gidding', which exists wholly in the present tense and renders experience as it is taking place. But this distinction permits and supports others. For one thing, the speaker in 'Burnt Norton' recounts not 'what has been', but rather 'what might have been', and the poetry thus becomes speculative and wishful, loaded with an intense nostalgia for something that never happened. The emotions of the child in this scene are distinguished from those of the narrator, but they are not defined with the same precision, being implied only in the dramatic situation. If one thinks of the child in a garden, aware of invisible presences, hearing the laughter of hidden children, it is easy to sympathize with the wonder and excitement that the poetry suggests. The point is that while in 'Burnt Norton' we are made to notice the personality and feelings of the speaker, this is much less the case with the winter scene in 'Little Gidding'. The later passage is mainly descriptive; the emotions of the protagonist are not directly presented, but seem rather to be embodied in the landscape he observes; as a result they can scarcely be characterized except, of course, to say that he is shaken and feels a quickening of life. But in this context, such an attitude of objective contemplation has considerable significance. It is, after all, very close to the final state of Christian beatitude.

One can also note that in the rose-garden the protagonist has no understanding of the vision granted him. Indeed, the point is that no explanation can be offered at this stage. When, for example, the speaker remarks that 'they were behind us, reflected in the pool', the reference remains obscure precisely because he does not know who 'they' are and can tell us nothing more about them. In 'Little Gidding', however, the meaning has been discovered. The kindling illumination taking place is framed within Christian theology – it is 'pentecostal' – and the protagonist recognizes its significance in his own life. It is the moment of baptism or rebirth, a crossing from the merely natural realm into a dimension of religious faith, or, as the poem puts it, 'This is the spring time / But not in time's convenant.'

Both the achieved faith and the symbolism of midwinter spring permit the protagonist to go much further than he could in the rose-garden. Since human experience is and must be limited to 'hints and guesses', he cannot in either scene know the final reality, but now he can at least posit it. For when, at the end of the passage in 'Little Gidding', the protagonist asks, 'Where is the summer, the unimaginable / Zero summer', he is, of course, speaking of God, and defining the final communion as an intensification of the experience he has already had, an experience which allows such antithetical extremes as winter and spring to meet at one point and which, within the symbols adopted, can be carried further only by forcing the antithetical terms until the cold of winter becomes zero and the spring turns into summer. Unlike midwinter spring, a 'Zero summer' is literally 'unimaginable'. It has no basis in possible conditions of climate. The answer to the question, 'Where is the Zero summer', must be that it is not in or of this world. But if the question is hypothetical and speculative, the hypothesis arises naturally from the description of midwinter spring and is justified by it.

The most important difference between the two scenes is also the most obvious, and we have touched on it repeatedly. If the protagonist in the rose-garden is a child, the garden itself – with its gate and box circle suggesting a seclusion and privacy that deepen as the dry pool is approached, with its bird that can speak, its unbodied companions and irrational excitement – suggests the child's world of fantasy. In the same way, the winter landscape objectifies the consciousness of an old man now incapable of sensory response ('no earth smell / Or smell of living thing'), 'dumb' and frozen.

The association here of winter, old age, and darkness ('the dark time of year'), laces out beyond the *Four Quartets* to recall much of Eliot's poetry since the opening lines of *The Waste Land* and even before. And, of course, it is central to the *Four Quartets*. Among the more relevant sections is the moving close of 'East Coker', where the protagonist bravely declares that 'Old men ought to be explorers' and goes on to recognize that the exploration must be through 'dark cold and empty desolation'. Here, of course, the poetry specifically anticipates the sea of time pictured in 'The Dry Salvages'. It also harks back to that 'darkness of God' which 'East Coker' especially defines and which can be a prelude to religious happiness. But in a more personal and dramatic sense, it refers to 'the dark cold and empty desolation' of old age which the protagonist, being old, is compelled to explore. The hope is to find through the darkness 'a further union, a deeper communion', and it is this hope that is answered at the start of 'Little Gidding'.

Finally, if the events in the enclosed rose-garden, the sudden blaze of light in the presence of ghostly figures, can be explained as an optical illusion and as the working of a child's imagination, the parallel experience in 'Little Gidding' possesses an unchallengeable authority and a new meaning. The illumination takes place in an open landscape, on the road to a church. It is no longer merely private, no longer questionable, no longer, in fact, something wholly given. The roadway suggests a pilgrimage or deliberate journey, and the pentecostal vision coming at the end of the journey in association with the church is both given and achieved. Moreover, the church here is not merely a symbol of Christian faith, but of faith as it binds the protagonist in society with other men, both living and dead. Therefore, if the midwinter scene in 'Little Gidding' restores the moment in the rose-garden, it does so in a way that subsumes many of the leading themes of the *Four Quartets*, including the struggle of the protagonist not only to come to a wholehearted religious commitment, but also to find through faith a means of attachment to the lives of other people and a reconciliation to life in time, a need especially urgent since the protagonist is himself an old man who is learning that 'time is no healer'.

(*Modern Language Quarterly*, 1962)

SELECT BIBLIOGRAPHY

R. P. Blackmur, *Language as Gesture* (Allen & Unwin, 1954; Harcourt Brace, 1954). Contains 'Unappeasable and Peregrine: Behaviour in the *Four Quartets*', a glittering performance in Blackmur's late style, which is less a critical essay than a ceremonious paraphrase.

R. L. Brett, *Reason and Imagination* (Oxford U.P., 1960). Contains a philosophically orientated discussion of the *Quartets*; Professor Brett has returned to the subject in 'Mysticism and Incarnation in *Four Quartets*' in *English*, Autumn 1966.

Northrop Frye, *T. S. Eliot* (Oliver & Boyd, 1963; Barnes & Noble, 1966). Relates the *Quartets* to the archetypal patterns and transformations in the whole body of Eliot's poetry and plays.

Helen Gardner, *The Art of T. S. Eliot* (Cresset Press and Dutton, 1949; sixth impression, with new preface, 1968). The whole book is primarily directed towards the study of the *Quartets* and is of appropriate interest, in addition to the chapter reprinted in the present volume.

Herbert Howarth, *Notes on Some Figures Behind T. S. Eliot* (Chatto & Windus and Houghton, 1965). Contains a good deal of biographical and anecdotal material, some of it pointing to the sources of parts of the *Quartets*.

F. R. Leavis, *Education and the University* (Chatto & Windus, 1943). Contains, as Appendix 1, 'T. S. Eliot's Later Poetry', an enthusiastic review of the first three *Quartets*, reprinted from *Scrutiny*, Summer 1942. See also Leavis's 'Poet as Executant', a short review of the gramophone records of Eliot reading the *Quartets*, which Leavis finds a deplorable rendering; first published in *Scrutiny* in 1947, and reprinted in volume I of *A Selection from Scrutiny*, compiled by F. R. Leavis (Cambridge U.P., 1968).

Kathleen Nott, *The Emperor's Clothes* (Heinemann, 1953; Indiana U.P., paperback, 1958). A sharp attack on the Christian literary revival of the 1940s, of which the *Quartets* were once seen as forming part.

Raymond Preston, *Four Quartets Rehearsed* (Sheed & Ward and Haskell, 1946). A short explicatory book on the *Quartets*, concentrating on the religious elements.

Grover Smith, *T. S. Eliot's Poetry and Plays* (Chicago U.P., 1956). An indispensable and exhaustive work on the literary sources and analogues of Eliot's poetry.

T. S. Eliot: A Study of His Writings by Several Hands, ed. B. Rajan (Dennis Dobson & Russell, 1947). Contains a number of relevant essays, including Helen Gardner, '*Four Quartets:* A Commentary' (subsequently developed into *The Art of T. S. Eliot*); B. Rajan, 'The Unity of the *Quartets*'; and Philip Wheelwright, 'Eliot's Philosophical Themes'.

Leonard Unger, *T. S. Eliot: Moments and Patterns* (Minnesota U.P. and Oxford U.P., 1966). Describes, among other things, the use in the *Quartets* of motifs from Eliot's earlier poetry.

Addendum (1979)

Michael Edwards, *Eliot: Language* (Aquila Publishing Co., 1975). A short book or long essay, full of aphoristic insights into the *Quartets*.

Helen Gardner, *The Composition of 'Four Quartets'* (Faber, 1978). A very illuminating account of how Eliot wrote the poems, based on a close study of manuscript drafts and early printed versions.

F. R. Leavis, *The Living Principle* (Chatto and Windus, 1975). Contains a long and detailed commentary of the *Quartets*, responding less favourably than Leavis once did.

NOTES ON CONTRIBUTORS

A. ALVEREZ, critic and poet, is author of *The Shaping Spirit* (1958), *Beyond All This Fiddle* (1968), *The Savage God* (1971) and studies of Donne and Beckett.

CURTIS BRADFORD was, at the time of his death, Professor of English at Grinnel College, Iowa; his publications include *Yeats at Work* (1964).

DONALD DAVIE is Professor of English at Vanderbilt University, having previously taught at Dublin, Cambridge, Essex and Stanford. He is author of *Articulate Energy* (1955), *Ezra Pound* (1965), and *Thomas Hardy and British Poetry* (1972); his *Collected Poems* were published in 1972.

DENIS DONOGHUE is Professor of English at University College, Dublin. He is author of several books on modern literature, of which the most recent is *The Sovereign Ghost* (1978).

R. W. FLINT is an American crtiic; he edited *F. T. Marinetti: Selected Writings* (1972) and is occasional contributor to *Kenyon Review*, *Sewanee Review*, *Commentary* and other magazines.

DAME HELEN GARDNER is Professor Emeritus of English at Oxford. Her works on Eliot include *The Art of T. S. Eliot* (1949) and *The Composition of 'Four Quartets'* (1978); among her other contributions to the study of English literature are editions of Donne's poetry and the new version of the *Oxford Book of English Verse*.

D. W. HARDING is Emeritus Professor of Psychology at the University of London, and a former editor of *Scrutiny*. He is author of *The Impulse to Dominate* (1941), *Social Psychology and Individual Values* (1953), *Experience into Words* (1963) and *Words into Rhythm: English Speech Rhythms in Verse and Prose* (1976).

HUGH KENNER is Professor of English at Johns Hopkins University, Maryland. He has written books on Chesterton, Pound, Wyndham Lewis, Joyce and Beckett and in 1960 published *The Invisible Poet: T. S. Eliot.*

F. R. LEAVIS (1895–1978) has had a strong influence on literary criticism; his publications include *The Great Tradition* (1948), *English Literature in Our Time and The University* (1969), *Never Shall My Sword* (1972), *The Living Principle* (1975), and *Thoughts, Words and Creativity* (1976).

WILLIAM F. LYNCH is an American Jesuit critic and teacher; his books include *The Image Industries* (1959), *Christ and Apollo* (1960), *Images of Hope* (1966) and *Christ and Prometheus* (1970).

MARSHALL MCLUHAN is Professor of English, University of Toronto. He is the author of *The Mechanical Bride* (1951), *The Gutenberg Galaxy* (1962) and *Understanding Media* (1964).

F. O. MATTHIESSEN was an American critic and author of *The Achievement of T. S. Eliot* (1935), *American Renaissance* (1941) and *Henry James: the major phase* (1944). He died in 1948.

GEORGE ORWELL was an English novelist and essayist who died in 1950. His books include *Homage to Catalonia* (1938), *Animal Farm* (1945) and *Nineteen Eighty-Four* (1949).

DAVID PERKINS is Professor of English at Harvard, and author of *Quest for Permanence* (1959), *Wordsworth and the Poetry of Sincerity* (1964), and a *History of Modern Poetry* (1976).

KARL SHAPIRO is Professor of English, University of California. In addition to *In Defense of Ignorance* (1960), he has written *Poems of a Jew* (1958) and a *A Primer for Poets* (1965).

C. K. STEAD is Professor of English at the University of Auckland. In addition to *The New Poetic* (1964) he has edited

New Zealand Short Stories (1966). He is the editor of *Measure for Measure* in the present series.

JAMES JOHNSON SWEENEY has had a distinguished career as director of art galleries in America. He has published several volumes of literary and art criticism, including *Vision and Image* (1968).

MORRIS WEITZ is an American philosopher with a particular interest in aesthetics. He is the editor of *Problems of Aesthetics* (1959) and author of *Hamlet and the Philosophy of Literary Criticism* (1964).

INDEX

WITHDRAWN